D

REVISE EDEXCEL

AS Mathematics
C1 C2 M1 S1 D1

REVISION GUIDE

Author: Harry Smith

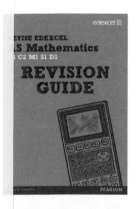

THE REVISE EDEXCEL SERIES
Available in print or online

Online editions for all titles in the Revise Edexcel series are available Spring 2014. Presented on our ActiveLearn platform, you can view the full book and customise it by adding notes, comments and weblinks.

Print editions

AS Maths Revision Guide	9781447961642
AS Maths Revision Workbook	9781447961680

Online editions

AS Maths Revision Guide	9781447961659
AS Maths Revision Workbook	9781447961697

This Revision Guide is designed to complement your classroom and home learning, and to help prepare you for the exam. It does not include all the content and skills needed for the complete course.

To find out more visit:
www.pear‌... mathsrevision

059374

ALWAYS LEARNING

PEARSON

Contents

A small bit of small print

Edexcel publishes Sample Assessment Material and the Specification on its website. This is the official content and this book should be used in conjunction with it. The questions in *Now try this* have been written to help you practise every topic in the book. Remember: the real exam questions may not look like this.

Index laws

You need to be able to work with algebraic expressions confidently for all your AS units. Make sure you know how to use these six index laws.

 1 $a^m \times a^n = a^{m+n}$ $x^5 \times x^{-2} = x^3$

2 $\dfrac{a^m}{a^n} = a^{m-n}$ $\dfrac{x^8}{x^6} = x^2$

 3 $(a^m)^n = a^{mn}$ $(x^4)^3 = x^{12}$

4 $a^{-n} = \dfrac{1}{a^n}$ $5^{-2} = \dfrac{1}{5^2} = \dfrac{1}{25}$

5 $a^{\frac{1}{n}} = \sqrt[n]{a}$ $49^{\frac{1}{2}} = 7$

$27^{\frac{1}{3}} = 3$

$2 \times 2 \times 2 \times 2 = 16$ so $\sqrt[4]{16} = 2$ ⟵ $16^{\frac{1}{4}} = 2$

6 $a^{\frac{m}{n}} = (\sqrt[n]{a})^m$ $27^{-\frac{2}{3}} = \left(27^{\frac{1}{3}}\right)^{-2}$

$= \left(\sqrt[3]{27}\right)^{-2}$

Do these calculations one step at a time.

$= 3^{-2} = \dfrac{1}{3^2} = \dfrac{1}{9}$

Worked example

Given that $\dfrac{10x - 5x^{\frac{7}{2}}}{\sqrt{x}}$ can be written in the form $10x^p - 5x^q$, write down the value of p and the value of q.   **(2 marks)**

$\dfrac{10x}{x^{\frac{1}{2}}} - \dfrac{5x^{\frac{7}{2}}}{x^{\frac{1}{2}}} = 10x^{1-\frac{1}{2}} - 5x^{\frac{7}{2}-\frac{1}{2}}$

$= 10x^{\frac{1}{2}} - 5x^3$

$p = \frac{1}{2}$ and $q = 3$

The fraction acts like a bracket, so you need to divide **both** terms in the denominator by $\sqrt{x}$. Write down the values of p and q when you've finished.

Golden rule

Convert all roots into fractional powers before applying the other index laws.

$\sqrt{x} = x^{\frac{1}{2}}$ $\sqrt[3]{x} = x^{\frac{1}{3}}$

Powers and roots

Remember you can't use a calculator in your C1 exam. Learn:

✓ square numbers up to 15^2

✓ cube numbers up to 5^3

✓ corresponding square and cube roots.

Worked example

Find the value of $125^{-\frac{1}{3}}$ **(2 marks)**

$125^{-\frac{1}{3}} = \dfrac{1}{125^{\frac{1}{3}}}$

$= \dfrac{1}{\sqrt[3]{125}}$

$= \dfrac{1}{5}$

Apply the index laws one at a time.

Now try this

1. Simplify $x\left(4x^{-\frac{1}{2}}\right)^3$ **(2 marks)**

2. Simplify $\left(9y^{10}\right)^{\frac{3}{2}}$ **(2 marks)**

3. Write $\dfrac{5 + 2\sqrt{x}}{x^2}$ in the form $5x^p + 2x^q$, where p and q are constants.   **(2 marks)**

There are full worked solutions to all the Now try this questions on page 140.

Remember that a constant doesn't have to be an integer.

Expanding and factorising

In your C1 exam, you might have to MULTIPLY OUT (or EXPAND) a product of THREE brackets, or FACTORISE a CUBIC expression.

Expanding brackets

To expand the product of two factors, you have to multiply EVERY TERM in the first factor by EVERY TERM in the second factor.

There are 2 terms in the first factor and 3 terms in the second factor, so there will be $2 \times 3 = 6$ terms in the expanded expression BEFORE you collect like terms.

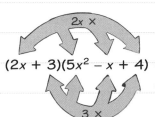

$$(2x + 3)(5x^2 - x + 4) = 10x^3 - 2x^2 + 8x + 15x^2 - 3x + 12$$
$$= 10x^3 + 13x^2 + 5x + 12$$

Simplify your expression by collecting like terms:
$-2x^2 + 15x^2 = 13x^2$

Worked example

Show that $(3 + 2\sqrt{x})^2$ can be written as $9 + k\sqrt{x} + 4x$, where k is a constant to be found. **(2 marks)**

$(3 + 2\sqrt{x})(3 + 2\sqrt{x}) = 9 + 6\sqrt{x} + 6\sqrt{x} + 4x$
$$= 9 + 12\sqrt{x} + 4x$$

$k = 12$

Remember that $\sqrt{x} \times \sqrt{x} = x$.
$(2\sqrt{x})^2 = 2\sqrt{x} \times 2\sqrt{x} = 4\sqrt{x}\sqrt{x}$
$$= 4x$$

If you have to find a constant, it's a good idea to write down the value of the constant when you have finished your working.

Factorising

Factorising is the opposite of expanding brackets.

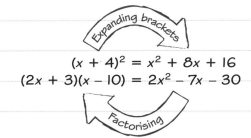

$(x + 4)^2 = x^2 + 8x + 16$
$(2x + 3)(x - 10) = 2x^2 - 7x - 30$

Worked example

Factorise completely $x^3 + x^2 - 6x$ **(3 marks)**

$x^3 + x^2 - 6x = x(x^2 + x - 6)$
$$= x(x + 3)(x - 2)$$

Start by taking the common factor, x, out of every term. You are left with a quadratic expression, which you can factorise into two linear factors.

Now try this

1. Given that $(x + 2)(x + 1)^2 = x^3 + bx^2 + cx + d$ where b, c and d are constants, find the values of b, c and d. **(3 marks)**

   Multiply out $(x + 1)^2$ first to get $(x + 2)(x^2 + 2x + 1)$.

2. Factorise completely $3x^3 - 2x^2 - x$ **(3 marks)**

3. Factorise completely $25x^2 - 16$ **(2 marks)**

   This is a difference of two squares:
   $a^2 - b^2 = (a + b)(a - b)$

Surds

You can use surds to give answers as exact numbers. You can't use a calculator in your C1 exam so you need to be able to work with surds confidently.

Golden rules

These are the two golden rules for simplifying surds:

1
$$\sqrt{ab} = \sqrt{a} \times \sqrt{b}$$
$$\sqrt{8} = \sqrt{4} \times \sqrt{2} = 2\sqrt{2}$$

2
$$\sqrt{\frac{a}{b}} = \frac{\sqrt{a}}{\sqrt{b}} \qquad \sqrt{\frac{3}{25}} = \frac{\sqrt{3}}{\sqrt{25}} = \frac{\sqrt{3}}{5}$$

Worked example

Write $\sqrt{45}$ in the form $k\sqrt{5}$, where k is an integer.   **(2 marks)**

$$\sqrt{45} = \sqrt{9 \times 5}$$
$$= \sqrt{9} \times \sqrt{5}$$
$$= 3\sqrt{5}$$

$k = 3$

Worked example

Simplify $\sqrt{27} + \sqrt{48}$, giving your answer in the form $a\sqrt{3}$, where a is an integer.

(2 marks)

$$\sqrt{27} + \sqrt{48} = \sqrt{9} \times \sqrt{3} + \sqrt{16} \times \sqrt{3}$$
$$= 3\sqrt{3} + 4\sqrt{3}$$
$$= 7\sqrt{3}$$

$\sqrt{a} + \sqrt{b}$ is **not** equal to $\sqrt{a + b}$.

You know you need to write the answer in the form $a\sqrt{3}$ so write each surd in the form $k\sqrt{3}$. You need to take a factor of 3 out of each number:

$27 = 9 \times 3$ so $\sqrt{27} = \sqrt{9 \times 3}$
$48 = 16 \times 3$ so $\sqrt{48} = \sqrt{16 \times 3}$

Rationalising the denominator

You can rationalise the denominator of a fraction by removing any surds in the denominator.

$$\overset{\times\,(4+\sqrt{11})}{\frac{1}{4 - \sqrt{11}}} = \frac{4 + \sqrt{11}}{(4 - \sqrt{11})(4 + \sqrt{11})} = \frac{4 + \sqrt{11}}{5}$$

$\times (4 + \sqrt{11})$

$(4 - \sqrt{11})(4 + \sqrt{11}) = 16 - 4\sqrt{11} + 4\sqrt{11} - 11$
$$= 5$$

To work out what to multiply the top and bottom by, look at the denominator of the original fraction. Swap a plus for a minus, or swap a minus for a plus.

Worked example

Express $\dfrac{14}{3 + \sqrt{2}}$ in the form $a + b\sqrt{2}$, where a and b are integers.   **(2 marks)**

$$\frac{14}{3 + \sqrt{2}} = \frac{14(3 - \sqrt{2})}{(3 + \sqrt{2})(3 - \sqrt{2})}$$
$$= \frac{14(3 - \sqrt{2})}{9 + 3\sqrt{2} - 3\sqrt{2} - 2}$$
$$= \frac{\overset{2}{\cancel{14}}(3 - \sqrt{2})}{\underset{1}{\cancel{7}}}$$
$$= 6 - 2\sqrt{2}$$

$a = 6$ and $b = -2$

If the denominator is in the form $p + \sqrt{q}$ then multiply the numerator and denominator of the fraction by $p - \sqrt{q}$.

Now try this

1. Expand and simplify $(7 + \sqrt{2})(7 - \sqrt{2})$
                                                        (2 marks)

2. Write $\sqrt{98}$ in the form $a\sqrt{2}$, where a is an integer.   **(1 mark)**

3. Simplify the following, giving your answers in the form $a + b\sqrt{5}$, where a and b are integers.

   (a) $\dfrac{8}{3 + \sqrt{5}}$ **(2 marks)** (b) $\dfrac{4 + \sqrt{5}}{2 - \sqrt{5}}$ **(4 marks)**

Quadratic equations

Quadratic equations can be written in the form $ax^2 + bx + c = 0$ where a, b and c are constants. The solutions of a quadratic equation are sometimes called the ROOTS of the equation.

Solution by factorising

You can follow these steps to solve some quadratic equations.

1. REARRANGE the equation into the form $ax^2 + bx + c = 0$

2. FACTORISE the left-hand side.

3. Set each factor EQUAL TO ZERO and solve to find two values of x.

> The first solution is the value of x which makes the $(2x + 3)$ factor equal to 0.

Worked example

Solve $2(x + 1)^2 = 3x + 5$ **(4 marks)**

$$2(x^2 + 2x + 1) = 3x + 5$$
$$2x^2 + 4x + 2 = 3x + 5$$
$$2x^2 + x - 3 = 0$$
$$(2x + 3)(x - 1) = 0$$

$2x + 3 = 0$ or $x - 1 = 0$

$x = -\dfrac{3}{2}$ $x = 1$

Worked example

$x^2 + 6x - 2 = (x + a)^2 + b$, where a and b are constants.

(a) Find the values of a and b. **(3 marks)**

$$x^2 + 6x - 2 = (x + 3)^2 - 3^2 - 2$$
$$= (x + 3)^2 - 9 - 2$$
$$= (x + 3)^2 - 11$$

$a = 3$ and $b = -11$

(b) Hence, or otherwise, show that the roots of
$$x^2 + 6x - 2 = 0$$
are $c \pm \sqrt{11}$, where c is an integer to be found. **(2 marks)**

$(x + 3)^2 - 11 = 0$ $(+ 11)$

$(x + 3)^2 = 11$ $(\sqrt{\ })$

$x + 3 = \pm\sqrt{11}$ (-3)

$x = -3 \pm \sqrt{11}$

$c = -3$

Completing the square

You can write a quadratic expression in the form $(x + p)^2 + q$ using these two identities:

1 $x^2 + 2bx + c = (x + b)^2 - b^2 + c$

2 $x^2 - 2bx + c = (x - b)^2 - b^2 + c$

You can use this method to solve any quadratic equation without using a calculator.

> Write the left-hand side in completed square form, and use inverse operations to solve the equation. Remember that any positive number has **two** square roots: one positive and one negative. You need to use the $\pm$ symbol when you take square roots of both sides of the equation.

Now try this

1. Solve the equation $2(x - 3)^2 + 3x = 14$ **(3 marks)**

> $x^2 - 10x + 7 = (x - 5)^2 - 5^2 + 7$

2. (a) Show that $x^2 - 10x + 7$ can be written as $(x + p)^2 + q$, where p and q are integers to be found. **(2 marks)**

   (b) Hence solve the equation $x^2 - 10x + 7 = 0$, giving your answer in the form $x = a \pm b\sqrt{2}$, where a and b are integers to be found. **(3 marks)**

> You could also solve this by substituting $a = 1$, $b = -10$ and $c = 7$ into the quadratic formula, $x = \dfrac{-b \pm \sqrt{b^2 - 4ac}}{2a}$, then simplifying.

The discriminant

The discriminant of a quadratic expression $ax^2 + bx + c$ is the value $b^2 - 4ac$. You can use the discriminant to work out whether a quadratic equation has any REAL ROOTS or REAL SOLUTIONS. There are three possible conditions for the discriminant.

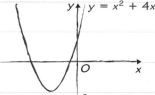 **$b^2 - 4ac > 0$**

$y = x^2 + 4x + 2$

Discriminant $= 4^2 - 4 \times 1 \times 2$
$= 8 > 0$

TWO DISTINCT REAL ROOTS

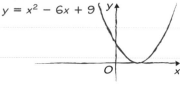 **$b^2 - 4ac = 0$**

$y = x^2 - 6x + 9$

Discriminant $= (-6)^2 - 4 \times 1 \times 9$
$= 0$

TWO EQUAL REAL ROOTS

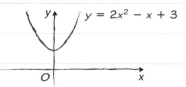 **$b^2 - 4ac < 0$**

$y = 2x^2 - x + 3$

Discriminant $= (-1)^2 - 4 \times 2 \times 3$
$= -23 < 0$

NO REAL ROOTS

Worked example

The equation $x^2 + 4qx + 2q = 0$, where q is a non-zero constant, has <u>equal roots</u>.
Find the value of q.   **(4 marks)**

$$b^2 - 4ac = 0$$
$$(4q)^2 - 4 \times 1 \times (2q) = 0$$
$$16q^2 - 8q = 0$$
$$q(16q - 8) = 0$$
$$q = 0 \qquad 16q - 8 = 0 \text{ so } q = \frac{1}{2}$$

Follow these steps.

1. Work out the values of a, b and c:
   $a = 1$, $b = 4q$ and $c = 2q$.

2. Find an expression for the discriminant $(b^2 - 4ac)$ in terms of q.

3. Set the discriminant equal to 0, because there are two **equal** roots.

4. Solve this **new** equation to work out two possible values for q.

You are told that q is non-zero, so the correct solution is $q = \frac{1}{2}$.

EXAM ALERT!

The equation must be in the form $ax^2 + bx + c = 0$ before you work out the values of a, b and c. Always write down the condition for the discriminant that you are using, and use **brackets** when you substitute.

Students have struggled with this topic in recent exams – be prepared!

Worked example

The equation $2x^2 - kx + 6 = k$ has <u>no real solutions</u> for x. Show that $k^2 + 8k - 48 < 0$
                    (3 marks)

$$2x^2 - kx + 6 - k = 0$$
$$b^2 - 4ac < 0$$
$$(-k)^2 - 4 \times 2 \times (6 - k) < 0$$
$$k^2 + 8k - 48 < 0$$

Now try this

1. Find the value of the discriminant of $3x^2 - 2x - 5$ **(1 mark)**

2. The equation $px^2 + 2x - 3 = 0$, where p is a constant, has equal roots.
   Find the value of p.   **(3 marks)**

   The expression $(k + p)^2$ must always have a positive value.

3. $f(x) = x^2 + (k + 5)x + 2k$, where k is a constant.
   (a) Find the discriminant of $f(x)$ in terms of k.   **(2 marks)**
   (b) Show that the discriminant can be written in the form $(k + p)^2 + q$, where p and q are integers to be found.   **(2 marks)**
   (c) Show that, for all values of k, the equation $f(x) = 0$ has distinct real roots.   **(2 marks)**

Sketching quadratics

When you SKETCH a graph you need to show its key features. You don't need to use graph paper for a sketch, but you should still draw your axes and any straight lines using a RULER.

Factorised quadratics

On a sketch you usually show the points where the graph crosses the axes.

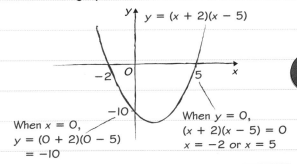

When x = 0,
$y = (0 + 2)(0 - 5)$
$= -10$

When y = 0,
$(x + 2)(x - 5) = 0$
$x = -2$ or $x = 5$

$y = 4x - x^2$, so the coefficient of x^2 is **negative**.

Negative coefficients

If the coefficient of x^2 is NEGATIVE the graph will be an 'upside down' U-shape. You can check the coefficient of x by multiplying out the brackets.

Worked example

Sketch the curve with equation $y = x(4 - x)$ **(3 marks)**

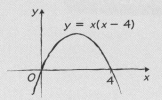

Worked example

Sketch the curve with equation $y = (x + 2)^2 + 1$
Label the minimum point and any points where the curve crosses the coordinate axes.   **(3 marks)**

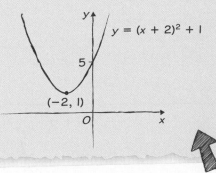

To work out the point where the curve crosses the y-axis, substitute $x = 0$ into the equation.

Sketching $y = (x + a)^2 + b$

If a quadratic is written in COMPLETED SQUARE form then you can find the position of its VERTEX easily.

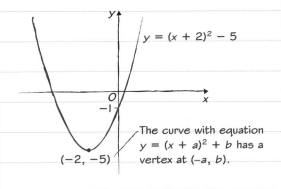

The curve with equation $y = (x + a)^2 + b$ has a vertex at $(-a, b)$.

Now try this

1. On separate diagrams, sketch the graphs of

   (a) $y = (x - 2)^2$ **(3 marks)**

   (b) $y = (x - 2)^2 + k$, where k is a positive constant.   **(2 marks)**

   Show on each sketch the turning point and the coordinates of any points where the graph meets the axes.

2. $x^2 + 6x + 15 = (x + a)^2 + b$

   (a) Find the values of a and b.   **(2 marks)**

   (b) Sketch the graph of $y = x^2 + 6x + 15$, labelling the minimum point and any points of intersection with the axes.   **(3 marks)**

   (c) Find the value of the discriminant of $x^2 + 6x + 15$. Explain how the sign of the discriminant relates to your sketch in part (b).   **(2 marks)**

There is more about the discriminant on page 5.

Simultaneous equations

If a pair of simultaneous equations involves an x^2 or a y^2 term, you need to solve them using SUBSTITUTION. Remember to NUMBER the equations to keep track of your working.

Rearrange the linear equation to make y the subject.

$$y = x^2 - 2x - 7 \qquad ①$$
$$x - y = -3 \qquad ②$$

From ②:
$$y = x + 3 \qquad ③$$

Each solution for x has a corresponding value of y. Substitute to find the values of y.

$$x + 3 = x^2 - 2x - 7$$ Substitute $x + 3$ for y in equation ①.
$$0 = x^2 - 3x - 10$$
$$0 = (x - 5)(x + 2)$$
$$x = 5 \text{ or } x = -2$$

The solutions are $x = 5$, $y = 8$ and $x = -2$, $y = 1$.

Worked example

Solve the simultaneous equations

$$x - 2y = 1 \qquad ①$$
$$x^2 + y^2 = 13 \qquad ②$$

(6 marks)

From ①: $x = 1 + 2y \qquad ③$

Substitute $1 + 2y$ for x in ②:

$$(1 + 2y)^2 + y^2 = 13$$
$$1 + 4y + 4y^2 + y^2 = 13$$
$$5y^2 + 4y - 12 = 0$$
$$(5y - 6)(y + 2) = 0$$
$$y = \frac{6}{5} \qquad\qquad \text{or} \qquad\qquad y = -2$$
$$x = 1 + 2\left(\frac{6}{5}\right) = \frac{17}{5} \qquad x = 1 + 2(-2) = -3$$

Solutions: $x = \frac{17}{5}$, $y = \frac{6}{5}$ and $x = -3$, $y = -2$

You can substitute for x or y. It is easier to substitute for x because there will be no fractions.

Use brackets to make sure that the whole expression is squared.

Rearrange the quadratic equation for y into the form $ay^2 + by + c = 0$

Factorise the left-hand side to find two solutions for y.

Remember that there will be **two pairs** of solutions. Each value of y will produce a corresponding value of x. You need to find **four** different values in total **and** pair them up correctly.

Thinking graphically

The solutions to a pair of simultaneous equations correspond to the points where the graphs of the equations INTERSECT.
Because an equation involving x^2 or y^2 represents a CURVE, there can be more than one point of intersection. Each point has an x-value and a y-value. You can write the solutions using coordinates.

There is more on intersections of graphs on page 13.

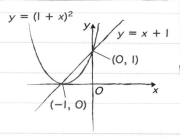
$y = (1 + x)^2$, $y = x + 1$, $(0, 1)$, $(-1, 0)$

Now try this

1. Solve the simultaneous equations
$$x + y = 5$$
$$x^2 + 2y^2 = 22 \qquad \textbf{(6 marks)}$$

You will need to write $x^2 - 6x + 7$ in completed square form. Have a look at page 4 for a reminder.

2. (a) By eliminating y from the simultaneous equations
$$y = x + 6$$
$$xy - 2x^2 = 7$$
show that $x^2 - 6x + 7 = 0$ **(2 marks)**

(b) Hence solve the simultaneous equations in part (a), giving your answers in the form $a \pm \sqrt{2}$, where a is an integer.   **(4 marks)**

Inequalities

You might need to find a set of values which SATISFY an inequality. If the inequality involves a QUADRATIC expression you should always SKETCH A GRAPH to help you answer the question.

This graph shows a sketch of $y = (x - 1)(x + 5)$.

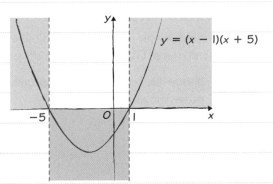

For these values of x, the curve is BELOW the x-axis, so $y < 0$.

The solution to $(x - 1)(x + 5) < 0$ is $-5 < x < 1$

For these values of x, the curve is ABOVE the x-axis, so $y > 0$.

The solution to $(x - 1)(x + 5) > 0$ is $x < -5$ or $x > 1$

There are two separate sets of values which satisfy this inequality. You need to give both sets of values, and write OR between them.

Worked example

Find the set of values for which

(a) $8x - 7 < 5x + 5$ **(2 marks)**

$8x < 5x + 12$

$3x < 12$

$x < 4$

(b) $2x^2 - 5x - 3 > 0$ **(4 marks)**

$(2x + 1)(x - 3) > 0$

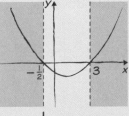

$x < -\dfrac{1}{2}$ or $x > 3$

(c) **both** $8x - 7 < 5x + 5$
and $2x^2 - 5x - 3 > 0$ **(3 marks)**

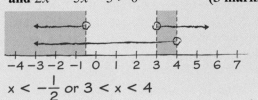

$x < -\dfrac{1}{2}$ or $3 < x < 4$

Quadratic inequalities

Follow these steps to solve any quadratic inequality:

1. Rearrange so one side is 0.

2. Factorise the other side.

3. Sketch the graph.

4. Write the solutions using $<$, $>$, $\leq$ or $\geq$.

EXAM ALERT!

Make sure you write **two separate** inequalities for your answer. You can't write $3 < x < -\frac{1}{2}$. It's not true, because 3 is larger than $-\frac{1}{2}$.

Students have struggled with this topic in recent exams – be prepared!

You need **both** inequalities to be true at the same time. Draw them both on a number line and look for the values where the inequalities **overlap**.

Now try this

1. Find the set of values of x for which
   $x(x - 5) < 14$ **(4 marks)**

   You need to expand the brackets and rearrange the inequality into the form $ax^2 + bx + c < 0$ first.

2. The equation $x^2 + (k - 3)x - 4k$ has two distinct real roots.

   (a) Show that k satisfies $k^2 + 10k + 9 > 0$ **(3 marks)**

   (b) Hence find the set of possible values for k. **(4 marks)**

Sketching cubics

CUBIC FUNCTIONS contain an x^3 term. You need to know the shapes of graphs of cubic functions and be able to sketch them.

Factorise then sketch

If a cubic equation is FACTORISED then you can work out the points where it crosses the x-axis easily. There are TWO special cases you need to know about for your C1 exam.

 If one factor is x then the curve will pass through the origin.

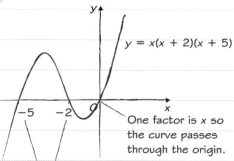

$y = x(x + 2)(x + 5)$

One factor is x so the curve passes through the origin.

The curve crosses the x-axis at the values of x which make each factor equal to 0.

 If one factor is REPEATED then the curve will JUST TOUCH the x-axis at the corresponding point.

The factor $(x + 1)$ is repeated, because it is SQUARED. So the curve just touches the x-axis at $x = -1$.

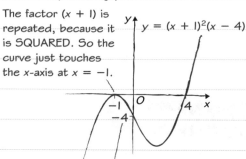

$y = (x + 1)^2(x - 4)$

You can work out the point where the curve crosses the y-axis by setting $x = 0$:
$$y = (0 + 1)^2(0 - 4) = 1^2 \times (-4) = -4$$

Worked example

(a) Factorise completely $x^3 - 8x^2 + 16x$ **(3 marks)**

$$x(x^2 - 8x + 16) = x(x - 4)^2$$

(b) Hence sketch the curve with equation $y = x^3 - 8x^2 + 16x$, showing the points where the curve meets the coordinate axes.   **(3 marks)**

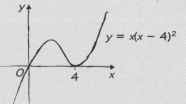

$y = x(x - 4)^2$

Negative coefficients

If the coefficient of x^3 is negative, the shape of the curve will be 'upside down'.

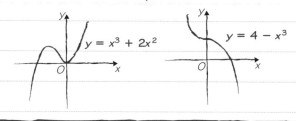

$y = x^3 + 2x^2$

$y = 4 - x^3$

The factorised equation has a factor of x so the curve will pass through the origin. It also has a **repeated** factor of $(x - 4)$ so the curve will just touch the x-axis at the point $x = 4$.

Now try this

1. Sketch the graph of $y = x^2(3 - x)$ **(3 marks)**

> Be careful! The coefficient of x^3 is negative.

2. (a) Factorise completely $x^3 - 9x$ **(3 marks)**

    (b) Hence sketch the curve $y = x^3 - 9x$ **(3 marks)**

3. Sketch the graph of $y = (2x - 1)(x - 3)^2$, showing clearly the coordinates of the points where the curve meets the coordinate axes.   **(4 marks)**

> You need to show the coordinates of the point where the graph meets the y-axis as well.

Transformations 1

You can change the equation of a graph to translate it, stretch it or reflect it. These tables show you how you can use functions to transform the graph of $y = f(x)$.

Function	$y = f(x) + a$	$y = f(x + a)$	$y = af(x)$
Transformation of graph	Translation $\begin{pmatrix} 0 \\ a \end{pmatrix}$	Translation $\begin{pmatrix} -a \\ 0 \end{pmatrix}$	Stretch in the vertical direction, scale factor a
Useful to know	$f(x) + a \rightarrow$ move UP a units $f(x) - a \rightarrow$ move DOWN a units	$f(x + a) \rightarrow$ move LEFT a units $f(x - a) \rightarrow$ move RIGHT a units	x-values stay the same
Example	$y = f(x) + 3$, $y = f(x)$	$y = f(x + 5)$, $y = f(x)$	$y = 3f(x)$, $y = f(x)$

Function	$y = f(ax)$	$y = -f(x)$	$y = f(-x)$
Transformation of graph	Stretch in the horizontal direction, scale factor $\frac{1}{a}$	Reflection in the x-axis	Reflection in the y-axis
Useful to know	y-values stay the same	'$-$' outside the bracket	'$-$' inside the bracket
Example	$y = f(2x)$, $y = f(x)$	$y = f(x)$, $y = -f(x)$	$y = f(-x)$, $y = f(x)$

Worked example

The diagram shows a sketch of a curve with equation $y = f(x)$.

On the same diagram sketch the curve with equation

(a) $y = f(x + 3)$　　　　　**(3 marks)**

(b) $y = -f(x)$.　　　　　**(3 marks)**

Show clearly the coordinates of any maximum or minimum points, and any points of intersection with the axes.

> Everything in blue is part of the answer.

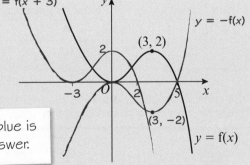

Now try this

The diagram shows a sketch of a curve C with equation $y = f(x)$.
On separate diagrams sketch the curve with equation

(a) $y = 2f(x)$　　　**(3 marks)**　　　(b) $y = f(-x)$　　　**(3 marks)**

(c) $y = f(x + k)$, where k is a constant and $0 < k < 4$　　　**(4 marks)**

On each diagram show the coordinates of any maximum or minimum points, and any points of intersection with the x-axis.

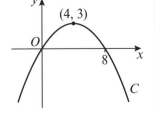

Transformations 2

You need to be able to spot transformed functions from their equations, and sketch transformations involving ASYMPTOTES.

Functions and equations

Curve C below has equation $y = x^3 - 3x^2 - 2$. You can sketch the curves of other equations by transforming curve C.

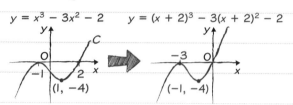

$y = f(x)$
$y = x^3 - 3x^2 - 2$

$y = f(x + 2)$
$y = (x + 2)^3 - 3(x + 2)^2 - 2$

Asymptotes

An asymptote is a line which a curve approaches, but never reaches. You draw asymptotes on graphs with DOTTED LINES.

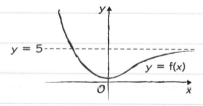

This curve has an asymptote at $y = 5$. When you transform a graph, its asymptotes are transformed as well.

Transformation	New asymptote
$y = f(x) - 1$	$y = 4$
$y = 2f(x)$	$y = 10$
$y = f(x + 4)$	$y = 5$

The graph is translated 4 units to the left, so the horizontal asymptote does not change.

Worked example

The diagram shows a sketch of the curve with equation $y = f(x)$ where

$$f(x) = \frac{2x}{x + 1}, x \neq -1$$

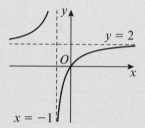

The curve has asymptotes with equations $y = 2$ and $x = -1$

(a) Sketch the curve with equation $y = f(x + 2)$ and state the equations of its asymptotes.   **(3 marks)**

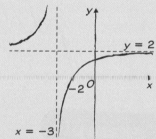

(b) Find the coordinates of the points where the curve in part (a) crosses the coordinate axes.   **(3 marks)**

$$f(x + 2) = \frac{2(x + 2)}{(x + 2) + 1} = \frac{2x + 4}{x + 3}$$

When $x = 0$, $y = \frac{4}{3}$

$(-2, 0)$ and $(0, \frac{4}{3})$

Now try this

The diagram shows a curve C with equation $y = f(x)$, where

$$f(x) = \frac{(x + 2)^2}{x + 1}, x \neq -1$$

(a) Sketch the curve with equation $y = f(x + 1)$ and state the new equation of the asymptote $x = -1$ **(3 marks)**

(b) Write down the coordinates of the points where the curve meets the coordinate axes.   **(3 marks)**

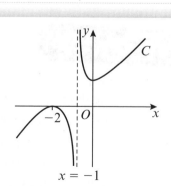

Sketching $y = \dfrac{k}{x}$

The graph of $y = \dfrac{k}{x}$ is called a RECIPROCAL graph.
You need to know the shape of the reciprocal graph, and its key features.

Positive or negative?

The shape of a reciprocal graph is different for positive and negative values of k.

 $k > 0$　 **$k < 0$**

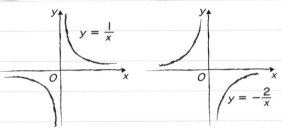

The figure shows a sketch of the curve $y = \dfrac{6}{x}$

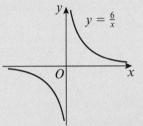

(a) On a separate diagram, sketch the curve with equation $y = \dfrac{6}{x - 3}$, showing any points at which the curve crosses the coordinate axes.　**(3 marks)**

When $x = 0$, $y = \dfrac{6}{-3} = -2$

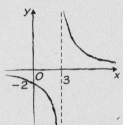

(b) Write down the equation of the asymptotes of the curve in part (a).　**(2 marks)**

$y = 0$ and $x = 3$

Translations

Reciprocal graphs have two ASYMPTOTES.

For $y = \dfrac{k}{x}$ the asymptotes are the x- and y-axes.

There is more about asymptotes and translations on page 11.

If the graph is TRANSLATED then the asymptotes are also translated:

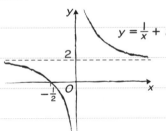

This is a translation of $y = \dfrac{1}{x}$ by vector $\begin{pmatrix} 0 \\ 2 \end{pmatrix}$.

$y = f(x) \rightarrow y = f(x) + 2$

So the new asymptotes are $x = 0$ (the y-axis) and $y = 2$.

The transformation from $y = \dfrac{6}{x}$ to

$y = \dfrac{6}{x - 3}$ is the translation $\begin{pmatrix} 3 \\ 0 \end{pmatrix}$.

1. Sketch the graph of $y = -\dfrac{4}{x}$　**(2 marks)**

The transformation is
$y = f(x) \rightarrow y = f(x + 1)$
Draw the new asymptote on your sketch before you draw your curve.

2. (a) Sketch the graph of $y = \dfrac{3}{x}$　**(2 marks)**

(b) On a separate diagram, sketch the graph of $y = \dfrac{3}{x + 1}$, showing any points at which the curve crosses the coordinate axes.　**(3 marks)**

(c) Write down the equations of the asymptotes of the curve in part (b).　**(2 marks)**

Intersecting graphs

The coordinates of the points where two graphs INTERSECT are the x- and y-values which satisfy BOTH equations at the same time. You can use algebra to find the points where two curves intersect.

The diagram shows the graphs of $y = -\dfrac{2}{x}$ and $y = 5 - 3x$.

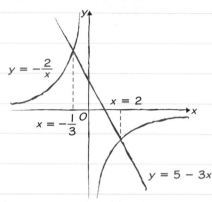

The x-coordinates at the points of intersection are the solutions to the equation

$$5 - 3x = -\frac{2}{x}$$
$$x(5 - 3x) = -2$$
$$5x - 3x^2 = -2$$
$$3x^2 - 5x - 2 = 0$$
$$(3x + 1)(x - 2) = 0$$
$$x = -\frac{1}{3} \quad \text{or} \quad x = 2$$

Worked example

(a) On the same axes, sketch the graph with the equation
   (i) $y = x(x + 1)(x - 4)$
   (ii) $y = \dfrac{2}{x}$ **(5 marks)**

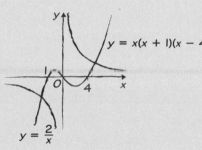

(b) Write down the number of real solutions to the equation $x(x + 1)(x - 4) = \dfrac{2}{x}$

(1 mark)

2

The points of intersection will be solutions to the equation $x^2(3 - x) = -4x$.

Worked example

(a) On the same axes, sketch the graph with the equation
   (i) $y = x^2(3 - x)$
   (ii) $y = -4x$ **(5 marks)**

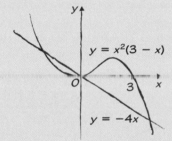

(b) Find the coordinates of the points of intersection. **(6 marks)**

$$3x^2 - x^3 = -4x$$
$$x^3 - 3x^2 - 4x = 0$$
$$x(x^2 - 3x - 4) = 0$$
$$x(x - 4)(x + 1) = 0$$
$$x = 0 \quad \text{or} \quad x = 4 \quad \text{or} \quad x = -1$$
$$y = 0 \qquad y = -16 \quad y = 4$$
$$(0, 0), \quad (4, -16), \quad (-1, 4)$$

Now try this

(a) On the same axes, sketch the graph with the equation
   (i) $y = x^2(x - 3)$
   (ii) $y = x(8 - x)$ **(6 marks)**
   Indicate all the points where the curves meet the x-axis.

(b) Use algebra to find the coordinates of the points of intersection. **(7 marks)**

There are three points of intersection: one at $(0, 0)$, one with a negative value of x and one with a positive value of x.

Equations of lines

The equation of a straight line can be written in the form $y = mx + c$, where m is the GRADIENT of the line, and c is the point where it crosses the y-axis. There are other useful ways to write the equation of a straight line.

Point and gradient

If a straight line has GRADIENT m and passes through the POINT (x_1, y_1), then you can write its equation as

$$y - y_1 = m(x - x_1)$$

This equation is NOT given in the formulae booklet, so you need to remember it.

If you are given two points on a line, (x_1, y_1) and (x_2, y_2), you can calculate the gradient using

$$m = \frac{y_2 - y_1}{x_2 - x_1}$$

Thinking in transformations

You can remember this equation by thinking of it as a TRANSLATION of the graph $y = mx$ by vector $\begin{pmatrix} x_1 \\ y_1 \end{pmatrix}$

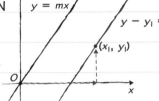

Worked example

The line L passes through the point $(-8, 5)$ and has gradient $\frac{1}{2}$. Find an equation for L in the form $ax + by + c = 0$, where a, b and c are integers. **(3 marks)**

$$y - y_1 = m(x - x_1)$$
$$y - 5 = \frac{1}{2}(x - (-8))$$
$$2y - 10 = x + 8$$
$$x - 2y + 18 = 0$$

EXAM ALERT!

If you are using a formula which is **not** in the booklet, always **write it down** before you substitute. Here, $m = \frac{1}{2}$, $x_1 = -8$ and $y_1 = 5$.

You need a, b and c to be integers, so multiply every term in your equation by 2 to remove the fraction. Then rearrange so one side is equal to 0.

> Students have struggled with this topic in recent exams – be prepared!

Worked example

You can draw a sketch to help you find the gradient, or use

$$m = \frac{y_2 - y_1}{x_2 - x_1}$$

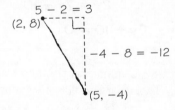

Write the equation as $y = -4x + c$ and substitute the values of x and y from either point on the graph to find c.

The line L passes through the points $(2, 8)$ and $(5, -4)$. Find an equation for L in the form $y = mx + c$ **(3 marks)**

$$m = \frac{y_2 - y_1}{x_2 - x_1} = \frac{-4 - 8}{5 - 2} = \frac{-12}{3} = -4$$
$$y = -4x + c$$
$$8 = -4(2) + c$$
$$c = 16 \quad \text{so} \quad y = -4x + 16$$

Now try this

1. The line L passes through the point $(6, -5)$ and has gradient $-\frac{1}{3}$. Find an equation for L in the form $ax + by + c = 0$, where a, b and c are integers. **(3 marks)**

2. The line L passes through $(-4, 2)$ and $(8, 11)$. Find an equation for L in the form $y = mx + c$, where m and c are constants. **(3 marks)**

3. The line $3y + 4x - k = 0$ passes through the point $(5, 1)$. Find
(a) the value of k **(1 mark)**
(b) the gradient of the line. **(2 marks)**

 To find the gradient, rearrange the equation into the form $y = mx + c$.

Parallel and perpendicular

PARALLEL lines have the same gradient. These three lines all have a gradient of 1.

PERPENDICULAR means at right angles. If a line has gradient m then any line perpendicular to it will have gradient $-\dfrac{1}{m}$

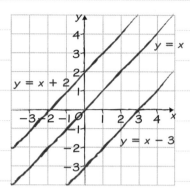

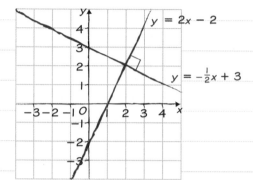

Worked example

P is the point $(3, -2)$ and Q is the point $(7, 6)$. The line L is perpendicular to PQ and passes through the midpoint of PQ. Find an equation for L in the form $ax + by + c = 0$, where a, b and c are integers. **(5 marks)**

Gradient of PQ $= \dfrac{6 - (-2)}{7 - 3} = \dfrac{8}{4} = 2$

So gradient of $L = -\dfrac{1}{2}$

Midpoint of PQ $= \left(\dfrac{3 + 7}{2}, \dfrac{-2 + 6}{2}\right)$

$= (5, 2)$

Equation of L: $\quad y - y_1 = m(x - x_1)$

$y - 2 = -\dfrac{1}{2}(x - 5)$

$2y - 4 = -x + 5$

$x + 2y - 9 = 0$

Worked example

The line L_1 has equation $7y + 2x - 3 = 0$. The line L_2 is perpendicular to L_1 and crosses the y-axis at $(0, 5)$. Find an equation for L_2 in the form $ax + by + c = 0$, where a, b and c are integers. **(3 marks)**

L_1: $7y = -2x + 3$

$y = -\dfrac{2}{7}x + \dfrac{3}{7}$

L_2 has gradient $\dfrac{7}{2}$

L_2: $\qquad y = \dfrac{7}{2}x + 5$

$2y = 7x + 10$

$7x - 2y + 10 = 0$

Start by finding the gradient of L_1. The easiest way to do this is to rearrange the equation into the form $y = mx + c$.

Find the gradient and the midpoint of PQ. The midpoint of the line segment joining (x_1, y_1) and (x_2, y_2) is $\left(\dfrac{x_1 + x_2}{2}, \dfrac{y_1 + y_2}{2}\right)$.

Now try this

1. The line L has equation $y = 10 - 3x$
   (a) Show that the point $P (4, -2)$ lies on L. **(1 mark)**

   (b) Find an equation of the line perpendicular to L which passes through P. Give your answer in the form $ax + by + c = 0$, where a, b and c are integers. **(3 marks)**

2. The line L_1 with equation $4x - 5y - 1 = 0$ crosses the x-axis at A. The line L_2 is perpendicular to L_2 and passes through A. Find the equation of L_2 in the form $y = mx + c$ **(4 marks)**

Substitute $y = 0$ into the equation of L_1 to work out the x-coordinate of A.

Lengths and areas

You might have to calculate the length of a line segment, or the area of a shape on a coordinate grid. It's always a good idea to DRAW SKETCHES to keep track of your working.

Worked example

P is the point $(2, 5)$ and Q is the point $(3, -2)$. The length of PQ is $a\sqrt{2}$, where a is an integer. Find the value of a.

(3 marks)

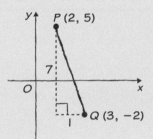

$AB^2 = 1^2 + 7^2$

$\quad = 50$

$AB = \sqrt{50}$

$\quad = \sqrt{25} \times \sqrt{2} = 5\sqrt{2}$

$a = 5$

(a) To work out the coordinates of the point where two lines intersect you need to solve their equations simultaneously.

Substitute $y = -x$ into the equation for L_2.

(b) The vertical height of triangle AOB is $\frac{5}{2}$. Substitute $y = 0$ into the equation for L_2 to find the coordinates of B, then use Area $= \frac{1}{2} \times$ base $\times$ height. You don't need to give any units when you're calculating lengths and areas on a graph.

Using a formula

If P has coordinates (x_1, y_1) and Q has coordinates (x_2, y_2), then the length of the line segment PQ is

$$\sqrt{(x_2 - x_1)^2 + (y_2 - y_1)^2}$$

Worked example

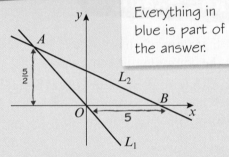

Everything in blue is part of the answer.

The line L_1 has equation $y = -x$, and the line L_2 has equation $3y + x - 5 = 0$

(a) Work out the coordinates of A. **(2 marks)**

$3(-x) + x - 5 = 0$

$\quad -2x - 5 = 0$

$\qquad x = -\frac{5}{2}, \; y = \frac{5}{2}$

A is the point $\left(-\frac{5}{2}, \frac{5}{2}\right)$

(b) Find the area of triangle AOB. **(3 marks)**

$3(0) + x - 5 = 0$

$\qquad x = 5$

B is the point $(5, 0)$.

Area $= \dfrac{1}{2} \times 5 \times \dfrac{5}{2} = \dfrac{25}{4}$

Now try this

The line L_1 has equation $x - 2y + 6 = 0$
L_1 crosses the x-axis at P and the y-axis at Q.

(a) Show that $PQ = 3\sqrt{5}$ **(3 marks)**

The line L_2 is perpendicular to L_1 and passes through Q.

(b) Find an equation for L_2. **(4 marks)**

L_2 crosses the x-axis at R.

(c) Find the area of the triangle PQR. **(4 marks)**

Draw a sketch to help you visualise the problem.

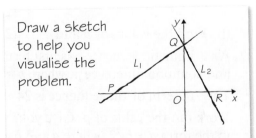

Arithmetic sequences

An arithmetic sequence is a sequence where the difference between consecutive terms is constant. You usually use a to represent the FIRST TERM and d to represent the COMMON DIFFERENCE. Here are two examples.

1 $\overbrace{11, \ 14, \ 17, \ 20, \ 23}^{+3 \ \ +3 \ \ +3 \ \ +3} \ldots$

$a = 11, \ d = 3,$ nth term $= 11 + 3(n - 1)$

2 $\overbrace{1, \ \tfrac{1}{2}, \ 0, \ -\tfrac{1}{2}, \ -1}^{-\frac{1}{2} \ -\frac{1}{2} \ -\frac{1}{2} \ -\frac{1}{2}} \ldots$

$a = 1, \ d = -\tfrac{1}{2},$ nth term $= 1 - \tfrac{1}{2}(n - 1)$

Finding the nth term

If an arithmetic sequence has first term a and common difference d, then the nth term, or GENERAL TERM is

$a + (n - 1)d$ This formula is given in the formulae booklet, but you should make sure you are CONFIDENT using it.

Worked example

The first term of an arithmetic sequence is a and the common difference is d.

The 13th term of the sequence is 8 and the 16th term of the sequence is $12\tfrac{1}{2}$

(a) Write down two equations for a and d.

(2 marks)

$a + (13 - 1)d = 8$ so $a + 12d = 8$ ①

$a + (16 - 1)d = 12\tfrac{1}{2}$ so $a + 15d = 12\tfrac{1}{2}$ ②

(b) Find the values of a and d.   **(2 marks)**

② − ①: $3d = 4\tfrac{1}{2}$

$d = 1\tfrac{1}{2}$

Substitute $d = 1\tfrac{1}{2}$ into ①: $a + 12\left(1\tfrac{1}{2}\right) = 8$

$a + 18 = 8$

$a = -10$

You could also work out the common difference by writing down a few terms of the sequence:

$\ldots, \ \ 8, \ \ ?, \ \ ?, \ \ 12\tfrac{1}{2}, \ \ldots$ $\overbrace{}^{+1\frac{1}{2} \ \ +1\frac{1}{2} \ \ +1\frac{1}{2}}$

There are three jumps between the 13th term and the 16th term. $12\tfrac{1}{2} - 8 = 4\tfrac{1}{2}$

So each jump is $4\tfrac{1}{2} \div 3 = 1\tfrac{1}{2}$.

Solve the two equations simultaneously to find a and d. Number each equation to keep track of your working.

You can work in decimals or mixed numbers. You could give your answer as $a = -10$, $d = 1.5$.

Now try this

1. The first term of an arithmetic sequence is a and the common difference is d.

   The 9th term of the sequence is 3 and the 11th term of the sequence is −4

   (a) Write down two equations for a and d.
   (2 marks)

   (b) Find the values of a and d.   **(2 marks)**

2. An arithmetic sequence has first term $p^2 + 1$ and common difference p, where $p > 0$

   The 7th term of the sequence is 24

   Work out the value of p. Give your answer in the form $a + b\sqrt{2}$, where a and b are integers.   **(5 marks)**

3. Beth is saving money for a deposit on a house. In the first month she saves £300. Each month she increases the amount she saves by £20

   (a) Show that in the fifth month Beth saves £380   **(1 mark)**

   (b) Find an expression in terms of n for the amount Beth saves in the nth month.
   (2 marks)

   Use the information given to write a quadratic equation involving p. You need the answer in surd form so solve your equation by completing the square. There is more about this on page 4.

Recurrence relationships

A recurrence relationship tells you how to find a term in the sequence if you know the PREVIOUS TERM. You need to be able to generate a sequence from a recurrence relationship.

You will usually be given the FIRST TERM, and the rule for finding the next term.

You can use any letter to represent a term in a sequence.

This number tells you the term number.

The FIRST TERM is 5.

$$x_1 = 5$$
$$x_{n+1} = 2x_n + 3, n \geqslant 1$$

The TERM-TO-TERM rule is 'multiply by 2 then add 3'.

The term numbers in a series are all positive integers.

So for this sequence:

$x_2 = 2x_1 + 3 = 2(5) + 3 = 13$
$x_3 = 2x_2 + 3 = 2(13) + 3 = 29$

... and so on.

You have to find each term in the sequence — there is no quick way to find the general term.

Worked example

A sequence of positive numbers is defined by
$$U_{n+1} = \sqrt{U_n^2 - 8}$$
$$U_1 = 6$$

(a) Find U_2, giving your answer in the form $2\sqrt{p}$, where p is a prime number. **(2 marks)**

$U_2 = \sqrt{6^2 - 8}$
$\quad = \sqrt{28}$
$\quad = 2\sqrt{7} \qquad p = 7$

(b) Show that $U_5 = 2$ **(2 marks)**

$U_3 = \sqrt{U_2^2 - 8} = \sqrt{28 - 8} = \sqrt{20}$
$U_4 = \sqrt{U_3^2 - 8} = \sqrt{20 - 8} = \sqrt{12}$
$U_5 = \sqrt{U_4^2 - 8} = \sqrt{12 - 8} = \sqrt{4} = 2$

Worked example

A sequence $a_1, a_2, a_3, \ldots$ is defined by $a_1 = k$, $a_{n+1} = 3a_n + 1, n \geqslant 1$, where k is a constant.

(a) Write down an expression for a_2 in terms of k. **(1 mark)**

$a_2 = 3a_1 + 1 = 3k + 1$

(b) Given that $\sum_{r=1}^{3} a_r = 44$, show that $k = 3$ **(4 marks)**

$a_1 = k$ and $a_2 = 3k + 1$
$a_3 = 3a_2 + 1 = 3(3k + 1) + 1 = 9k + 4$

$\sum_{r=1}^{3} a_r = a_1 + a_2 + a_3$

$\quad = k + (3k + 1) + (9k + 4) = 13k + 5$

$13k + 5 = 44$
$13k = 39$ so $k = 3$

Sigma notation

The Greek letter sigma ($\sum$) is used to show the SUM of a set of terms in a sequence. The numbers above and below the $\sum$ tell you which terms to ADD TOGETHER:

You are adding the first FOUR terms of the sequence.

$$\sum_{r=1}^{4} U_r = U_1 + U_2 + U_3 + U_4$$

Substitute values of r from 1 up to 4, and add the terms.

Write an expression for $\sum_{r=1}^{3} a_r$ in terms of k.

Now try this

1. A sequence $a_1, a_2, a_3, \ldots$ is defined by $a_1 = 5$, $a_{n+1} = 2a_n - 4, n \geqslant 1$

   (a) Find the values of a_2 and a_3. **(2 marks)**

   (b) Calculate the value of $\sum_{r=1}^{5} a_r$ **(3 marks)**

   Write a quadratic equation and solve it by factorising. Remember that p is positive.

2. A sequence $x_1, x_2, x_3, \ldots$ is defined by $x_1 = 2$, $x_{n+1} = px_n - 1, n \geqslant 1$ where p is a positive constant.

   (a) Write down an expression for x_2 in terms of p. **(1 mark)**

   (b) Show that $x_3 = 2p^2 - p - 1$ **(2 marks)**

   (c) Given that $x_3 = 9$, find the value of p. **(3 marks)**

Arithmetic series

In a series, the terms are always ADDED TOGETHER. A series is arithmetic if its terms have a common difference, like $8 + 10 + 12 + 14 + \dots$. Here is another example:

$$a + (n - 1)d = 20$$
$$70 - 5(n - 1) = 20$$

$$70 \xrightarrow{-5} 65 \xrightarrow{-5} 60 + \dots + 20 \qquad n = 11$$

You could use the formula on the right to work out the sum of this series.

Use $a = 70$, $d = -5$ and $n = 11$. The sum is:

$$\tfrac{1}{2}(11)[2(70) + (11 - 1)(-5)] = \tfrac{1}{2}(11)(90) = 495$$

Sum to n terms

If an ARITHMETIC series has first term a and common difference d, then the SUM of the first n terms is $\frac{1}{2}n[2a + (n - 1)d]$.

This formula is given in the booklet. But you also need to know its PROOF and this is NOT in the formula booklet. Look at the first Worked example below to see the proof in action.

Worked example

An arithmetic series has first term a and common difference d. Prove that the sum of the first n terms of the series, S, is

$$\tfrac{1}{2}n[2a + (n - 1)d] \qquad \textbf{(4 marks)}$$

$S = a + (a + d) + \dots + [a + (n - 1)d]$ ①

$S = [a + (n - 1)d] + \dots + (a + d) + a$ ②

① + ②:

$2S = [2a + (n - 1)d] + \dots + [2a + (n - 1)d]$

$2S = n[2a + (n - 1)d]$

$S = \tfrac{1}{2}n[2a + (n - 1)d]$

To prove this you need to write the sum FORWARDS and BACKWARDS.

You can then add pairs of terms to get an expression for $2S$:

$a \qquad + [a + (n - 1)d] = 2a + (n - 1)d$
$(a + d) \quad + [a + (n - 2)d] = 2a + (n - 1)d$
$(a + 2d) + [a + (n - 3)d] = 2a + (n - 1)d$

... and so on.

Every pair of terms adds up to $2a + (n - 1)d$, and there are n pairs, so

$2S = n[2a + (n - 1)d]$

Worked example

Substitute the values of a and d into the formula to get an expression for the sum in **terms of n**. Set this expression equal to 175 and simplify to get a quadratic equation in n.

An arithmetic series has first term 13 and common difference 4 The sum of the first n terms of the sequence is 175

(a) Show that n satisfies $2n^2 + 11n - 175 = 0$ **(3 marks)**

$a = 13$, $d = 4$, $S = 175$, $S_n = \tfrac{1}{2}n[2a - (n - 1)d]$

$\tfrac{1}{2}n[26 + 4(n - 1)] = 175$

$13n + 2n^2 - 2n = 175$

$2n^2 + 11n - 175 = 0$

Solve your quadratic equation by factorising. n is the number of terms in the series, so it must be a **positive integer**. This means you can ignore the negative solution.

(b) Hence find the value of n.   **(3 marks)**

$(2n + 25)(n - 7) = 0$

$n = -\tfrac{25}{2} \qquad n = 7$

Now try this

1. An arithmetic series has first term -3 and common difference d. The sum of the first 20 terms of the series is 320 Find the value of d.   **(4 marks)**

2. Prove that the sum of the first n natural numbers is $\frac{1}{2}n(n + 1)$ **(3 marks)**

You can't use the formula because it says 'prove'. Try to apply the technique in the first Worked example.

Sequence and series problems

You might have to solve a WORD PROBLEM involving SEQUENCES or SERIES.

Worked example

Nisha is buying a car. She pays for it monthly over 12 months. The garage offers two repayment plans. Both plans form an arithmetic sequence.

<u>Plan A:</u> First month payment £X
Payments decrease by £$2Y$ each month

<u>Plan B:</u> First month payment £$(X - 1100)$
Payments decrease by £Y each month

(a) Show that the **total** amount paid under Plan A for the 12-month period is £$(12X - 132Y)$

(2 marks)

$a = X, d = -2Y, n = 12$

$S_n = \frac{1}{2}n[2a + (n - 1)d]$

$= \frac{1}{2}(12)[2X - 2Y(12 - 1)]$

$= 6(2X - 22Y)$

$= 12X - 132Y$

(b) For the 12-month period, the **total** paid is the same for both plans. Find the value of Y.

(4 marks)

For Plan B, $S_n = \frac{1}{2}n[2a + (n - 1)d]$

$= \frac{1}{2}(12)[2(X - 1100) - Y(12 - 1)]$

$= 12X - 66Y - 13200$

$12X - 66Y - 13200 = 12X - 132Y$

$66Y = 13200$

$Y = 200$

(c) Under Plan A, Nisha's final payment would be £300. Work out the value of X. **(3 marks)**

$X + (12 - 1)(-400) = 300$

$X - 4400 = 300$

$X = 4700$

 The payments **decrease**, so the values of d in your arithmetic sequences will be **negative**.
For Plan A: $a = X$, $d = -2Y$ and $n = 12$
For Plan B: $a = (X - 1100)$,
$d = -Y$ and $n = 12$

 Write down the formula for the sum of the first n terms of an arithmetic series. This formula is given in the formula booklet. Then substitute for a, d and n and simplify your expression.

Write your expression for the total paid under Plan B, make it equal to $12X - 132Y$ and solve an equation to find Y.

EXAM ALERT!

The monthly payments **decrease** by $2Y$ each month, so $d = -400$. Make sure you use the formula for the nth term, not for the sum. Write an equation and solve it to find the value of X.

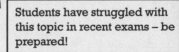 Students have struggled with this topic in recent exams – be prepared!

Now try this

Hanna is planning a training regime. On the first day she does 25 sit-ups. Each day she increases the number of sit-ups by 6

(a) Find an expression for the number of sit-ups Hanna does on the nth day of her regime. **(2 marks)**

(b) Show that the total number of sit-ups she had done after n days is $3n^2 + 22n$

(3 marks)

(c) On the nth day of her regime, Hanna does 79 sit-ups. How many sit-ups has she done in total in the n days of her regime? **(4 marks)**

Differentiation 1

You can DIFFERENTIATE a function to find its DERIVATIVE or GRADIENT FUNCTION.

The derivative is written as f'(x) or $\dfrac{dy}{dx}$

Differentiating x^n

$y = f(x)$ $y = x^n$

Differentiation

Multiply by the power ...

$\dfrac{dy}{dx} = f'(x)$ $\dfrac{dy}{dx} = nx^{n-1}$ ... then reduce the power by 1

This rule works for ANY value of n, including FRACTIONS and NEGATIVE numbers.

Golden rules

1 Write every term in a polynomial in the form ax^n BEFORE differentiating.

$\sqrt{x} \to x^{\frac{1}{2}}$ $\dfrac{6}{x^2} \to 6x^{-2}$

2 Constant terms differentiate to ZERO, and x terms differentiate to a CONSTANT.

$f(x) = 7 \to f'(x) = 0$ $f(x) = 3x + 1 \to f'(x) = 3$

Worked example

Given that $y = 3x^6 - 8 + \dfrac{1}{x^3}$, $x \neq 0$, find $\dfrac{dy}{dx}$ **(3 marks)**

$y = 3x^6 - 8 + x^{-3}$

$\dfrac{dy}{dx} = 18x^5 - 3x^{-4}$

Start by rewriting $\dfrac{1}{x^3}$ as x^{-3}. Remember that you are multiplying by -3 when you differentiate this term, so the new term is **negative**.

Worked example

Differentiate with respect to x

(a) $x^3 - 3\sqrt{x} + \dfrac{x}{7}$ **(3 marks)**

$f(x) = x^3 - 3x^{\frac{1}{2}} + \dfrac{1}{7}x$

$f'(x) = 3x^2 - \dfrac{3}{2}x^{-\frac{1}{2}} + \dfrac{1}{7}$

(b) $\dfrac{kx + 5}{x^2}$ **(3 marks)**

$f(x) = \dfrac{kx}{x^2} + \dfrac{5}{x^2} = kx^{-1} + 5x^{-2}$

$f'(x) = -kx^{-2} - 10x^{-3}$

EXAM ALERT!

With respect to x just means that x is the variable. You should treat any other letters in the function as **constants**.

It's OK to leave powers as **negative numbers** or **fractions** in your final answers. The answer to part (a) could be in either of these forms:

$3x^2 - \dfrac{3}{2}x^{-\frac{1}{2}} + \dfrac{1}{7}$ $3x^2 - \dfrac{3}{2\sqrt{x}} + \dfrac{1}{7}$

Students have struggled with this topic in recent exams – be prepared!

Now try this

1. Given that $y = \dfrac{(x + 3)^2}{x}$, $x \neq 0$, find $\dfrac{dy}{dx}$ **(4 marks)**

Multiply out the brackets, then write the function in the form $y = ax + b + cx^{-1}$ before differentiating.

2. (a) Write $\dfrac{2 + 5\sqrt{x}}{x}$ in the form $2x^p + 5x^q$, where p and q are constants. **(2 marks)**

(b) Given that $y = 3x^2 + 1 - \dfrac{2 + 5\sqrt{x}}{x}$, find $\dfrac{dy}{dx}$ **(4 marks)**

Differentiation 2

You can use the DERIVATIVE or GRADIENT FUNCTION to find the RATE OF CHANGE of a function, or the gradient of a curve.

This curve has equation $y = x^3 + 5x^2$. Its gradient function has equation $\frac{dy}{dx} = 3x^2 + 10x$. You can find the GRADIENT at any point on the graph by substituting the x-coordinate at that point into the gradient function.

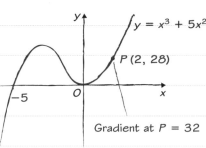

$y = x^3 + 5x^2$

$P(2, 28)$

Gradient at $P = 32$

At the point P:

$x = 2$

$\frac{dy}{dx} = 3(2)^2 + 10(2) = 12 + 20 = 32$

Worked example

$f(x) = (10 + 2\sqrt{x})^2,\ x > 0$

(a) Show that $f(x) = 100 + k\sqrt{x} + 4x$, where k is a constant to be found. **(2 marks)**

$f(x) = 10^2 + 20\sqrt{x} + 20\sqrt{x} + (2\sqrt{x})^2$

$\quad = 100 + 40\sqrt{x} + 4x \qquad k = 40$

(b) Find $f'(x)$. **(2 marks)**

$f(x) = 100 + 40x^{\frac{1}{2}} + 4x$

$f'(x) = 20x^{-\frac{1}{2}} + 4$

(c) Evaluate $f'(25)$. **(1 mark)**

$f'(25) = 20\left(25^{-\frac{1}{2}}\right) + 4$

$\qquad = 20\left(\frac{1}{5}\right) + 4$

$\qquad = 4 + 4 = 8$

Evaluating f'(x)

$f'(x)$ tells you the RATE OF CHANGE of the function for a given value of x. You can calculate $f'(x)$ for a given value of x by substituting that value of x into the derivative.

$25^{-\frac{1}{2}} = \frac{1}{25^{\frac{1}{2}}} = \frac{1}{\sqrt{25}} = \frac{1}{5}$

For a reminder about using the index laws to simplify powers have a look at page 1.

Second-order derivatives

You can differentiate TWICE to find the SECOND-ORDER derivative.

You write the second-order derivative as $\frac{d^2y}{dx^2}$ or $f''(x)$.

$y = 5x^3$

| Differentiate |

$\frac{dy}{dx} = 15x^2$

| Differentiate |

$\frac{d^2y}{dx^2} = 30x$

Worked example

Given that $y = 8\sqrt{x} - 3x^2 + 5x,\ x > 0$,

find $\dfrac{d^2y}{dx^2}$ **(4 marks)**

$y = 8x^{\frac{1}{2}} - 3x^2 + 5x$

$\frac{dy}{dx} = 4x^{-\frac{1}{2}} - 6x + 5$

$\frac{d^2y}{dx^2} = -2x^{-\frac{3}{2}} - 6$

Now try this

1. $f(x) = 3x^3 + 5x,\ x > 0$

   (a) Differentiate to find $f'(x)$. **(2 marks)**

   (b) Given that $f'(x) = 41$, find the value of x. **(3 marks)**

2. Given that $y = 2x^2 + 4x^{-2}$, find $\dfrac{d^2y}{dx^2}$ **(4 marks)**

3. The curve C has equation $y = x(x - 1)(x + 3)$

   (a) Find $\dfrac{dy}{dx}$ **(2 marks)**

   (b) Sketch C, showing each point where C meets the x-axis. **(3 marks)**

   (c) Find the gradient of C at each point where the curve meets the x-axis. **(2 marks)**

Tangents and normals

You can use DIFFERENTIATION to work out the equations of tangents and normals.

The curve drawn in black has equation

$$y = x^2 - 2x + 4$$

You can differentiate this to work out the gradient function:

$$\frac{dy}{dx} = 2x - 2$$

There is more about finding gradient functions on page 21.

At the point P (2, 4) the gradient of the curve is 2, so the gradient of the tangent is also 2.

The tangent passes through (2, 4) and it has equation $y = 2x$.

The normal is perpendicular to the tangent, so it has gradient $-\frac{1}{2}$.

The normal also passes through (2, 4) and it has equation $y = -\frac{1}{2}x + 5$.

There is more about parallel and perpendicular lines on page 15.

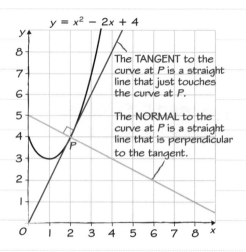

$y = x^2 - 2x + 4$

The TANGENT to the curve at P is a straight line that just touches the curve at P.

The NORMAL to the curve at P is a straight line that is perpendicular to the tangent.

Golden rules

If a curve has gradient m at point P:

 the TANGENT at P ALSO has gradient m

 the NORMAL at P has gradient $-\dfrac{1}{m}$

Follow these steps:

1. Differentiate to find the gradient function.

2. Substitute $x = 2$ into $\dfrac{dy}{dx}$. The gradient at point P is -1.

3. Use $y - y_1 = m(x - x_1)$ to find the equation of a straight line with gradient -1 that passes through (2, 3).

There is more on finding equations of straight lines on page 14.

Worked example

The curve C has equation

$$y = x^3 - 3x^2 - x + 9, \qquad x > 0$$

The point P with coordinates (2, 3) lies on C.

Find the equation of the tangent to C at P, giving your answer in the form $y = mx + c$, where m and c are constants. **(5 marks)**

$$\frac{dy}{dx} = 3x^2 - 6x - 1$$
$$= 3(2)^2 - 6(2) - 1$$
$$= 12 - 12 - 1$$
$$= -1$$
$$y - y_1 = m(x - x_1)$$
$$y - 3 = (-1)(x - 2)$$
$$y - 3 = -x + 2$$
$$y = -x + 5$$

Now try this

The curve C has equation $y = f(x)$, $x > 0$, where

$$\frac{dy}{dx} = \sqrt{x} + \frac{8}{x^2} - 5$$

Given that the point P (4, 11) lies on C, find the equation of the normal to C at point P, giving your answer in the form $ax + by + c = 0$ **(4 marks)**

You have been given $\dfrac{dy}{dx}$, so start by substituting the x-coordinate of P to find the gradient of the **tangent** at P. The **normal** will be perpendicular to this.

Integration

Integration is the OPPOSITE of differentiation. You can use this rule to integrate terms which are written in the form ax^n.

You INCREASE the power by I ...

... then DIVIDE by the NEW power.

This is the symbol for integration.

This rule DOESN'T work if the original power is −1

$$\int x^n dx = \frac{x^{n+1}}{n+1} + c, n \neq -1$$

You are integrating WITH RESPECT TO x.

You have to add the CONSTANT OF INTEGRATION.

To INTEGRATE a function, write each term in the form ax^n, then integrate one term at a time.

The constant of integration

When you DIFFERENTIATE, any CONSTANT TERMS disappear. So lots of functions have the same derivative.

$y = x^2 + 5$

$y = x^2$

$y = x^2 - 19$

Differentiate → $\frac{dy}{dx} = 2x$ **Integrate** → $y = x^2 + c$

When you integrate you don't know the constant. You write '+ c' at the end to show this. This is called INDEFINITE INTEGRATION.

Worked example

Find $\int(12x^3 + 6x - 15x^{\frac{2}{3}}) dx$, giving each term in its simplest form. **(5 marks)**

$\int\left(12x^3 + 6x - 15x^{\frac{2}{3}}\right) dx$

$= \frac{12x^4}{4} + \frac{6x^2}{2} - \frac{15x^{\frac{5}{3}}}{\left(\frac{5}{3}\right)} + c$

$= 3x^4 + 3x^2 - 9x^{\frac{5}{3}} + c$

Integrate term-by-term and don't forget to add the constant of integration.
For each term:
- increase the power by I
- divide by the **new** power.

$\frac{2}{3} + 1 = \frac{5}{3}$. Dividing by $\frac{5}{3}$ is the same as dividing by 5 then multiplying by 3.

Golden rules

1 Write every term in a polynomial in the form ax^n BEFORE integrating.

2 Remember to include the CONSTANT OF INTEGRATION.

3 Simplify any COEFFICIENTS if possible.

Worked example

Given that $y = \frac{1}{x^3} - 3x^5$, $x \neq 0$, find $\int y \, dx$ **(3 marks)**

$\int(x^{-3} - 3x^5) dx = \frac{x^{-2}}{-2} - \frac{3x^6}{6} + c$

$= -\frac{1}{2}x^{-2} - \frac{1}{2}x^6 + c$

Be careful with negative powers. For the first term, you have to **increase** the power of −3 by I to get −2, then divide by the **new power**, −2.

Now try this

1. Find $\int(1 - 3x^3) dx$ **(3 marks)**

2. Find $\int(3x + 1)^2 dx$ **(4 marks)**

3. Given that $y = 6x^2 + 5x\sqrt{x}$, $x > 0$, find $\int y \, dx$ **(3 marks)**

 Expand the brackets first.

Finding the constant

If you know ONE POINT on the original curve, or ONE VALUE of f(x), then you can calculate the constant of integration.

Using substitution

All three of these curves have the same gradient function:

$$\frac{dy}{dx} = 2x$$

But only one passes through the point $(2, -1)$. You can find its equation by integrating, then substituting $x = 2$ and $y = -1$ to find the value of c.

$$y = x^2 + c$$
$$-1 = 2^2 + c$$
$$c = -5$$
$$y = x^2 - 5$$

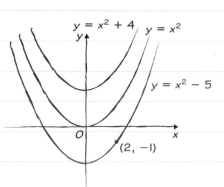

Worked example

$$\frac{dy}{dx} = 7 + \frac{1}{\sqrt{x}}, x > 0$$

Given that $y = 26$ at $x = 4$, find y in terms of x.   **(6 marks)**

$$\frac{dy}{dx} = 7 + x^{-\frac{1}{2}}$$

$$y = 7x + \frac{x^{\frac{1}{2}}}{\left(\frac{1}{2}\right)} + c$$

$$= 7x + 2x^{\frac{1}{2}} + c$$

$$26 = 7(4) + 2(4)^{\frac{1}{2}} + c$$

$$= 28 + 4 + c$$

$$c = -6$$

$$y = 7x + 2x^{\frac{1}{2}} - 6$$

Worked example

Given that $f(-1) = 9$ and $f'(x) = 6x^2 - 10x - 3$, find $f(x)$.   **(5 marks)**

$$f(x) = \frac{6x^3}{3} - \frac{10x^2}{2} - 3x + c$$

$$= 2x^3 - 5x^2 - 3x + c$$

$$f(-1) = 2(-1)^3 - 5(-1)^2 - 3(-1) + c$$

$$= -2 - 5 + 3 + c$$

$$= -4 + c$$

$$9 = -4 + c$$

$$c = 13$$

$$f(x) = 2x^3 - 5x^2 - 3x + 13$$

$f(-1) = 9$ is the same as saying that the curve with equation $y = f(x)$ passes through the point $(-1, 9)$.

Three key steps

1 Integrate, and remember to include the constant of integration.

2 Substitute the values of x and y you know and solve an equation to find c.

3 Write out the function including the constant of integration you've found.

Now try this

1. The curve C has equation $y = f(x)$, $x > 0$, and the point $(4, 17)$ lies on C.

   Given that $f'(x) = 3 - \dfrac{2 + 3\sqrt{x}}{x^2}$, find $f(x)$.   **(5 marks)**

2. $\dfrac{dy}{dx} = \dfrac{(x^2 + 5)^2}{x^2}$, $x \neq 0$

   (a) Show that $\dfrac{dy}{dx} = x^2 + 10 + 25x^{-2}$.   **(2 marks)**

   (b) Given that $y = -13$ at $x = 1$, find y in terms of x.   **(6 marks)**

You are the examiner!

CHECKING YOUR WORK is one of the key skills you will need for your C1 exam. All five of these students have made a key mistake in their working. Can you spot them all?

 1 Simplify $\dfrac{5 - 2\sqrt{3}}{\sqrt{3} - 1}$ giving your answer in the form $p + q\sqrt{3}$, where p and q are rational numbers. **(4 marks)**

$$\frac{5 - 2\sqrt{3}}{\sqrt{3} - 1} \times \frac{\sqrt{3} + 1}{\sqrt{3} + 1}$$

$$= \frac{5 - 2\sqrt{3}(\sqrt{3} + 1)}{(\sqrt{3})^2 - \sqrt{3} + \sqrt{3} - 1}$$

$$= \frac{5 - 6 - 2\sqrt{3}}{2}$$

$$= -\frac{1}{2} - \sqrt{3}$$

 2 The equation $x^2 + 3px + p = 0$, where p is a non-zero constant, has equal roots. Find the value of p. **(4 marks)**

$$b^2 - 4ac = 0$$
$$3p^2 - 4p = 0$$
$$p(3p - 4) = 0$$
$$\cancel{p = 0} \text{ or } \underline{p = \frac{4}{3}}$$

 3 Find the set of values of x for which
(a) $4x - 5 > 15 - x$ **(2 marks)**
(b) $x(x - 4) > 12$ **(4 marks)**

(a) $5x > 20$
   $x > 4$

(b) $x(x - 4) - 12 > 0$
   $x^2 - 4x - 12 > 0$
   $(x - 6)(x + 2) > 0$
   $x > 6$ or $x > -2$

 4 Find $\int(12x^5 - 8x^3 + 3)\,dx$, giving each term in its simplest form. **(4 marks)**

$$\int(12x^5 - 8x^3 + 3)\,dx = \frac{12x^6}{6} - \frac{8x^4}{4} + \frac{3x}{1}$$

$$= 2x^6 - 2x^4 + 3x$$

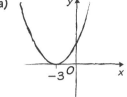 **5** On separate diagrams, sketch the graphs of
(a) $y = (x + 3)^2$ **(3 marks)**
(b) $y = (x + 3)^2 + k$ **(2 marks)**
Show on each sketch the coordinates of each point at which the graph meets the axes.

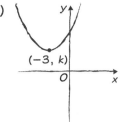

Checking your work

If you have any time left at the end of your exam, you should check back through your working.

☑ Check you have answered EVERY PART and given all the information asked for.

☑ Make sure you have given your answers in the CORRECT FORM.

☑ Double-check any numerical calculations, especially for SEQUENCES and SERIES.

☑ Make sure everything is EASY TO READ.

☑ Cross out any incorrect working with a SINGLE NEAT LINE and UNDERLINE the correct answer.

☑ Make sure any sketches are LABELLED.

Now try this

Find the mistake in each student answer on this page, and write out the correct working for each question. Turn over for the answers.

You are still the examiner!

BEFORE looking at this page, turn back to page 26 and try to spot the key mistake in each student's working. Use this page to CHECK your answers – the corrections are shown in red, and these answers are now 100% CORRECT.

 1 Simplify $\dfrac{5 - 2\sqrt{3}}{\sqrt{3} - 1}$ giving your answer in the form $p + q\sqrt{3}$, where p and q are rational numbers. **(4 marks)**

$$\dfrac{5 - 2\sqrt{3}}{\sqrt{3} - 1} \times \dfrac{\sqrt{3} + 1}{\sqrt{3} + 1}$$

$$= \dfrac{(5 - 2\sqrt{3})(\sqrt{3} + 1)}{(\sqrt{3})^2 - \sqrt{3} + \sqrt{3} - 1}$$

$$= \dfrac{5 - 6 - 2\sqrt{3}}{2} = \dfrac{3\sqrt{3} - 1}{2}$$

$$= -\dfrac{1}{2} - \sqrt{3} \qquad = -\dfrac{1}{2} + \dfrac{3}{2}\sqrt{3}$$

Top tip

Be really careful with your algebra. If you have to multiply a fraction by an expression, use brackets to make sure you multiply **every term**.

$(5 - 2\sqrt{3})(\sqrt{3} + 1) = 5\sqrt{3} - 2\sqrt{3}\sqrt{3} - 2\sqrt{3} + 5$
$\qquad\qquad\qquad = 3\sqrt{3} - 1$

Surds are covered on page 3.

 2 The equation $x^2 + 3px + p = 0$, where p is a non-zero constant, has equal roots. Find the value of p. **(4 marks)**

$b^2 - 4ac = 0$
$(3p)^2 - 4p = 0 \qquad\qquad 9p^2 - 4p = 0$
$\cancel{p(3p - 4) = 0} \qquad\qquad p(9p - 4) = 0$
$\cancel{p = 0}$ or $p = \dfrac{4}{3} \qquad \cancel{p = 0}$ or $p = \dfrac{4}{9}$

Top tip

Use **brackets** when you are substituting into any formula. And be especially careful when dealing with **squares**, **fractions** or **negative numbers**.

Look at page 5 for more on the discriminant.

Top tip

If you're doing **indefinite** integration you'll lose a mark if you forget the **constant of integration**.

For a reminder about integration, look at page 24.

 3 Find the set of values of x for which
(a) $4x - 5 > 15 - x$ **(2 marks)**
(b) $x(x - 4) > 12$ **(4 marks)**

(a) $5x > 20$
$\quad x > 4$

(b) $x(x - 4) - 12 > 0$
$\quad x^2 - 4x - 12 > 0$
$\quad (x + 6)(x - 2) > 0$
$\quad \cancel{x > -6 \text{ or } x > 2}$

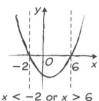

$x < -2$ or $x > 6$

 4 Find $\int(12x^5 - 8x^3 + 3)\,\mathrm{d}x$, giving each term in its simplest form. **(4 marks)**

$$\int(12x^5 - 8x^3 + 3)\,\mathrm{d}x = \dfrac{12x^6}{6} - \dfrac{8x^4}{4} + \dfrac{3x}{1} + c$$

$$= 2x^6 - 2x^4 + 3x + c$$

Top tip

If you are solving a quadratic inequality, always **draw a sketch** to identify the correct region.

There's more on quadratic inequalities on page 8.

5 On separate diagrams, sketch the graphs of
(a) $y = (x + 3)^2$ **(3 marks)**
(b) $y = (x + 3)^2 + k$ **(2 marks)**

Show on each sketch the coordinates of each point at which the graph meets the axes.

(a) 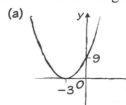 (b)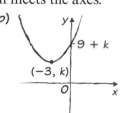

Top tip

Read the question carefully and make sure you are giving **all** the information asked for. When sketching a graph, you might have to label the points of intersection with **both** axes.

Sketching quadratics is covered on page 6, and transformations are covered on pages 10 and 11.

The factor theorem

In your C2 exam, you might need to use the factor theorem to help you FACTORISE POLYNOMIALS like these:

$f(x) = 2x^3 + 5x^2 - 15x + 10$

This is a CUBIC because the highest power of x is 3.

$f(x) = x^4 - 4x^3 + 2x^2 - 3$

This is a QUARTIC because the highest power of x is 4.

The factor theorem

If $f(x)$ is a polynomial and $f(p) = 0$, then $(x - p)$ is a FACTOR of $f(x)$.

✓ Only use this theorem with POLYNOMIALS.

✓ Watch out for the SIGN. If $f(-1) = 0$ then the factor would be $(x + 1)$.

✓ LEARN this rule – it's not in the formulae booklet.

Synthetic division with polynomials

If you have to COMPLETELY FACTORISE a CUBIC polynomial, you will usually need to find THREE LINEAR FACTORS. You can find the first one using the factor theorem. When you take this factor out, your other factor will be a QUADRATIC EXPRESSION. The safest way to find this is by using SYNTHETIC DIVISION.

To completely factorise $f(x) = 3x^3 - 17x^2 + 2x + 40$:

1. Use the factor theorem to find one factor: $f(5) = 0$, so $(x - 5)$ is a factor.
2. Use synthetic division to divide $3x^3 - 17x^2 + 2x + 40$ by $(x - 5)$:

To divide by $(x - p)$, write p here.

Write the coefficients of $f(x)$ on the top row.

```
5 | 3   -17    2    40
  |      15   -10  -40
  --------------------
    3    -2   -8    0
```

Write the coefficient of x^3 on the bottom row, then multiply by 5.

Add the result to the coefficient of x^2, and so on ...

These are the coefficients in the QUADRATIC factor. If $(x - p)$ is a factor of $f(x)$, this number will be zero.

3. The quadratic factor is $3x^2 - 2x - 8$. Factorise this to complete the factorisation.
4. So $3x^3 - 17x^2 + 2x + 40 = (x - 5)(3x^2 - 2x - 8) = (x - 5)(3x + 4)(x - 2)$.

Worked example

$f(x) = 2x^3 - x^2 - 15x + 18$

(a) Use the factor theorem to show that $(x + 3)$ is a factor of $f(x)$. **(2 marks)**

$f(-3) = 2(-3)^3 - (-3)^2 - 15(-3) + 18$
$\quad = -54 - 9 + 45 + 18 = 0$

So $(x + 3)$ is a factor.

(b) Factorise $f(x)$ completely. **(4 marks)**

Using synthetic division to divide $f(x)$ by $(x + 3)$:

```
-3 | 2    -1   -15   18
   |      -6    21  -18
   -------------------
     2    -7    6    0
```

So $\dfrac{2x^3 - x^2 - 15x + 18}{x + 3} = 2x^2 - 7x + 6$

$f(x) = (x + 3)(2x^2 - 7x + 6) = (x + 3)(2x - 3)(x - 2)$

Be careful with the sign (+ or –). The factor theorem says that $(x - p)$ is a factor if $f(p) = 0$, so you need to evaluate $f(-3)$. You need to write down that $(x + 3)$ is a factor at the end of your working.

You know that $(x + 3)$ is a factor, so divide $f(x)$ by $(x + 3)$ using **synthetic division**. You could check your answer by expanding the brackets:

$(x + 3)(2x^2 - 7x + 6)$

$= 2x^3 - 7x^2 + 6x + 6x^2 - 21x + 18$
$= 2x^3 - x^2 - 15x + 18$ ✓

You need to factorise $(2x^2 - 7x + 6)$ in the normal way. Look at page 2 for a reminder.

Now try this

1. (a) Use the factor theorem to show that $(x - 2)$ is a factor of $x^3 - 7x^2 - 14x + 48$ **(2 marks)**

   (b) Factorise $x^3 - 7x^2 - 14x + 48$ completely. **(4 marks)**

2. $f(x) = 2x^3 - 3x^2 - 65x - a$

   (a) Given that $(x + 4)$ is a factor of $f(x)$, find the value of a. **(3 marks)**

   (b) Factorise $f(x)$ completely. **(4 marks)**

The remainder theorem

If you DIVIDE a POLYNOMIAL by a LINEAR TERM which is NOT A FACTOR then there will be a remainder. You can use the remainder theorem to work out what that remainder will be.

Worked example

Find the remainder when $2x^3 + 5x^2 - 12x + 1$ is divided by

(i) $(x - 2)$ (ii) $(2x + 1)$ **(3 marks)**

(i) $f(2) = 2(2)^3 + 5(2)^2 - 12(2) + 1$

$= 16 + 20 - 24 + 1 = 13$

So remainder is 8.

(ii) $f\left(-\frac{1}{2}\right) = 2\left(-\frac{1}{2}\right)^3 + 5\left(-\frac{1}{2}\right)^2 - 12\left(-\frac{1}{2}\right) + 1$

$= -\frac{1}{4} + \frac{5}{4} + 6 + 1 = 8$

So remainder is 13.

The remainder theorem

If a polynomial f(x) is DIVIDED by ($ax - b$) then the REMAINDER will be $f\left(\frac{b}{a}\right)$.

✓ $x = \frac{b}{a}$ is the value of x which makes ($ax - b$) equal to ZERO. This is a useful way to remember the remainder theorem.

✓ Use the rule when dividing a POLYNOMIAL by a LINEAR EXPRESSION.

✓ The FACTOR THEOREM on page 28 is a special case of this theorem. If the remainder is 0, then ($ax - b$) is a FACTOR of f(x).

✓ LEARN this rule – it's not in the formula booklet.

(a) Using the remainder theorem, you know that f(-2) = 5. Work out f(-2) in terms of a and b and equate it to 5 to find the equation.

(b) Use the fact that f(1) = -1 to write a second equation involving a and b. You can solve your equations **simultaneously** to find the values of a and b.

Worked example

f(x) = $2x^3 + ax^2 + bx - 7$, where a and b are constants.

(a) Given that when f(x) is divided by ($x + 2$) the remainder is 5, show that $2a - b = 14$
     (2 marks)

$f(-2) = 2(-2)^3 + a(-2)^2 + b(-2) - 7$

$= -23 + 4a - 2b$

So $-23 + 4a - 2b = 5$

$4a - 2b = 28$

$2a - b = 14$ ①

(b) Given also that when f(x) is divided by ($x - 1$) the remainder is -1, find the values of a and b.   **(4 marks)**

$f(1) = 2(1)^3 + a(1)^2 + b(1) - 7 = a + b - 5$

So $a + b - 5 = -1$

$a + b = 4$ ②

① + ②: $3a = 18$

$a = 6$

From ②: $b = 4 - 6 = -2$

Golden rule

If a polynomial has TWO UNKNOWNS and you are given TWO REMAINDER FACTS then you will have to solve SIMULTANEOUS EQUATIONS to find the unknown coefficients.

Being given a FACTOR is like being given a remainder fact. If ($ax - b$) is a factor, then the remainder when f(x) is divided by ($ax - b$) is ZERO, so $f\left(\frac{b}{a}\right) = 0$.

Now try this

1. f(x) = $kx^3 + 2x^2 - 7x + 19$

When f(x) is divided by ($x + 3$) the remainder is 4

(a) Show that $k = 2$ **(3 marks)**

(b) Find the remainder when f(x) is divided by
(i) $(x - 2)$
(ii) $(2x + 5)$ **(3 marks)**

2. f(x) = $x^4 - 2x^3 + ax + b$, where a and b are constants.

When f(x) is divided by ($x + 1$) the remainder is -2

When f(x) is divided by ($x - 2$) the remainder is 4

Find the values of a and b.   **(7 marks)**

Equation of a circle

A circle with centre (a, b) and radius r has equation

$$(x - a)^2 + (x - b)^2 = r^2$$

Be really careful with the right-hand side. It is the radius SQUARED.

You need to LEARN this equation as it's not given in the formulae booklet.

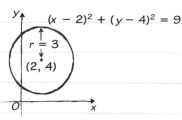
$(x - 2)^2 + (y - 4)^2 = 9$
$r = 3$
$(2, 4)$

Worked example

A circle C has centre $(3, 1)$ and passes through the point $(-2, 5)$.

(a) Find an equation for C.   **(4 marks)**

$r = \sqrt{(x_2 - x_1)^2 + (y_2 - y_1)^2}$

$\quad = \sqrt{(-2 - 3)^2 + (5 - 1)^2} = \sqrt{41}$

$(x - a)^2 + (y - b)^2 = r^2$
$(x - 3)^2 + (y - 1)^2 = 41$

(b) Verify that the point $(7, -4)$ also lies on C.
          (1 mark)

$(x - 3)^2 + (y - 1)^2 = (7 - 3)^2 + (-4 - 1)^2$

$\quad = 4^2 + (-5)^2 = 16 + 25 = 41$

So point $(7, -4)$ lies on C.

The radius of the circle, r, is the length of the line segment between $(3, 1)$ and $(-2, 5)$. For a reminder about finding the length of a line segment have a look at page 16.

EXAM ALERT!

Just because you **can** use a calculator in your C2 exam, it doesn't mean you always should! Don't write your radius as a decimal. If you leave it in the form $\sqrt{41}$ it will be exact when you square it to write your equation.

> Students have struggled with this topic in recent exams – be prepared!

(a) You need to rearrange the equation into the form $(x - a)^2 + (x - b)^2 = r^2$
This is a bit like **completing the square**. Have a look at page 4 for a recap.
$x^2 - 6x = (x - 3)^2 - 3^2$
$y^2 + 2y = (y + 1)^2 - 1^2$

Remember that the right-hand side of the equation is r^2, so the radius is 5, not 25.

(b) Substitute $x = 0$ into the equation to find the points where C crosses the y-axis.

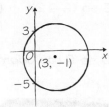
3
O $(3, -1)$
-5

Worked example

The circle C has equation $x^2 + y^2 - 6x + 2y - 15 = 0$

(a) Find the coordinates of the centre of C and the radius of C.   **(4 marks)**

$\quad\quad x^2 - 6x + y^2 + 2y - 15 = 0$
$(x - 3)^2 - 3^2 + (y + 1)^2 - 1^2 - 15 = 0$
$\quad\quad (x - 3)^2 + (y + 1)^2 - 25 = 0$
$\quad\quad\quad (x - 3)^2 + (y + 1)^2 = 5^2$

C has centre $(3, -1)$ and radius 5.

(b) Find the coordinates of the points where C crosses the y-axis.   **(2 marks)**

When $x = 0$, $(0 - 3)^2 + (y + 1)^2 = 25$

$\quad\quad\quad\quad (y + 1)^2 = 16$

$\quad\quad\quad\quad y + 1 = \pm 4$

$\quad\quad\quad\quad y = -5$ or 3

C crosses the y-axis at $(0, -5)$ and $(0, 3)$.

Now try this

$A(-6, 0)$ and $B(2, 4)$ are the endpoints of a diameter of the circle C. Find

(a) the length of AB **(2 marks)**

(b) the coordinates of the midpoint of AB **(2 marks)**

(c) an equation for the circle C.   **(2 marks)**

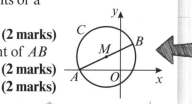
C B
M
A O x

You will need these two key **diameter** facts to solve this problem:

1. The **midpoint** of any diameter of a circle is the centre of the circle.

2. The diameter is **twice** the radius.

Have a look at page 15 for a reminder about midpoints.

Circle properties

You might need to solve circle problems involving SEMICIRCLES, TANGENTS and CHORDS.
Here are the three key facts you might need to use.

1 **Angles in a semicircle**

The angle in a semicircle is always a right angle.

2 **Chord and radius**

The angle between a TANGENT and a RADIUS is always a right angle.

3 **Perpendicular to a chord**

The PERPENDICULAR to a chord from the centre of the circle BISECTS that chord.

M is the midpoint of *VW*.

Worked example

The line *L*, with equation $x + 3y - 12 = 0$ is a tangent to the circle *C* with centre *A*. It touches the circle at the point *B*(4, 6).

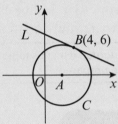

(a) Find an equation of the straight line through *A* and *B*. **(3 marks)**

$y = -\frac{1}{3}x + 4$ so *L* has gradient $-\frac{1}{3}$

So line through A and B has gradient 3.

$y - y_1 = m(x - x_1)$

$y - 6 = 3(x - 4)$

$y = 3x - 6$

(b) Given that *A* lies on the *x*-axis, find the coordinates of *A*. **(1 mark)**

At A, $y = 0$ so $0 = 3x - 6$ so $x = 2$

A has coordinates (2, 0).

Worked example

The circle *C* has equation $(x - 2)^2 + (y - 1)^2 = 25$
The points *P*(−1, 5) and *Q*(5, −3) lie on the circle.

(a) Show that *PQ* is a diameter of *C*. **(2 marks)**

Midpoint of $PQ = \left(\left(\frac{-1 + 5}{2}\right), \left(\frac{5 + (-3)}{2}\right)\right)$

$= (2, 1)$

which is the centre of *C*, so *PQ* is a diameter.

(b) The point *R* has coordinates (6, *a*), where $a > 0$ and the angle $PRQ = 90°$. Find the coordinates of *R*. **(4 marks)**

R lies on the circle because $\angle PRQ = 90°$.

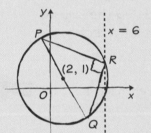

It can help to draw a sketch.

$x = 6$ so $(6 - 2)^2 + (y - 1)^2 = 25$

$(y - 1)^2 = 9$

$y = -2$ or 4

$a > 0$ so R has coordinates (6, 4).

A tangent is perpendicular to a radius, so the straight line through *A* and *B* is perpendicular to *L*. Remember that if a line has gradient *m*, then any line perpendicular to it will have gradient $-\frac{1}{m}$.

Look at page 15 for a recap.

Now try this

The circle *C* has centre (5, −2) and radius 10
(a) Write down an equation for *C*. **(2 marks)**
(b) Verify that the point (−1, 6) lies on *C*. **(1 mark)**
(c) Find an equation of the tangent to *C* at the point (−1, 6), giving your answer in the form $ax + by + c = 0$, where *a*, *b* and *c* are integers. **(4 marks)**

Geometric sequences

To get from one term to the next in a geometric sequence you multiply by the same number each time. You usually use a to represent the FIRST TERM and r to represent the COMMON RATIO. So the sequence is of the form a, ar, ar^2, ..., ar^{n-1}, ... Here are two examples.

1
$\overset{\times 2}{\frown}\ \overset{\times 2}{\frown}\ \overset{\times 2}{\frown}\ \overset{\times 2}{\frown}$
3,   6,   12,   24,   48 ...
$a = 3$, $r = 2$, nth term $= 3 \times 2^{n-1}$

2
$\overset{\times(-\frac{1}{2})}{\frown}\ \overset{\times(-\frac{1}{2})}{\frown}\ \overset{\times(-\frac{1}{2})}{\frown}\ \overset{\times(-\frac{1}{2})}{\frown}$
80,   −40,   20,   −10,   5 ...
$a = 80$, $r = -\frac{1}{2}$, nth term $= 80 \times \left(-\frac{1}{2}\right)^{n-1}$

General term

If a geometric sequence has first term a and common ratio r, then the nth term is

$$u_n = ar^{n-1}$$

This is how the formula will appear in the formulae booklet.

Worked example

The fifth term of a geometric sequence is 324 and the eighth term is 12

(a) Show that the common ratio is $\frac{1}{3}$ **(2 marks)**

$ar^4 = 324$ ①
$ar^7 = 12$ ②
② ÷ ①: $r^3 = \dfrac{1}{27}$
$r = \dfrac{1}{3}$

(b) Find the first term of the sequence.   **(2 marks)**

$a\left(\dfrac{1}{3}\right)^4 = 324$

$\dfrac{1}{81}a = 324$

$a = 26244$

To get from the fifth term to the eighth term you multiply by r three times, so in total you have multiplied by r^3:

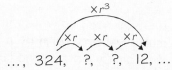

..., 324, ?, ?, 12, ...

Use the formula for the nth term to write two equations. Divide one equation by the other to eliminate a, then take the cube root of both sides to work out r. You can substitute your value of r into one of your equations to find the value of a.

In a **geometric** sequence the **ratio** between consecutive terms is constant. This gives you this useful relationship:

$$\frac{u_2}{u_1} = \frac{u_3}{u_2} = \frac{u_4}{u_3} = \ldots$$

Substituting $u_1 = 9$, $u_2 = k$ and $u_3 = (k + 4)$ into this relationship gives you a quadratic equation, which you can solve to find two possible values of k.

Worked example

The first three terms of a geometric sequence are 9, k and $(k + 4)$ respectively. Find the two possible values of k. **(5 marks)**

$$\frac{k}{9} = \frac{(k + 4)}{k}$$
$$k^2 = 9(k + 4)$$
$$k^2 - 9k - 36 = 0$$
$$(k - 12)(k + 3) = 0$$
$$k = 12 \text{ or } k = -3$$

Now try this

1. A geometric sequence has first term $a = 420$ and common ratio $r = \frac{5}{6}$
   Find the 20th term of the sequence. Give your answer to 3 significant figures. **(2 marks)**

   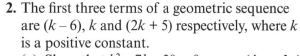
   In part (c), the common ratio will be $\dfrac{k}{k - 6}$

2. The first three terms of a geometric sequence are $(k - 6)$, k and $(2k + 5)$ respectively, where k is a positive constant.
   (a) Show that $k^2 - 7k - 30 = 0$ **(4 marks)**
   (b) Hence show that $k = 10$ **(2 marks)**
   (c) Write down the common ratio for this sequence. **(1 mark)**

Geometric series

In a series, the terms are ADDED TOGETHER. The terms in a geometric series have a COMMON RATIO. You write a for the FIRST TERM and r for the common ratio. Here are two examples.

①
$$\overset{\times 3}{\frown}\ \overset{\times 3}{\frown}\ \overset{\times 3}{\frown}\ \overset{\times 3}{\frown}$$
$$2 + 6 + 18 + 54 + 162 + \dots$$
$a = 2$ and $r = 3$
The sum of the first 5 terms is $S_5 = 242$.

②
$$\overset{\times\left(-\frac{1}{2}\right)}{\frown}\ \overset{\times\left(-\frac{1}{2}\right)}{\frown}\ \overset{\times\left(-\frac{1}{2}\right)}{\frown}$$
$$30 - 15 + 7.5 - 3.75 + \dots$$
$a = 30$ and $r = -\frac{1}{2}$. When r is negative, the terms ALTERNATE between $+$ and $-$. You can still use the formula to work out S_n:

$$S_4 = \frac{30\left[1 - \left(-\frac{1}{2}\right)^4\right]}{1 - \left(-\frac{1}{2}\right)} = 18.75$$

Sum to n terms

If a GEOMETRIC series has first term a and common ratio r, then the SUM of the first n terms is

$$S_n = \frac{a(1 - r^n)}{1 - r} \quad \text{or} \quad S_n = \frac{a(r^n - 1)}{r - 1}$$

You can use either of these versions. The first one appears in the formulae booklet. You also need to know its PROOF and this is NOT in the formulae booklet. Look at the Worked example below to see the proof in action.

Worked example

To prove this you need to write out S_n and then **multiply every term by r.** If you subtract rS_n from S_n most of the terms cancel:

$$a + \cancel{ar} + \cancel{ar^2} + \dots + \cancel{ar^{n-2}} - \cancel{ar^{n-1}}$$
$$- \cancel{ar} - \cancel{ar^2} - \dots - \cancel{ar^{n-2}} - \cancel{ar^{n-1}} - ar^n$$

You are left with $S_n - rS_n = a - ar^n$. You can factorise the left-hand side and divide by $(1 - r)$ to get S_n on its own.

A geometric series has first term a and common ratio r. Prove that the sum of the first n terms of the series, S_n, is $\dfrac{a(1 - r^n)}{1 - r}$ **(4 marks)**

$$S_n = a + ar + ar^2 + \dots + ar^{n-1} \quad ①$$
$$rS_n = ar + ar^2 + \dots + ar^{n-1} + ar^n \quad ②$$
$$① - ②: \quad S_n - rS_n = a - ar^n$$
$$S_n(1 - r) = a(1 - r^n)$$
$$S_n = \frac{a(1 - r^n)}{1 - r}$$

Worked example

Find $\displaystyle\sum_{k=1}^{10} 50(2^k)$ **(3 marks)**

$$\sum_{k=1}^{10} 50(2^k) = 100 + 200 + 400 + \dots + 51200$$

So $a = 100$ and $r = 2$

$$S_{10} = \frac{100(1 - 2^{10})}{1 - 2} = 102300$$

For a reminder about **sigma notation** have a look at page 18. It's a good idea to write out a few terms to check that you have the correct values for a and r. You can enter the calculation in one go on your calculator using the  and ▣ keys.

Now try this

You can't use the formula. Try to apply the technique in the first Worked example.

1. A geometric series has first term $a = 7$ and common difference $r = \frac{3}{2}$. Find the sum of the first 20 terms of the series, giving your answer to the nearest whole number. **(2 marks)**

2. In the geometric series $1 + 2 + 4 + 8 + \dots$ each term is twice the previous term. Prove that the sum of the first n terms of this series is $2^n - 1$ **(4 marks)**

Infinite series

This diagram shows the GEOMETRIC SERIES $1 + \frac{1}{2} + \frac{1}{4} + \ldots$ with first term 1 and common ratio $\frac{1}{2}$.

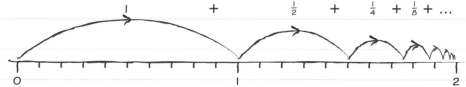

$$1 \qquad + \qquad \frac{1}{2} \qquad + \qquad \frac{1}{4} + \frac{1}{8} + \ldots$$

The sum gets closer and closer to 2, but never reaches it. You say that the SUM TO INFINITY of this series is 2. You write the sum to infinity as S_∞.

Sum to infinity

For a geometric series with first term a and common difference r, the sum to infinity is

$S_\infty = \dfrac{a}{1 - r}$ where $-1 < r < 1$.

In the example above, $a = 1$ and $r = \frac{1}{2}$,

so $S_\infty = \dfrac{1}{1 - \frac{1}{2}} = 2$

Convergent series

The sum to infinity of a geometric series ONLY EXISTS if the series is convergent. This only happens if the common ratio, r, is between -1 and 1.

In the formulae booklet this condition is written as $|r| < 1$.

Be careful – the inequalities are strict. Geometric series with $r > 1$, $r = 1$, $r < -1$ or $r = -1$ ARE NOT CONVERGENT, so S_∞ doesn't exist.

In the example above, $r = \frac{1}{2}$ so the series is convergent.

Worked example

Find the sum to infinity of the geometric series
$\frac{3}{5} + \frac{6}{15} + \frac{12}{45} + \ldots$ **(3 marks)**

$a = \dfrac{3}{5}$, $r = \dfrac{6}{15} \div \dfrac{3}{5} = \dfrac{2}{3}$

$S_\infty = \dfrac{\frac{3}{5}}{1 - \frac{2}{3}} = \dfrac{9}{5}$

> You need to find the values of a and r before you can use the formula for S_∞. a is the first term and r is the common ratio, so
> $r = \dfrac{u_2}{u_1} = \dfrac{6}{15} \div \dfrac{3}{5}$. You can check your value of r using u_2 and u_3:
> $\dfrac{u_3}{u_2} = \dfrac{12}{45} \div \dfrac{6}{15} = \dfrac{2}{3}$ ✓

Worked example

The first term of a geometric series is 80 and the sum to infinity is 50. Find the common ratio, r.   **(3 marks)**

$\dfrac{80}{1 - r} = 50$

$80 = 50(1 - r)$

$50r = -30$

$r = -\dfrac{3}{5}$

> Use the formula for S_∞ to write an equation and solve it to find r. Remember that r can be positive as well as negative. This is the convergent geometric series
>
> $80 - 48 + \dfrac{144}{5} - \dfrac{432}{25} + \ldots$
>
> which has sum to infinity $\dfrac{80}{1 - \left(-\frac{3}{5}\right)} = 50$

Now try this

1. Find the sum to infinity of the geometric series
$$15 + 12 + 9.6 + \ldots \qquad \textbf{(3 marks)}$$

2. The first term of a geometric series is 2 and the common ratio is k. The sum to infinity of the series is $3k + 4$, where k is a constant. Find the value of k.   **(5 marks)**

> Use the formula for S_∞ to write a quadratic equation involving k. Remember that in order for the sum to infinity to exist, k must be between -1 and 1.

Binomial expansion

The binomial expansion is a formula that lets you EXPAND BRACKETS easily. There are two versions of the binomial expansion given in the formulae booklet. This one is the most useful for your C2 exam:

$$(a + b)^n = a^n + \binom{n}{1} a^{n-1}b + \binom{n}{2} a^{n-2}b^2 + \ldots + \binom{n}{r} a^{n-r}b^r + \ldots + b^n \quad (n \in \mathbb{N})$$

where $\binom{n}{r} = {}^nC_r = \dfrac{n!}{r!(n-r)!}$ ——— This means n FACTORIAL. $n! = n \times (n-1) \times \ldots \times 3 \times 2 \times 1$

The expansion is valid as long as n is a POSITIVE INTEGER.

$\binom{n}{r}$ or ${}^nC_r$ means n CHOOSE r – use the [nCr] key on your calculator to work it out.

Worked example

Find the first 3 terms, in ascending powers of x, of the binomial expansion of $(2 - 3x)^6$. Give each term in its simplest form. **(4 marks)**

$a = 2, b = -3x$

$(a + b)^6 = a^6 + \binom{6}{1} a^5b + \binom{6}{2} a^4b^2 + \ldots$

$(2 - 3x)^6 = 2^6 + \binom{6}{1} \times 2^5 \times (-3x) + \binom{6}{2} \times 2^4 \times (-3x)^2 + \ldots$

$= 64 - 576x + 2160x^2 + \ldots$

EXAM ALERT!

Be careful if either a or b is negative. Always use brackets if you are substituting anything more complicated than a positive whole number.

Students have struggled with this topic in recent exams – be prepared!

$b = px$, so in the third term you need to square **all** of px.
$(px)^2 = p^2x^2$.

To work out $\binom{10}{2}$ or ${}^{10}C_2$ on your calculator,

type 10 [nCr] 2 [=].

Make sure you **simplify** each term as much as possible. Don't leave any powers of numbers or multiplication signs in your final answer.

You could also answer part (a) by using the expansion for $(1 + x)^n$ given in the formulae booklet. Replace n with 10, and x with px.

Worked example

(a) Find the first 3 terms, in ascending powers of x, of the binomial expansion of $(1 + px)^{10}$, where p is a non-zero constant. Give each term in its simplest form. **(2 marks)**

$a = 1, b = px$

$(a + b)^{10} = a^{10} + \binom{10}{1} a^9b + \binom{10}{2} a^8b^2 + \ldots$

$(1 + px)^{10} = 1^{10} + \binom{10}{1} \times 1^9 \times px + \binom{10}{2} \times 1^8 \times (px)^2 + \ldots$

$= 1 + 10px + 45p^2x^2 + \ldots$

(b) Given that the coefficient of x^2 is 9 times the coefficient of x, find the value of p. **(2 marks)**

$45p^2 = 9(10p)$ so $45p^2 - 90p = 0$

$45p(p - 2) = 0$

~~$p = 0$~~ $\underline{p = 2}$

Now try this

1. Find the first 4 terms, in ascending powers of x, of each of these binomial expansions, giving each term in its simplest form.

    (a) $(1 + 3x)^9$ **(3 marks)**

    (b) $(2 + 5x)^4$ **(4 marks)**

    (c) $(3 - x)^{12}$ **(4 marks)**

2. (a) Find the first 3 terms, in ascending powers of x, of the binomial expansion of $(2 + kx)^5$, where k is a constant. **(4 marks)**

    (b) Given that the coefficient of x is 48, find the value of k. **(2 marks)**

    (c) Write down the coefficient of x^2 **(1 mark)**

Solving binomial problems

You can use the binomial expansion to make APPROXIMATIONS or to solve harder problems.

Worked example

Find the coefficient of x^5 in the binomial expansion of $\left(6 - \dfrac{x}{3}\right)^9$ **(2 marks)**

$a = 6$, $b = -\dfrac{x}{3}$, $n = 9$ so x^r term $= \dbinom{n}{r}a^{n-r}b^r$

x^5 term $= \dbinom{9}{5} \times 6^4 \times \left(-\dfrac{x}{3}\right)^5$

$= 126 \times 1296 \times \left(-\dfrac{1}{243}\right)x^5$

$= -672x^5$

The coefficient of x^5 is -672.

You can use this part of the binomial expansion of $(a + b)^n$ in the formulae booklet to find the x^r term without finding every term up to it:

$$\ldots + \binom{n}{r}a^{n-r}b^r + \ldots$$

The x part of each term comes from $b = -\dfrac{x}{3}$, so use $r = 5$ to get the x^5 term. Be careful with the fraction part:

$$\left(-\dfrac{x}{3}\right) = \left(-\dfrac{1}{3}\right)^5 x^5$$

Binomial approximations

You can use a binomial expansion to ESTIMATE values. This is especially useful if x is SMALL. If x is less than 1, then LARGER POWERS of x get SMALLER. By ignoring large powers of x you can find a simple approximation. For example:

$(1 + x)^{100} \approx 1 + 100x + 4950x^2$

This means 'is approximately equal to'.

Write down the value of x you need to substitute. You can check your answer with a calculator. $1.05^6 = 1.340095\ldots$ ✓

Worked example

The first 4 terms of the binomial expansion of $\left(1 + \dfrac{x}{2}\right)^6$ are given below.

$\left(1 + \dfrac{x}{2}\right)^6 = 1 + 3x + \dfrac{15}{4}x^2 + \dfrac{5}{2}x^3 + \ldots$

Use the expansion to estimate the value of $(1.05)^6$ **(3 marks)**

If $x = 0.1$, then $\dfrac{x}{2} = 0.05$ and $\left(1 + \dfrac{x}{2}\right)^6 = (1.05)^6$

$(1.05)^6 \approx 1 + 3 \times (0.1) + \dfrac{15}{4} \times (0.1)^2 + \dfrac{5}{2} \times (0.1)^3 + \ldots$

$= 1 + 0.3 + 0.0375 + 0.0025 + \ldots$

$= 1.34$

Worked example

The first 4 terms of the binomial expansion of $(2 - x)^7$ are given below.

$(2 - x)^7 = 128 - 448x + 672x^2 + 560x^3 + \ldots$

If x is small, so that x^2 and higher powers can be ignored, show that $(1 + x)(2 - x)^7 \approx 128 - 320x$ **(2 marks)**

$(1 + x)(128 - 448x + \ldots)$

$= 128 + 128x - 448x - 448x^2 + \ldots$

$= 128 - 320x$ ignoring x^2 and higher powers

You are going to **ignore** x^2 and higher powers, so you only need to consider the first two terms of the expansion of $(2 - x)^7$. All the other terms would give you x^2 or higher terms when the brackets are multiplied out.

Now try this

1. In the binomial expansion of $(1 + 2x)^{30}$, the coefficients of x^3 and x^4 are p and q respectively.
   (a) Show that $p = 32\,480$ **(1 mark)**
   (b) Find the value of $\left(\dfrac{q}{p}\right)$ **(2 marks)**

2. (a) Find the first 4 terms, in ascending powers of x, of the binomial expansion of $\left(1 + \dfrac{x}{4}\right)^{12}$ **(4 marks)**
   (b) Use your expansion to estimate the value of $(1.025)^{12}$, giving your answer to 4 decimal places. **(3 marks)**

Radians, arcs and sectors

If you have to solve LENGTH or AREA problems involving circles and triangles in your C2 exam, any angles will usually be measured in RADIANS.

There are π radians in a semicircle, or 2π radians in a full turn.

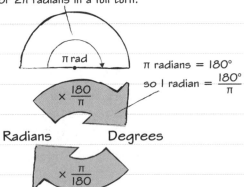

π rad

π radians = 180°

so 1 radian = $\frac{180°}{\pi}$

$\times \frac{180}{\pi}$

Radians   Degrees

$\times \frac{\pi}{180}$

Writing radians

Make sure you know whether you are working in RADIANS or DEGREES. These two angles are measured in radians.

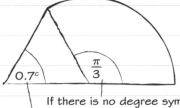

0.7ᶜ $\frac{\pi}{3}$

If there is no degree symbol then the angle is definitely in radians.

This means 0.7 radians. This angle could also be written as 0.7 rad.

Radians in length and area formulae

Radians are really useful for working out ARC LENGTHS and SECTOR AREAS. Here are two formulae that ONLY WORK if the angle θ is measured in RADIANS.

1 **Arc length $\ell = r\theta$**

This is the Greek letter θ. It is sometimes used to represent an unknown ANGLE.

2 **Sector area $A = \frac{1}{2}r^2\theta$**

NEITHER of these formulae is in the booklet, so make sure you LEARN them.

Worked example

The diagram shows ABC, a sector of a circle with centre A and radius 9 cm.

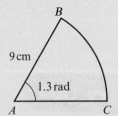

9 cm

1.3 rad

A C

B

Given that the size of $\angle BAC$ is 1.3 radians, find

(a) the length of the arc BC **(2 marks)**

$\ell = r\theta = 9 \times 1.3 = 11.7\,\text{cm}$

(b) the area of the sector ABC.   **(2 marks)**

$A = \frac{1}{2}r^2\theta = \frac{1}{2} \times 9^2 \times 1.3 = 52.65\,\text{cm}^2$

The angle, **θ**, is given in radians, so you can use the formulae for arc length and sector area given above.

EXAM ALERT!

Remember to **write out the formula** first. That way, you will get some credit even if you make a mistake when you're substituting your values.

Now try this

The diagram shows a sector OAB of a circle with radius 12 cm and centre O.
The length of the arc AB is 27 cm. Find

(a) the size of $\angle AOB$ in radians   **(2 marks)**

(b) the area of the sector.   **(2 marks)**

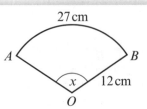

27 cm

A B

x 12 cm

O

Cosine rule

The cosine rule applies to ANY TRIANGLE. You usually use the cosine rule when you know TWO SIDES and the ANGLE BETWEEN THEM (SAS) or when you are given THREE SIDES and you want to work out an ANGLE (SSS).

1 $a^2 = b^2 + c^2 - 2bc\cos A$

This version is in the formulae booklet – use it to find a missing side.

2 $\cos A = \dfrac{b^2 + c^2 - a^2}{2bc}$

LEARN this version – it's useful for finding a missing angle.

Using a calculator

If you're using the sine rule or cosine rule you need to make sure that your CALCULATOR is in the correct mode (DEGREES or RADIANS).

This calculator is in radians mode.

$\sin^{-1}(0.5)$ $\dfrac{1}{6}\pi$ Your calculator might give angles in radians in terms of π.

On some calculators you need to press SHIFT and SETUP to change between degrees and radians mode.

Worked example

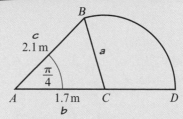

The diagram shows a triangle ABC and a sector BCD of a circle with centre C.
Find the length of BC. **(3 marks)**

$a^2 = b^2 + c^2 - 2bc\cos A$

$BC^2 = 1.7^2 + 2.1^2 - 2 \times 1.7 \times 2.1 \times \cos\dfrac{\pi}{4}$

$= 2.2512...$

$BC = 1.50\,\text{m (3 s.f.)}$

Everything in blue is part of the answer.

You know two sides and the angle between them (SAS) so you can use the cosine rule to find the opposite side. If the angle on the diagram is given in terms of π then it is in **radians**. Make sure your calculator is set to radians before working out $\cos\dfrac{\pi}{4}$.

Worked example

In the triangle ABC, $AB = 15$ cm, $BC = 9$ cm and $CA = 10$ cm. Find the size of angle C, giving your answer to the nearest degree. **(3 marks)**

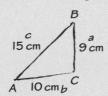

$\cos C = \dfrac{a^2 + b^2 - c^2}{2ab}$

$= \dfrac{9^2 + 10^2 - 15^2}{2 \times 9 \times 10} = -0.2444...$

$C = \cos^{-1}(-0.2444...) = 104°$

If no diagram is given in the question you can sketch one. You know three sides (SSS) so you can use the cosine rule to find any angle in the triangle. Be careful with the order. You add the squares of the sides **adjacent** to the angle, and subtract the square of the **opposite** side.

Now try this

The diagram shows two triangles PQR and PRS.
$\angle RSP = 0.8$ radians. Find

(a) the length of PR **(3 marks)**

(b) the size of $\angle PQR$, giving your answer in radians to 3 significant figures. **(3 marks)**

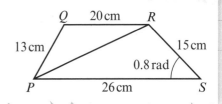

Sine rule

You need to LEARN the sine rule for your C2 exam. It applies to ANY TRIANGLE. The sine rule is useful when you know TWO ANGLES, or when you know a side and the OPPOSITE angle.

1 $\dfrac{a}{\sin A} = \dfrac{b}{\sin B} = \dfrac{c}{\sin C}$

This version is useful for finding a missing side.

2 $\dfrac{\sin A}{a} = \dfrac{\sin B}{b} = \dfrac{\sin C}{c}$

Use this version to find a missing angle.

Worked example

In the triangle PQR,
$PQ = 4$ cm,
$\angle PQR = 1.5$ radians and
$\angle QPR = 0.8$ radians.
Find the length of
the side PR.

(3 marks)

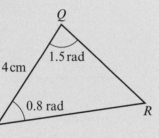

$\angle QRP = \pi - 1.5 - 0.8 = 0.8415\ldots$

$\dfrac{PR}{\sin(1.5)} = \dfrac{4}{\sin(0.8415\ldots)}$

$PR = \dfrac{4 \times \sin(1.5)}{\sin(0.8415\ldots)} = 5.35$ cm (3 s.f.)

Using radians

Most LENGTH and AREA problems in your C2 exam will use angles measured in RADIANS. Remember these key facts.

✓ Angles in a triangle add up to π radians.

✓ A right angle is $\dfrac{\pi}{2}$ radians.

There is more about measuring angles in radians on page 37.

The sine rule uses **opposite** sides and angles, so use the fact that the angles in a triangle add up to π radians (or 180°) to work out $\angle QRP$ first.

Two values

If you know $\sin x$, you might be asked to find TWO POSSIBLE VALUES for x. Use this rule for angles measured in RADIANS:

$$\sin x = \sin(\pi - x)$$

There is more about this on pages 42 and 44.

This sketch shows you why there are two possible values of x:

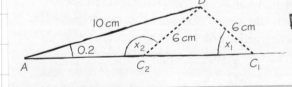

Worked example

In the triangle ABC, $AB = 10$ cm, $BC = 6$ cm, $\angle BAC = 0.2$ radians and $\angle ACB = x$ radians.

(a) Find the value of $\sin x$, giving your answer to 3 decimal places. **(3 marks)**

$\dfrac{\sin x}{10} = \dfrac{\sin(0.2)}{6}$

$\sin x = \dfrac{10 \times \sin(0.2)}{6} = 0.331$ (3 d.p.)

(b) Given that there are two possible values of x, find these values of x, correct to 2 decimal places. **(3 marks)**

$x_1 = \sin^{-1}(0.331) = 0.34$ radians (2 d.p.)
$x_2 = \pi - x_1 = \pi - 0.34 = 2.80$ radians (2 d.p.)

Now try this

In the triangle ABC, $BC = 13$ cm, $\angle ABC = \dfrac{\pi}{3}$ radians, and $\angle ACB = \dfrac{\pi}{5}$ radians. Find the length of AC. **(3 marks)**

Start by finding the size of $\angle CAB$.

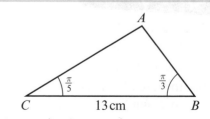

Areas of triangles

You can use this formula to find the area of ANY triangle if you know two sides and the angle between them (SAS):

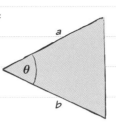

Area = $\frac{1}{2}ab\sin\theta$

This formula is not in the booklet so you need to LEARN it.

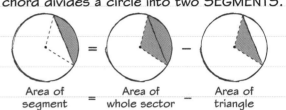

Areas of segments

A chord divides a circle into two SEGMENTS.

Area of segment = Area of whole sector − Area of triangle

Worked example

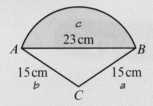

In the diagram CAB is a sector of a circle with centre C and radius 15 cm. The chord AB is 23 cm long.

(a) Find the size of $\angle ACB$, giving your answer in radians to 3 decimal places. **(3 marks)**

$\cos C = \dfrac{a^2 + b^2 - c^2}{2ab} = \dfrac{15^2 + 15^2 - 23^2}{2 \times 15 \times 15}$

$\qquad = -0.1755\ldots$

$C = \cos^{-1}(-0.1755\ldots) = 1.7472\ldots$

$\qquad\qquad\qquad = 1.747$ radians (3 d.p.)

(b) Calculate the area of the sector CAB, in cm², correct to 1 decimal place. **(2 marks)**

$A = \dfrac{1}{2}r^2\theta = \dfrac{1}{2} \times 15^2 \times 1.7472\ldots$

$\quad = 196.56\ldots = 196.6$ cm² (1 d.p.)

(c) Hence calculate the shaded area, in cm², correct to 1 decimal place. **(3 marks)**

Area of $\angle ABC = \dfrac{1}{2}ab\sin\theta$

$\qquad = \dfrac{1}{2} \times 15 \times 15 \times \sin(1.7472)$

$\qquad = 110.75\ldots = 110.8$ cm² (1 d.p.)

Shaded area $= 196.56\ldots - 110.75\ldots$

$\qquad\qquad = 85.8$ cm² (1 d.p.)

EXAM ALERT!

Don't try and learn a single formula for the area of a segment. You might get caught out with areas like these, which aren't segments:

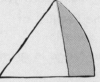

It's much safer and more useful to remember **how to work it out** using the formulae for the **area of a sector** and the **area of a triangle**.

> Students have struggled with this topic in recent exams – be prepared!

For a reminder about using the **cosine rule** to find a missing angle, look at page 38. To find the area of the shaded **segment**, subtract the area of the triangle from the area of the sector. You can revise areas of sectors on page 37.

BC and AD are parallel, so $\angle BCA = \angle CAD$. For part (b), work out $\angle ABC$ using the **sine rule**, then use the fact that the angles in a triangle add up to π radians to find $\angle BAC$. For a reminder about using the sine rule, look at page 39.

Now try this

The diagram shows the cross-section of a tent.
The lines BC and AD are parallel. ACD is a sector of a circle with centre A and radius 2.08 m. Find

(a) the area of the sector ACD in m² to 2 decimal places **(2 marks)**

(b) the size of $\angle BAC$ in radians, to 2 decimal places **(3 marks)**

(c) the area of the entire cross-section $ABCD$ of the tent, in m², to 2 decimal places. **(3 marks)**

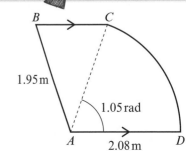

Trigonometric graphs

You need to be able to sketch the graphs of SIN, COS and TAN, and TRANSFORMATIONS of them. If you want to recap transformations of graphs from C1, have a look at pages 10 and 11.

$y = \sin x$ and $y = \cos x$

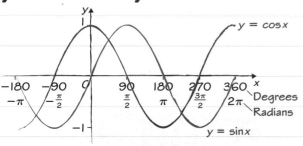

$y = \tan x$

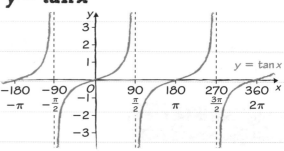

Sketching trig graphs

If you have to sketch a trigonometric graph in your C2 exam, make sure you:

- ✓ pay attention to the RANGE of values for x in the question
- ✓ use RADIANS if the range is given in radians
- ✓ label multiples of $\frac{\pi}{2}$ or 90° on the x-axis
- ✓ put a scale on the y-axis to show the MAX and MIN for $\sin x$ and $\cos x$
- ✓ draw the ASYMPTOTES for $\tan x$.

You can write $\cos \frac{\pi}{6}$ exactly as a surd. There is more about this on page 44. The graph of $y = \left(\cos x + \frac{\pi}{6}\right)$ is a **translation** of $y = \cos x$. The graph moves $\frac{\pi}{6}$ units to the **left**.

Worked example

(a) Sketch, for $0 \leqslant x \leqslant 2\pi$, the graph of
$$y = \cos\left(x + \frac{\pi}{6}\right)$$
(2 marks)

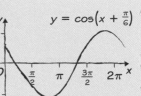

b) Write down the exact coordinates of the points where the graph meets the coordinate axes.
(3 marks)

When $x = 0$, $y = \cos \frac{\pi}{6} = \frac{\sqrt{3}}{2}$, so $\left(0, \frac{\sqrt{3}}{2}\right)$

When $y = 0$, $0 = \cos\left(x + \frac{\pi}{6}\right)$:

$\frac{\pi}{2} - \frac{\pi}{6} = \frac{\pi}{3}$, so $\left(\frac{\pi}{3}, 0\right)$

and $\frac{3\pi}{2} - \frac{\pi}{6} = \frac{4\pi}{3}$, so $\left(\frac{4\pi}{3}, 0\right)$

Worked example

The diagram shows a sketch of $y = \sin(ax - b)$, where $a > 0$ and $0 < b < 2\pi$.

Given that the curve cuts the x-axis at the points $P\left(\frac{6\pi}{5}, 0\right)$ and $Q\left(\frac{16\pi}{5}, 0\right)$, find a and b.
(4 marks)

$\sin\left(a\left(\frac{6\pi}{5}\right) - b\right) = 0$ and $\sin\left(a\left(\frac{16\pi}{5}\right) - b\right) = 0$

$a\left(\frac{6\pi}{5}\right) - b = 0$ ①

$a\left(\frac{16\pi}{5}\right) - b = \pi$ ②

② − ①: $2\pi a = \pi$ so $a = \frac{1}{2}$

Substituting into ①: $\frac{1}{2}\left(\frac{6\pi}{5}\right) - b = 0$ so $b = \frac{3\pi}{5}$

If $\sin(ax - b) = 0$, then $ax - b = 0$, or π, or 2π and so on. You can use these facts to write two equations and solve them **simultaneously** to find a and b.

Now try this

(a) On separate diagrams, sketch, for $0 \leqslant x \leqslant 2\pi$, the graphs of

  (i) $y = \sin(2x)$

  (ii) $y = \tan\left(x + \frac{\pi}{2}\right)$ **(4 marks)**

(b) Write down the coordinates of any points where the curves meet the coordinate axes and the equations of any asymptotes. **(6 marks)**

Trigonometric equations 1

You can solve an equation involving SIN, COS or TAN. You need to be really careful because these equations can have MULTIPLE SOLUTIONS. You will be given a RANGE (or INTERVAL) of values for x. This could be in DEGREES or RADIANS. You need to find values of x that are in that range.

Using graphs to find solutions

This graph shows the solutions to the equation $\cos x = -\frac{1}{2}$ in the range $-180° \leqslant x \leqslant 360°$.

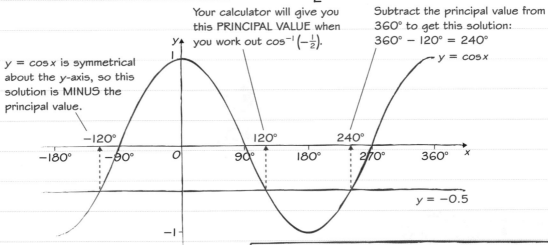

Your calculator will give you this PRINCIPAL VALUE when you work out $\cos^{-1}\left(-\frac{1}{2}\right)$.

Subtract the principal value from 360° to get this solution: $360° - 120° = 240°$

$y = \cos x$ is symmetrical about the y-axis, so this solution is MINUS the principal value.

$y = -0.5$

Worked example

Solve $3\tan x = 5$ in the interval $0 \leqslant x < 360°$. Give your answers to 1 decimal place.

(3 marks)

$\tan x = \dfrac{5}{3}$

$\tan^{-1}\left(\dfrac{5}{3}\right) = 59.036...°$

Work to 3 d.p. then round your **final** answer.

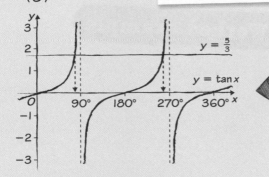

$180° + 59.036...° = 239.036...°$

$x = 59.0°, 239.0°$ (1 d.p.)

Using a CAST diagram

A CAST diagram tells you which trigonometric ratios are POSITIVE in which QUADRANT.

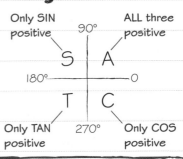

Only SIN positive — 90° — ALL three positive

S | A

180° ——— 0

T | C

Only TAN positive — 270° — Only COS positive

Use your calculator to find the **principal value** of x. You can find the other solution by sketching a graph or by drawing straight lines like this on a CAST diagram. You know that tan x is **positive**, so the other solution must be in the **third quadrant**.

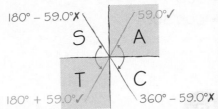

$180° - 59.0°$ ✗ $59.0°$ ✓

S | A

T | C

$180° + 59.0°$ ✓ $360° - 59.0°$ ✗

Tan x is ONLY positive for angles in the first and third quadrants. So you can REJECT the angles in the second and fourth quadrants.

Now try this

1. (a) Sketch the graph of $y = \sin x$ in the interval $0 \leqslant x < 360°$. **(2 marks)**

   (b) Find the values of x in the interval $0 \leqslant x \leqslant 360°$ for which $\sin x = -0.3$. Give your answers correct to 1 decimal place. **(3 marks)**

2. Solve, for $-\pi \leqslant \theta < \pi$, the equation

   (a) $3\cos \theta = 1$ **(3 marks)**

   (b) $\tan \theta + 2 = 0$ **(3 marks)**

   There will be **two solutions** to each equation. Find one using your calculator, then sketch the graph to find the other.

Trigonometric identities

You might need to use one of these two trigonometric identities to SIMPLIFY a trig equation before solving it. They are true for ALL VALUES of x or θ.

 $\tan \theta \equiv \dfrac{\sin \theta}{\cos \theta}$

$sin^2\theta$ means $(\sin\theta)^2$.

 $\sin^2\theta + \cos^2\theta \equiv 1$

Quadratic equations

If an equation involves $\sin^2\theta$ and $\sin\theta$ (or $\cos^2\theta$ and $\cos\theta$) then it is a quadratic. You can solve it by factorising:

$2\sin^2\theta - 3\sin\theta - 2 = 0$

$(2\sin\theta + 1)(\sin\theta - 2) = 0$

$\sin\theta = -\dfrac{1}{2} \qquad \sin\theta = 2$

No solutions exist to $\sin\theta = 2$, so you would only solve $\sin\theta = -\dfrac{1}{2}$.

Golden rules

When finding solutions to QUADRATIC TRIGONOMETRIC equations, remember these golden rules:

1 Write everything in terms of $\sin^2\theta$ and $\sin\theta$ (or $\cos^2\theta$ and $\cos\theta$).

2 Solutions to $\sin x = k$ and $\cos x = k$ ONLY EXIST if $-1 \leqslant k \leqslant 1$. Solutions to $\tan x = k$ exist for ANY VALUE of k.

Worked example

(a) Show that the equation $5\cos x = 1 + 2\sin^2 x$ can be written in the form
$2\cos^2 x + 5\cos x - 3 = 0$ **(2 marks)**

$5\cos x = 1 + 2\sin^2 x$

$5\cos x = 1 + 2(1 - \cos^2 x)$

$5\cos x = 1 + 2 - 2\cos^2 x$

$2\cos^2 x + 5\cos x - 3 = 0$

(b) Solve this equation for $0 \leqslant x < 360°$. **(3 marks)**

$(2\cos x - 1)(\cos x + 3) = 0$

$\cos x = \dfrac{1}{2} \qquad \cos x = -3$

$\cos^{-1}\left(\dfrac{1}{2}\right) = 60°$

$-60° + 360° = 300°$

$x = 60°, 300°$

You can use $\sin^2 x + \cos^2 x = 1$ to rewrite $\sin^2 x$ in terms of $\cos^2 x$:

$\sin^2 x = 1 - \cos^2 x$

You can then rearrange to get a quadratic equation in $\cos x$. You might find it easier to factorise if you write it as:

$2C^2 + 5C - 3 = 0 \rightarrow (2C - 1)(C + 3) = 0$

If $\cos x + 3 = 0$ then $\cos x = -3$, which has **no solutions**, so you can ignore the second factor.

Worked example

Given that $\sin\theta = 4\cos\theta$, find the value of $\tan\theta$. **(1 mark)**

$\dfrac{\sin\theta}{\cos\theta} = 4$ so $\tan\theta = 4$

Start by writing $\tan x$ as $\dfrac{\sin x}{\cos x}$

Now try this

1. Find all the solutions, in the interval $0 \leqslant x < 2\pi$, of the equation
$$3\cos^2 x - 9 = 11\sin x$$
giving each solution correct to 3 decimal places. **(6 marks)**

Use $\cos^2 x = 1 - \sin^2 x$ to get a quadratic equation in $\sin x$.

2. (a) Show that the equation $5\sin x = 2\tan x$ can be written in the form
$$\sin x(5\cos x - 2) = 0$$ **(2 marks)**

(b) Solve, for $0 \leqslant x < 360°$, $5\sin x = 2\tan x$ **(4 marks)**

Either $\sin x = 0$, or $5\cos x - 2 = 0$. Both these factors will give you solutions.

Trigonometric equations 2

You need to be careful if a trigonometric equation involves a FUNCTION of x or θ.

Worked example

Find the exact solutions of the equation
$$\cos(2\theta - 50°) = 0.5$$
in the interval $0 \leq \theta < 180°$.   **(4 marks)**

$0 \leq \theta < 180°$ so $-50° \leq 2\theta - 50° < 310°$

Let $Z = 2\theta - 50°$

$\cos Z = 0.5$, $-50° \leq Z < 310°$

So $Z = \cos^{-1}(0.5) = 60°$ in range ✓

or $Z = -60°$ not in range ✗

or $Z = 360° - 60° = 300°$ in range ✓

or $Z = 360° + 60° = 720°$ not in range ✗

So $2\theta - 50° = 60°$ or $300°$

So $\theta = 55°$ or $175°$

Transforming the range

The safest way to solve an equation involving sin, cos or tan of $(ax + b)$ is to TRANSFORM THE RANGE of values for x into a range of values for $(ax + b)$.

$$\times 2 \quad \overset{\displaystyle 0 \leq \theta < 180°}{\underset{\displaystyle 0 \leq 2\theta < 360°}{}} \quad \times 2$$

$$-50° \quad \searrow \quad \swarrow \quad -50°$$

$$-50° \leq 2\theta - 50° < 310°$$

If $Z = 2\theta - 50°$, you need to find all the values of Z such that $\cos Z = 0.5$ in the range $-50° \leq Z < 310°$. You can then find the corresponding value of θ for each solution.

The graph of $y = \sin(3x)$ is a horizontal stretch of the graph of $y = \sin x$ with scale factor $\frac{1}{3}$.

This sketch shows the solutions of the equation.

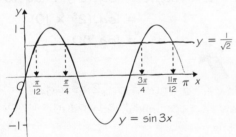

Make sure you remember to transform your solutions for $3x$ back into solutions for x at the end, and double check that they all lie within $0 \leq x < \pi$.

Worked example

Solve, for $0 \leq x < \pi$, the equation $\sin(3x) = \frac{1}{\sqrt{2}}$, giving your answers in terms of π.   **(6 marks)**

$0 \leq x < \pi$ so $0 \leq 3x < 3\pi$

Let $Z = 3x$

$\sin Z = \frac{1}{\sqrt{2}}$, $0 \leq Z < 3\pi$

So $Z = \sin^{-1}\left(\frac{1}{\sqrt{2}}\right) = \frac{\pi}{4}$ in range ✓

or $Z = \frac{\pi}{4} + 2\pi = \frac{9\pi}{4}$ in range ✓

or $Z = \frac{\pi}{4} + 4\pi = \frac{17\pi}{4}$ not in range ✗

or $Z = \pi - \frac{\pi}{4} = \frac{3\pi}{4}$ in range ✓

or $Z = \pi - \frac{\pi}{4} + 2\pi = \frac{11\pi}{4}$ in range ✓

or $Z = \pi - \frac{\pi}{4} + 4\pi = \frac{19\pi}{4}$ not in range ✗

So $3x = \frac{\pi}{4}$ or $\frac{9\pi}{4}$ or $\frac{3\pi}{4}$ or $\frac{11\pi}{4}$

So $x = \frac{\pi}{12}$ or $\frac{3\pi}{4}$ or $\frac{\pi}{4}$ or $\frac{11\pi}{12}$

Now try this

1. Solve, for $0 \leq x < 360°$

   (a) $\sin(x - 40°) = -\frac{1}{2}$ **(4 marks)**

   (b) $\cos(2x) = \frac{\sqrt{3}}{2}$ **(4 marks)**

2. Find the exact solutions of the equation
$$\cos\left(2x - \frac{\pi}{6}\right) = \frac{1}{2}$$
in the interval $0 \leq x < \pi$.   **(6 marks)**

Start by transforming the range:
$$0 \leq x < \pi$$
$$-\frac{\pi}{6} \leq 2x - \frac{\pi}{6} < \frac{11\pi}{6}$$

You need to give exact values so write them in terms of π. Your calculator should give you $\cos^{-1}\left(\frac{1}{2}\right) = \frac{\pi}{3}$.

Logarithms

Logarithms (or LOGS) are a way of writing facts about POWERS. These two statements mean the same thing:

You say 'log to the base a of b equals x'.

$$\log_a b = x \longleftrightarrow a^x = b$$

a is the BASE of the logarithm.

For example: $\log_3 9 = 2 \longleftrightarrow 3^2 = 9$

Remembering the order

The key to being confident in log questions is remembering the BASIC DEFINITION.
Start at the BASE, and work in a CIRCLE.

... to get b

$$\log_a b = x$$

Raise a to the power x...

Laws of logarithms

Learn these four key laws for manipulating expressions involving logs. These laws all work for logarithms with THE SAME BASE.

   $\log_a x + \log_a y = \log_a (xy)$

$\log_4 8 + \log_4 2 = \log_4 16 = 2$ (since $4^2 = 16$)

   $\log_a x - \log_a y = \log_a \left(\dfrac{x}{y}\right)$

$\log_9 18 - \log_9 6 = \log_9 3 = \frac{1}{2}$ (since $9^{\frac{1}{2}} = 3$)

   $\log_a \left(\dfrac{1}{x}\right) = -\log_a x$

$\log_8 \left(\dfrac{1}{2}\right) = -\log_8 2 = -\dfrac{1}{3}$

   $\log_a (x^n) = n \log_a x$

$\log_5 (25^3) = 3 \log_5 25 = 3 \times 2 = 6$

Worked example

Find

(a) the positive value of x such that

$\log_x 49 = 2$ **(2 marks)**

$x^2 = 49$

$x = 7$

(b) the value of y such that $\log_5 y = -2$ **(2 marks)**

$5^{-2} = y$

$y = \dfrac{1}{25}$

Write down the corresponding power fact. Remember:
$\log_a b = x \longleftrightarrow a^x = b$

Worked example

Express $3 \log_a 2 + \log_a 10$ as a single logarithm to base a.   **(3 marks)**

$3 \log_a 2 + \log_a 10 = \log_a (2^3) + \log_a 10$

$\qquad\qquad\qquad\quad = \log_a (2^3 \times 10)$

$\qquad\qquad\qquad\quad = \log_a 80$

Use law 4 to write $3 \log_a 2$ as $\log_a (2^3)$, then use law 1 to combine the two logarithms.

Changing the base

You can change the base of a logarithm using this formula:

$$\log_a x = \frac{\log_b x}{\log_b a}$$

For example: $\log_9 27 = \dfrac{\log_3 27}{\log_3 9} = \dfrac{3}{2}$

Now try this

1. Find

   (a) the value of y such that $\log_3 y = -1$ **(2 marks)**

   (b) the value of p such that $\log_p 8 = 3$ **(2 marks)**

   (c) the value of $\log_4 8$ **(2 marks)**

Use the change of base formula to write $\log_a b$ in terms of logs to the base b.

2. Express as a single logarithm to base a

   (a) $2 \log_a 5$ **(2 marks)**

   (b) $\log_a 2 + \log_a 9$ **(2 marks)**

   (c) $3 \log_a 4 - \log_a 8$ **(3 marks)**

3. Show that for all positive values of a and b,

   $(\log_a b)(\log_b a) = 1$ **(2 marks)**

Equations with logs

If you see an equation involving LOGARITHMS in your C2 exam, you will probably need to rearrange it using the LAWS OF LOGARITHMS, which are covered on page 45.

Two steps to solving log equations

Follow these two steps to solve most log equations in your C2 exam:

 Group the log terms on one side, then use the laws of logs on page 45 to write them as a SINGLE LOGARITHM.

 Rewrite $\log_a f(x) = k$ as $f(x) = a^k$ and solve the equation to find x.

Undefined logs

The value $\log_a b$ is ONLY DEFINED for $b > 0$. You can't calculate $\log_a 0$ or the log of any negative number. If an equation contains $\log_a x$ or $\log_a kx$ then IGNORE any solutions where $x \leq 0$.

If there are solutions to ignore in an exam question, you will usually be given a RANGE of possible values for x.

Worked example

Solve the equation $2\log_5 x - \log_5 3x = 2$ **(4 marks)**

$\log_5 x^2 - \log_5 3x = 2$

$\log_5 \left(\dfrac{x^2}{3x}\right) = 2$

$\dfrac{x^2}{3x} = 5^2 = 25$

$x^2 = 75x$

$x^2 - 75x = 0$

$x(x - 75) = 0$ so $\cancel{x = 0}$ or $\underline{x = 75}$

Follow the two steps given above:

1. Rearrange the left-hand side into a single logarithm.

2. Write the corresponding power fact:
$\log_5 f(x) = 2 \rightarrow f(x) = 5^2$

You need to solve two **simultaneous equations**. You can ignore the negative square root because p and q are positive.

Worked example

Given that $0 < x < 2$ and $\log_3 (2 - x) - 2\log_3 x = 1$, find the value of x.   **(6 marks)**

$\log_3 (2 - x) - \log_3 (x^2) = 1$

$\log_3 \left(\dfrac{2 - x}{x^2}\right) = 1$

$\dfrac{2 - x}{x^2} = 3$

$2 - x = 3x^2$

$3x^2 + x - 2 = 0$

$(3x - 2)(x + 1) = 0$

$x = \dfrac{2}{3}$ $x = \cancel{-1}$

Ignore this solution because $0 < x < 2$.

Worked example

p and q are positive constants, with
$$p = 5q \quad \text{①}$$
$$\log_5 p + \log_5 q = 2 \quad \text{②}$$
Find the exact values of p and q.   **(6 marks)**

From ②: $\log_5 (pq) = 2$

Substituting ①: $\log_5 (5q^2) = 2$

$5q^2 = 5^2 = 25$

$q^2 = 5$

$q = \sqrt{5}$

Substituting into ①: $p = 5\sqrt{5}$

Now try this

1. Solve $\log_2 (x + 1) - \log_2 x = \log_2 5$ **(3 marks)**

2. Solve the equation $\log_6 (x - 1) + \log_6 x = 1$ **(4 marks)**

3. Solve $\log_3 (x - 1) = -1$ **(2 marks)**

4. Find the values of x such that
$2\log_4 x - \log_4 (x - 3) = 2$ **(5 marks)**

Exponential equations

You can find unknown powers in equations using the log functions on your CALCULATOR. Make sure you WRITE DOWN any logarithms you are working out.

 If your calculator has this key, you can work out logs to any base.

 This key means $\log_{10}$. You can TAKE LOGS of both sides of an equation and solve it using this key.

Worked example

(a) Solve the equation $4^x = 13$, giving your answer to 3 significant figures. **(3 marks)**

$x = \log_4 13 = 1.85$ (3 s.f.)

(b) Find, to 3 significant figures, the value of y for which $5^y = 4$ **(3 marks)**

$\log(5^y) = \log 4$

$y \log 5 = \log 4$

$y = \dfrac{\log 4}{\log 5} = 0.861$ (3 s.f.)

Make sure you **write down** the logarithm you need to find even if you are working it out on your calculator in one go. Part (a) shows a method using the [log■] key. Part (b) shows a method by **taking logs** of both sides and using the laws of logs. This works for any base, so you can use the [log] key on your calculator.

Use the fact that $5^{2x} = (5^x)^2$ to write a **quadratic equation** in 5^x. For a reminder on the **laws of indices** have a look at page 1. It might help to write the equation as $Y^2 - 3Y + 2 = 0$, with $Y = 5^x$.

Factorising gives you two values for 5^x. Each of these gives you a value for x. Remember that $\log_a 1 = 0$ for any base, so $\log_5 1 = 0$.

Worked example

Solve the equation
$$5^{2x} - 3(5^x) + 2 = 0$$
giving your answers to 2 decimal places where appropriate. **(6 marks)**

$(5^x)^2 - 3(5^x) + 2 = 0$

$(5^x - 2)(5^x - 1) = 0$

$5^x = 2$ $5^x = 1$

$x = \log_5 2 = 0.43$ (2 d.p.) $x = \log_5 1 = 0$

Exponential graphs

You need to be able to sketch the graph of $y = a^x$.
You can only sketch this graph if a is a POSITIVE number.

✓ Passes through (0, 1).
✓ $y = 0$ is an ASYMPTOTE.
✓ If $a > 1$ graph curves UPWARDS.
✓ If $0 < a < 1$ graph curves DOWNWARDS.

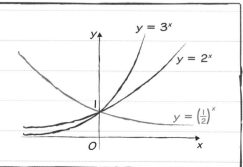

Now try this

1. Find, to 3 significant figures
   (a) the value of b for which $2^b = 15$ **(3 marks)**
   (b) the value of x for which $6^x = 0.4$ **(3 marks)**

2. (a) Solve the equation $3^{2x} + 3^x = 6$, giving your answer to 2 decimal places. **(6 marks)**
   (b) Explain why there is only one solution to the equation $3^{2x} + 3^x = 6$ **(1 mark)**

3. Sketch the graph of $y = 6^x, x \in \mathbb{R}$, showing the coordinates of any points at which the graph crosses the coordinate axes. **(2 marks)**

$x \in \mathbb{R}$ means for all real values of x. That means **all** the positive and negative numbers and zero.

Series and logs

You can use LOGARITHMS to answer questions about GEOMETRIC SEQUENCES and SERIES. If you need a reminder on geometric series, look at pages 32 and 33. For more on logs, look at page 45.

Modelling with geometric sequences

A car costs £16 000 new and depreciates in value by 20% each year. Its value each year produces a geometric sequence with first term $a = 16\,000$, and common ratio $r = 0.8$, or $\dfrac{4}{5}$

You can use LOGS to work out how many years it takes until the car is worth less than £4000. After n years the car is worth $16\,000 \times (0.8)^{n-1}$. You need this value to be less than £4000, so

$16\,000 \times (0.8)^{n-1} < 4000$

$(0.8)^{n-1} < 0.25$ — Don't try to write $\log_{0.8} 0.25 < n-1$ and use the $\boxed{\log_\square \square}$ key on your calculator – it's safer to TAKE LOGS of both sides.

$\log (0.8)^{n-1} < \log 0.25$

$(n-1)\log 0.8 < \log 0.25$

$n - 1 > \dfrac{\log 0.25}{\log 0.8}$ — $\log 0.8$ is NEGATIVE so when you divide both sides by $\log 0.8$ you have to REVERSE the inequality.

$n > 7.212\ldots$ — n must be a whole number, so the answer is $n = 8$.

Worked example

A geometric series has first term 5 and common ratio $\frac{3}{2}$. Find the smallest value of n for which the sum of the first n terms of the series exceeds 12 000 **(4 marks)**

$a = 5,\ r = 1.5,\ S_n = \dfrac{a(1 - r^n)}{1 - r}$

$\dfrac{5(1 - 1.5^n)}{1 - 1.5} > 12000$

$5(1 - 1.5^n) < -6000$

$1 - 1.5^n < -1200$

$1.5^n > 1201$

$\log (1.5^n) > \log 1201$

$n\log 1.5 > \log 1201$

$n > \dfrac{\log 1201}{\log 1.5} = 17.488$

$n = 18$

EXAM ALERT!

Be really careful with **inequalities**.
- If you multiply or divide by a negative number, change the direction of the inequality sign.
- If $a < 1$ then $\log a$ is **negative**.
- Check that your answer makes sense. You're usually looking for the next integer **greater than** the value you calculate.
- Double-check whether you should be using the formula for the **nth term**, ar^{n-1}, or the formula for the **sum to n terms**, $\dfrac{a(1 - r^n)}{1 - r}$

Students have struggled with this topic in recent exams – be prepared!

Now try this

1. A biologist models the number of trout after n years as $200 \times (1.4)^{n-1}$. Her model predicts that after k years, the number of trout in the lake will exceed 600

   (a) Show that $k > \dfrac{\log 3}{\log 1.4} + 1$ **(2 marks)**

   (b) Find the smallest possible value of k. **(2 marks)**

2. A geometric series has first term 4 and common ratio $\frac{9}{10}$. Find the smallest value of n for which the sum of the first n terms of the series exceeds 30 **(4 marks)**

Stationary points 1

You can use CALCULUS to find the stationary points of a GRAPH or FUNCTION in your C2 exam.
You need to be confident with DIFFERENTIATION – have a look at pages 21 and 22 for a reminder.

Using differentiation

The stationary points of a graph or function are the points where the DERIVATIVE, $\frac{dy}{dx}$ or f'(x), is equal to ZERO.

This graph has stationary points at P and Q. The slope of the curve is 0 at both points.

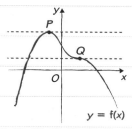

$y = f(x)$

Worked example

Find the coordinates of the stationary point on the curve with equation $y = 3x^2 + 12x + 5$

(4 marks)

$$\frac{dy}{dx} = 6x + 12$$

When $\frac{dy}{dx} = 0$, $6x + 12 = 0$

$$6x = -12$$

$$x = -2$$

So $y = 3 \times (-2)^2 + 12 \times (-2) + 5 = -7$

Stationary point is $(-2, -7)$.

To find the coordinates of the stationary point using calculus:

1. Differentiate to find $\frac{dy}{dx}$.
2. Set $\frac{dy}{dx} = 0$.
3. Solve the equation to find the value or values of x.
4. Find the corresponding value of y for each value of x.

Worked example

The diagram shows part of the curve with equation $y = 3x + \dfrac{12}{x^2} - 15$

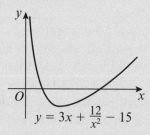

$y = 3x + \dfrac{12}{x^2} - 15$

Use calculus to show that y is increasing for $x > 2$

(4 marks)

$y = 3x + 12x^{-2} - 15$

$\dfrac{dy}{dx} = 3 - 24x^{-3} = 3 - \dfrac{24}{x^3}$

If $x > 2$ then $x^3 > 8$ and $\dfrac{24}{x^3} < 3$

So $3 - \dfrac{24}{x^3} > 0$

So if $x > 2$, $\dfrac{dy}{dx} > 0$ therefore y is increasing.

Increasing and decreasing functions

You can use the derivative to decide if a function is increasing or decreasing in a given interval:

☑ If f'(x) > 0 for $a < x < b$ then f(x) is INCREASING in the interval $a < x < b$.

☑ If f'(x) < 0 for $a < x < b$ then f(x) is DECREASING in the interval $a < x < b$.

The sign of f'(x) (+ or –) must be the same in the whole interval, otherwise the function is neither decreasing nor increasing.

Now try this

1. Find the coordinates of the stationary point on the curve C with equation $y = x^2 - 8x + 3$
(4 marks)

2. Use calculus to find the x-coordinates of the stationary points on the curve with equation $y = x^3 - 5x^2 + 8x + 1$ **(4 marks)**

You need to show that the **derivative** is **positive** for all values of x in the range given.

There are two stationary points. Differentiate, then solve a quadratic equation by factorising.

Stationary points 2

There are different types of stationary points on graphs. You need to be able to decide on the NATURE of a particular point. You can do this by finding the value of the SECOND DERIVATIVE, $\dfrac{d^2y}{dx^2}$ or $f''(x)$ at that point.

Maximum or minimum?

 If $\dfrac{dy}{dx} = 0$ and $\dfrac{d^2y}{dx^2} < 0$ then the stationary point is a MAXIMUM.

At P, $\dfrac{dy}{dx} = 3 \times (-2)^2 - 12 = 0$ and $\dfrac{d^2y}{dx^2} = 6 \times (-2) = -12 < 0$ so P is a MAXIMUM.

 If $\dfrac{dy}{dx} = 0$ and $\dfrac{d^2y}{dx^2} > 0$ then the stationary point is a MINIMUM.

At Q, $\dfrac{dy}{dx} = 3 \times (2)^2 - 12 = 0$ and $\dfrac{d^2y}{dx^2} = 6 \times (2) = 12 > 0$ so Q is a MINIMUM.

$\dfrac{dy}{dx} = 3x^2 - 12 \qquad \dfrac{d^2y}{dx^2} = 6x$

For a reminder about finding $\dfrac{d^2y}{dx^2}$ have a look at page 22.

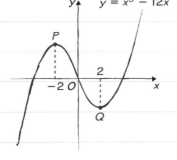

Worked example

The curve C has equation $y = 12\sqrt{x} - 2x$, $x > 0$

(a) Use calculus to find the coordinates of the turning point of C. **(4 marks)**

$y = 12x^{\frac{1}{2}} - 2x$

$\dfrac{dy}{dx} = 6x^{-\frac{1}{2}} - 2 = \dfrac{6}{\sqrt{x}} - 2$

When $\dfrac{dy}{dx} = 0$, $\dfrac{6}{\sqrt{x}} - 2 = 0$

$\qquad\qquad 6 = 2\sqrt{x}$

$\qquad\qquad x = 9$

So $y = 12\sqrt{9} - 2 \times 9 = 18$

Turning point is $(9, 18)$.

(b) Find $\dfrac{d^2y}{dx^2}$ **(2 marks)**

$\dfrac{d^2y}{dx^2} = -3x^{-\frac{3}{2}}$

(c) State the nature of the turning point. **(1 mark)**

At turning point, $x = 9$, so $\dfrac{d^2y}{dx^2} = -3 \times 9^{-\frac{3}{2}}$

$\qquad\qquad\qquad = -\dfrac{1}{9}$

$\dfrac{d^2y}{dx^2} < 0$ so the turning point is a maximum.

Points of inflexion

A stationary point that is neither a minimum nor a maximum is called a point of inflexion. The curve $y = x^3$ has a point of inflexion at $x = 0$.

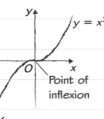

If $\dfrac{dy}{dx} = \dfrac{d^2y}{dx^2} = 0$ AND $\dfrac{d^3y}{dx^3}$ is NOT ZERO at a point P, then P is a point of inflexion.

You can find $\dfrac{d^3y}{dx^3}$ by differentiating $\dfrac{d^2y}{dx^2}$ again with respect to x.

A turning point is a stationary point which is a **local maximum** or a **local minimum**.

For part (c), work out the value of $\dfrac{d^2y}{dx^2}$ when $x = 9$. Write down whether it is greater or less than 0 and state whether the turning point is a maximum or a minimum.

Now try this

The diagram shows a sketch of the curve with equation $y = 5x^2 - 3x - x^3$

The curve has stationary points at A and B.

(a) Use calculus to find the coordinates of A and B. **(6 marks)**

(b) Find the value of $\dfrac{d^2y}{dx^2}$ at B, and hence verify that B is a maximum. **(2 marks)**

Max and min problems

You can use CALCULUS to solve real-life problems involving maximums and minimums.

Worked example

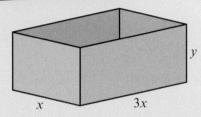

A cardboard box is made in the shape of an open-topped cuboid, with volume $18\,000\,\text{cm}^3$. The base of the cuboid has width $x\,\text{cm}$ and length $3x\,\text{cm}$. The height of the cuboid is $y\,\text{cm}$.

(a) Show that the area, $A\,\text{cm}^2$, of cardboard needed to make the box is given by

$$A = 3x^2 + \frac{48\,000}{x}$$ **(4 marks)**

Volume $= 3x^2 y = 18000$

$y = \dfrac{6000}{x^2}$

$A = 3x^2 + 2 \times xy + 2 \times 3xy$

$\quad = 3x^2 + 8xy$

$\quad = 3x^2 + 8x\left(\dfrac{6000}{x^2}\right)$

$\quad = 3x^2 + \dfrac{48000}{x}$

(b) Use calculus to find the value of x for which A is stationary. **(4 marks)**

$\dfrac{dA}{dx} = 6x - \dfrac{48000}{x^2}$

When $\dfrac{dA}{dx} = 0$, $6x - \dfrac{48000}{x^2} = 0$

$\qquad\qquad 6x^3 = 48000$

$\qquad\qquad x^3 = 8000$

$\qquad\qquad x = 20$

(c) Show that A is a minimum at this point. **(2 marks)**

$\dfrac{d^2A}{dx^2} = 6 + \dfrac{96000}{x^3}$

When $x = 20$, $\dfrac{d^2A}{dx^2} = 6 + \dfrac{96000}{20^3} = 18 > 0$

So A is a minimum.

(d) Calculate the value of A at this point. **(2 marks)**

$A = 3x^2 + \dfrac{48000}{x} = 3 \times (20)^3 + \dfrac{48000}{20}$

$\qquad = 26400$

This is the least area of carboard needed to make the box.

(a) Use the information given about the volume of the cuboid to write y in terms of x. Then write A in terms of x and y, and substitute your first expression to get A in terms of **x only.**

(b) Because A is a function of x only, you can **differentiate with respect to x** to find $\dfrac{dA}{dx}$. You can find the stationary (or turning) point of A by setting this equal to 0 and solving to find x.

(c) You need to find $\dfrac{d^2A}{dx^2}$ to determine the **nature** of the stationary point. For a reminder about this have a look at page 50.

Now try this

1. An oil well produces x barrels of oil each day. It models its profit, $£P$ each day, using the formula $P = 80x - \dfrac{x^2}{50}$

   (a) Find $\dfrac{dP}{dx}$ **(2 marks)**

   (b) Hence show that P has a stationary point at $x = 2000$ and use calculus to determine the nature of that stationary point. **(4 marks)**

2. The diagram shows a container in the shape of an open-topped cylinder, with height $x\,$m and radius $r\,$m. The cylinder has a capacity of $100\,\text{m}^3$.

   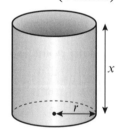

   (a) Show that the area of sheet metal, $A\,\text{m}^2$, needed to make the tank is given by $A = \pi r^2 + \dfrac{200}{r}$ **(4 marks)**

   (b) Use calculus to find the value of r for which A is stationary. **(4 marks)**

   (c) Prove that this value of r gives a minimum value of A. **(2 marks)**

   (d) Hence calculate the minimum area of sheet metal needed to make the tank. **(2 marks)**

For part (a), start by writing x in terms of r. When you differentiate, remember that π is a **constant**. For a reminder about differentiating with constants look at page 21.

Definite integration

In your C2 exam, you might have to find an integral with LIMITS. This is called definite integration. You should make sure you are confident with INDEFINITE INTEGRATION before revising this – check page 24 for a reminder.

Evaluating a definite integral

A definite integral has a NUMERICAL ANSWER.

Integrate $(6x + 1)$ in the normal way and write the integral in SQUARE BRACKETS. You can IGNORE the constant of integration.

UPPER LIMIT of the integral

Write the limits next to the square brackets.

$$\int_2^5 (6x + 1)\,dx = [3x^2 + x]_2^5$$

LOWER LIMIT of the integral

$$= (3 \times 5^2 + 5) - (3 \times 2^2 + 2)$$

$$= 80 - 14$$

$$= 66$$

EVALUATE the integral at the UPPER LIMIT...

... and SUBTRACT the value of the integral at the LOWER LIMIT.

Worked example

Use calculus to find the value of

$$\int_1^9 (2x + 6\sqrt{x})\,dx \qquad \text{(5 marks)}$$

$$\int_1^9 \left(2x + 6x^{\frac{1}{2}}\right)dx = \left[x^2 + 4x^{\frac{3}{2}}\right]_1^9$$

$$= \left(9^2 + 4 \times 9^{\frac{3}{2}}\right) - \left(1^2 + 4 \times 1^{\frac{3}{2}}\right)$$

$$= 189 - 5$$

$$= 184$$

If you are using calculus to do definite integration you will usually need to give an exact answer. If your answer isn't a whole number or a fraction, write it in simplified surd form.

$$2\sqrt{12} = 2\sqrt{4 \times 3} = 2\sqrt{4}\sqrt{3} = 4\sqrt{3}$$

Have a look at page 3 for a reminder about surds.

Worked example

Find the exact value of $\int_1^{12} \left(\frac{1}{\sqrt{x}}\right)dx$ **(4 marks)**

$$\int_1^{12} \left(x^{-\frac{1}{2}}\right)dx = \left[2x^{\frac{1}{2}}\right]_1^{12}$$

$$= (2\sqrt{12}) - (2\sqrt{1})$$

$$= 4\sqrt{3} - 2$$

Now try this

 Start by writing $\frac{6}{x^2}$ as $6x^{-2}$.

1. Use calculus to find the exact value of

$$\int_1^3 \left(3x^2 - 7 + \frac{6}{x^2}\right)dx \qquad \text{(5 marks)}$$

2. Given that $f(x) = \frac{6}{x^3} - \frac{2}{\sqrt{x}}$, find $\int_1^2 f(x)\,dx$, giving your answer in the form $a - b\sqrt{2}$, where a and b are constants. **(5 marks)**

Be careful when you are subtracting the value of the integral at $x = 1$. Use brackets to make sure you don't make a mistake with negative numbers.

Area under a curve

You can use DEFINITE INTEGRATION to find the area between a curve and the x-axis. The area between the curve $y = f(x)$, the x-axis and the lines $x = a$ and $x = b$ is given by

$$A = \int_a^b f(x)\, dx$$

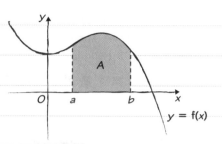

Look at page 52 for a reminder about definite integration.

Worked example

The diagram shows part of the curve with equation $y = (x + 3)(1 - x)$

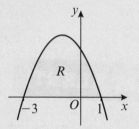

Use calculus to find the exact area of the shaded region, R. **(5 marks)**

$y = 3 - 2x - x^2$

$$\int_{-3}^{1} (3 - 2x - x^2)\, dx = \left[3x - x^2 - \frac{x^3}{3}\right]_{-3}^{1}$$

$$= (3 - 1 - \tfrac{1}{3}) - (-9 - 9 + 9)$$

$$= \frac{5}{3} - (-9) = 10\frac{2}{3}$$

Area of $R = 10\frac{2}{3}$

The curve crosses the x-axis at −3 and 1. So the **limits** for your **definite integral** will be −3 and 1. Always put the **right-hand** boundary as the **upper limit** and the left-hand boundary as the **lower limit**. You can give your exact answer as a fraction, mixed number or decimal.

Worked example

The diagram shows part of the curve with equation $y = x^2(x - 6)$

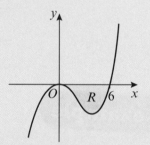

Find the area of the shaded region, R. **(6 marks)**

$y = x^3 - 6x^2$

$$\int_0^6 (x^3 - 6x^2)\, dx = \left[\frac{x^4}{4} - 2x^3\right]_0^6$$

$$= (324 - 432) - (0 - 0)$$

$$= -108$$

Area of $R = 108$

Negative areas

When you use a DEFINITE INTEGRAL to find an area BELOW the x-axis, the answer will be NEGATIVE. If you are asked to find an area, make sure you give your final answer as a POSITIVE number.

Now try this

The diagram shows part of the curve C with equation $y = x(x - 2)(x - 4)$

Use calculus to find the total area of the shaded region, between $x = 1$ and $x = 4$ and bounded by C, the x-axis, and the line $x = 1$ **(9 marks)**

Be careful with this question – you can't just find $\int_1^4 y\, dx$ because an area **below** the x-axis will produce a **negative** integral. You need to work out **two separate** definite integrals to find these two areas, then add the areas together:

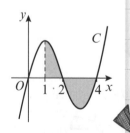

$$A_1 = \int_1^2 y\, dx$$

$$A_2 = -\int_2^4 y\, dx$$

Total area $= A_1 + A_2$

More areas

You can use areas of TRIANGLES and TRAPEZIUMS, together with DEFINITE INTEGRATION, to find areas enclosed by curves and straight lines. Here are three examples.

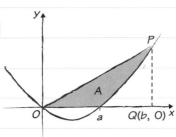

$$A = \boxed{OPQR} - \left| \int_o^a f(x)\,dx \right| \qquad A = \left| \int_a^b f(x)\,dx \right| - \boxed{PQR} \qquad A = \boxed{OPQ} -$$

Worked example

The diagram shows part of the curve C with equation $y = \dfrac{8}{x^2} + x - 2$, $x > 0$

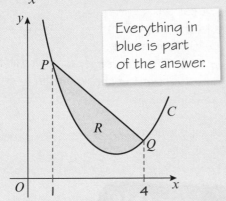

> Everything in blue is part of the answer.

The points P and Q lie on the curve and have x-coordinates 1 and 4 respectively.
The region R is bounded by the curve and the line segment PQ. Find the exact area of R.

(8 marks)

When $x = 1$, $y = 8 + 1 - 2 = 7$
So coordinates of P are (1, 7).

When $x = 4$, $y = \dfrac{1}{2} + 4 - 2 = 2\dfrac{1}{2}$
So coordinates of Q are (4, 2.5).

Area of trapezium $= \dfrac{1}{2}(7 + 2.5)(4 - 1)$

$\qquad\qquad\qquad = 14.25$

$\displaystyle\int_1^4 (8x^{-2} + x - 2)\,dx = \left[-8x^{-1} + \dfrac{1}{2}x^2 - 2x \right]_1^4$

$\qquad = (-2 + 8 - 8) - \left(-8 + \dfrac{1}{2} - 2\right)$

$\qquad = -2 - \left(-9\dfrac{1}{2}\right)$

$\qquad = 7.5$

So area of $R = 14.25 - 7.5 = 6.75$.

If you have to find the area between a curve and a line like this, **plan your answer** before you start. Work out how you can use triangles, trapeziums and rectangles to work out the area.

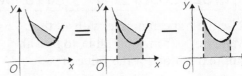

Before you can work out the area of the trapezium, you need to know the y-coordinates of P and Q. It's sometimes easier to work in decimals rather than fractions.

Use the formula $A = \dfrac{1}{2}(a + b)h$ to work out the area of the trapezium. Then work out $\displaystyle\int_1^4 y\,dx$ and subtract it from the area of the trapezium, to find the shaded area.

Now try this

The straight line with equation $y = x$ cuts the curve with equation $y = x(5 - x)$ at the points O and A.

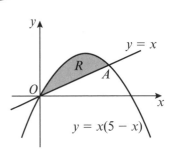

(a) Find the coordinates of A. **(2 marks)**

(b) Use calculus to find the exact area of the shaded region R. **(7 marks)**

The trapezium rule

There are some definite integrals that are difficult or even impossible to evaluate using calculus. You can use a NUMERICAL METHOD called the trapezium rule to find an APPROXIMATION.

The formulae booklet contains this formula for using the trapezium rule with n STRIPS.

Numerical integration

The trapezium rule: $\int_a^b y\,dx \approx \frac{1}{2}h\{(y_0 + y_n) + 2(y_1 + y_2 + \ldots + y_{n-1})\}$, where $h = \dfrac{b-a}{n}$

$y_0, y_1, y_2, \ldots$ and so on are values of y which you will calculate in a table of values. There are $n + 1$ values for y in total.

Worked example

$y = \sqrt{5^x + 2}$

(a) Complete the table below, giving the values of y to 3 decimal places.   **(2 marks)**

x	0	0.5	1	1.5	2
y	1.732	2.058	2.646	3.630	5.196

(b) Use the trapezium rule, with all the values of y from your table, to find an approximation for the value of

$$\int_0^2 \sqrt{5^x + 2}\,dx \qquad \textbf{(4 marks)}$$

$n = 4, a = 0, b = 2$

$h = \dfrac{2-0}{4} = 0.5$

$\int_0^2 y\,dx \approx \dfrac{1}{2} \times 0.5[(1.732 + 5.196)$

$\qquad + 2(2.058 + 2.646 + 3.630)]$

$\qquad = 5.899$

Use your calculator to work out the missing values in the table. Make sure you give your answers to the degree of accuracy asked for in the question. This is the trapezium rule with **four strips** so $n = 4$. The answer is an approximation of the area shaded in this diagram.

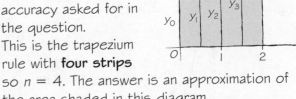
$y = \sqrt{5^x + 2}$

Work out h first. There are five values in the table, so $n = 5 - 1 = 4$.

Now try this

The diagram shows part of the curve C with equation $y = x\sqrt{5 - x}, x \leqslant 5$

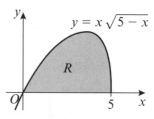
$y = x\sqrt{5 - x}$

(a) Complete the table below, giving the values of y to 3 decimal places where appropriate.   **(2 marks)**

x	0	1	2	3	4	5
y	0		3.464			0

(b) Use the trapezium rule, with all the values of y from your table, to find an approximation for the area of the shaded region, R.   **(4 marks)**

Trapezium rule checklist

When substituting into the trapezium rule remember:

- ✓ a and b are the limits of the integral.
- ✓ n is ONE LESS than the number of x-values in your table.
- ✓ Work out h first.
- ✓ Make sure EVERYTHING is multiplied by $\frac{1}{2}h$ – you need brackets within brackets.
- ✓ The first bracket contains the FIRST and LAST values of y.
- ✓ The second bracket (the one multiplied by 2) contains EVERY OTHER value for y.

You are the examiner!

CHECKING YOUR WORK is one of the key skills you will need for your C2 exam. All five of these students have made a key mistake in their working. Can you spot them all?

1   A circle has centre $(-1, 7)$ and passes through the point $(0, 0)$.
Find an equation for C. **(4 marks)**

$r = \sqrt{(-1)^2 + 7^2} = \sqrt{50} = 5\sqrt{2}$
$(x + 1)^2 + (y - 7)^2 = 5\sqrt{2}$

2   Find the first 3 terms, in ascending powers of x, of the binomial expansion of $(3 - x)^6$ and simplify each term. **(4 marks)**

$(3 - x)^6 = 3^6 + \binom{6}{1} \times 3^5 \times -x$
$\qquad\qquad + \binom{6}{2} \times 3^4 \times -x^2 \dots$
$\qquad = 729 - 1458x - 1215x^2 \dots$

3   Solve, for $0 \leqslant x < 180°$, $\cos(3x - 10°) = -0.4$ giving your answers to 1 decimal place.
You should show each step in your working. **(7 marks)**

$\cos^{-1}(-0.4) = 113.57\dots°$
$3x - 10° = 113.57\dots°$
$3x = 123.57\dots°$
$x = 41.2°$ (1 d.p.)

4   Given that $0 < x < 4$ and
$\qquad \log_5(4 - x) - 2\log_5 x = 1$,
find the value of x. **(6 marks)**

$\log_5\left(\dfrac{4 - x}{2x}\right) = 1$
$\dfrac{4 - x}{2x} = 5$
$4 - x = 10x$
$11x = 4$
$x = \dfrac{4}{11}$

5   Find the coordinates of the stationary point on the curve with equation $y = 2x^2 - 12x$ **(4 marks)**

$\dfrac{dy}{dx} = 4x - 12$
At the stationary point, $\dfrac{dy}{dx} = 0$
So $4x - 12 = 0$
$\qquad 4x = 12$
$\qquad x = 3$

Checking your work

If you have any time left at the end of your exam, you should check back through your working.

☑ Check you have answered EVERY PART and given all the information asked for.

☑ Double-check any numerical calculations, especially on BINOMIAL and TRAPEZIUM RULE questions.

☑ Make sure everything is EASY TO READ.

☑ If the RANGE for a trig equation is in RADIANS, make sure your answers (and calculator) are in radians.

☑ Cross out any incorrect working with a SINGLE NEAT LINE and UNDERLINE the correct answer.

Now try this

Find the mistake in each student's answer on this page, and write out the correct working for each question. Turn over for the answers.

You are still the examiner!

BEFORE looking at this page, turn back to page 56 and try to spot the key mistake in each student's working. Use this page to CHECK your answers – the corrections are shown in red, and these answers are now 100% CORRECT.

1 A circle has centre $(-1, 7)$ and passes through the point $(0, 0)$.
Find an equation for C. **(4 marks)**

$r = \sqrt{(-1)^2 + 7^2} = \sqrt{50} = 5\sqrt{2}$

$(x - a)^2 + (y - b)^2 = r^2$

$(x + 1)^2 + (y - 7)^2 = \cancel{5\sqrt{2}} = 50$

Top tip

The right-hand side of the circle equation is **r squared**. It's a good idea to **write out** the formula before you substitute.

Equation of a circle is on page 30.

2 Find the first 3 terms, in ascending powers of x, of the binomial expansion of $(3 - x)^6$ and simplify each term. **(4 marks)**

$(3 - x)^6 = 3^6 + \binom{6}{1} \times 3^5 \times (-x)$

$\qquad + \binom{6}{2} \times 3^4 \times (-x)^2 \dots$

$\qquad = 729 - 1458x + 1215x^2 \dots$

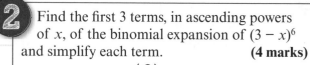

Top tip

The **binomial expansion** in the formulae booklet is for $(a + b)^n$. If b is **negative** you need to use brackets when you substitute. The terms will **alternate** between + and −.

Have a look at page 35 for a reminder.

3 Solve, for $0 \leqslant x < 180°$, $\cos(3x - 10°) = -0.4$ giving your answers to 1 decimal place.
You should show each step in your working. **(7 marks)**

$\cos^{-1}(-0.4) = 113.57\dots° \quad 0 \leqslant x < 180°$

$3x - 10° = 113.57\dots° \quad -10° \leqslant 3x - 10° < 530°$

$3x = 123.57\dots° \quad \text{Let } Z = 3x - 10°$

$x = 41.2° \text{ (1 d.p.)} \quad \cos Z = -0.4, -10° \leqslant Z < 530°$

So $Z = \cos^{-1}(-0.4) = 113.57\dots°$

or $Z = 360° - 113.57\dots° = 246.43\dots°$

or $Z = 113.57\dots° + 360° = 473.57\dots°$

$3x - 10° = 113.57\dots°, 246.43\dots°, 473.57\dots°$

$x = 41.2°, 85.5°, 161.2°$ (1 d.p.)

Top tip

Make sure you find **all** the solutions in the range given. If you are solving $\cos f(x) = k$ you will need to **transform the range** first.

There's more on this on page 44.

4 Given that $0 < x < 4$ and
$\log_5(4 - x) - 2\log_5 x = 1$,
find the value of x. **(6 marks)**

$\log_5\left(\dfrac{4 - x}{2x}\right) = \cancel{1} \qquad \log_5(4 - x) - \log_5 x^2 = 1$

$\cancel{\dfrac{4 - x}{2x} = 5} \qquad \log_5\left(\dfrac{4 - x}{x^2}\right) = 1$

$\cancel{4 - x = 10x} \qquad \dfrac{4 - x}{x^2} = 5$

$\cancel{11x = 4} \qquad 4 - x = 5x^2$

$\cancel{x = \dfrac{4}{11}} \qquad 5x^2 + x - 4 = 0$

$(5x - 4)(x + 1) = 0$

$x = \dfrac{4}{5}$ because x cannot equal -1 as

$\log_5(-1)$ is not defined.

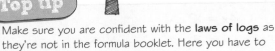

Top tip

Make sure you are confident with the **laws of logs** as they're not in the formula booklet. Here you have to write $2\log_5 x$ as $\log_5 x^2$ first.

Revise this topic on page 45.

5 Find the coordinates of the stationary point on the curve with equation $y = 2x^2 - 12x$ **(4 marks)**

$\dfrac{dy}{dx} = 4x - 12$

At the stationary point, $\dfrac{dy}{dx} = 0$

So $4x - 12 = 0$

$\qquad 4x = 12$

$\qquad x = 3$

So $y = 2 \times 3^2 - 12 \times 3 = 18 - 36 = -18$

Coordinates of stationary point are $(3, -18)$.

Top tip

Read the question carefully – if it asks for the **coordinates** of a point you need to find values for x **and** y.

Look at page 49 for more on stationary points.

Constant acceleration 1

For your M1 exam, there are FIVE formulae you need to learn for the motion of a particle in a STRAIGHT LINE with constant acceleration. They are covered here and on page 59.

Constant acceleration formulae

Here are the first two formulae you need to learn for motion in a straight line with constant acceleration.

 $v = u + at$ Look at the diagram on the right to see what each letter represents.

 $s = \frac{1}{2}(u + v)t$

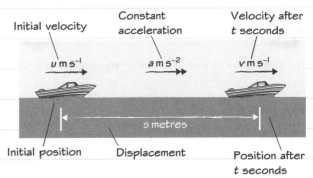

Worked example

In taking off, an aircraft moves on a straight runway AB of length 1.2 km. The aircraft moves from A with initial speed $2\,\text{m s}^{-1}$. It moves with constant acceleration and 20 s later it leaves the runway at C with speed $74\,\text{m s}^{-1}$. Find

(a) the acceleration of the aircraft   **(2 marks)**

$s = ?, u = 2, v = 74, a = ?, t = 20$

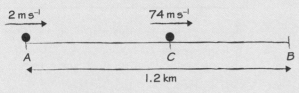

$v = u + at$

$74 = 2 + a \times 20$

$20a = 72$

$a = 3.6\,\text{m s}^{-2}$

(b) the distance CB.   **(4 marks)**

$s = ?, u = 2, v = 74, a = 3.6, t = 20$

$s = \frac{1}{2}(u + v)t$

$AC = \frac{1}{2}(2 + 74) \times 20$

$= 760\,\text{m}$

$CB = 1200\,\text{m} - 760\,\text{m} = 440\,\text{m}$

Using *SUVAT*

The constant acceleration formulae are sometimes called the *SUVAT* formulae. In the exam you should write down all five letters.

- ✓ Write in any values you KNOW.
- ✓ Put a QUESTION MARK next to the value you want to find.
- ✓ CROSS OUT any values you don't need for that question.

This will help you choose which formula to use.

EXAM ALERT!

When you are using the *suvat* formulae **always** write down the formula **before** you substitute in.

> Students have struggled with this topic in recent exams – be prepared!

Read the question carefully. The distance AB is 1.2 km, but the aircraft does not take off at B. If you have to solve a constant acceleration question involving **three points** like this one, it's a good idea to draw a quick sketch to help you see what is going on. In part (b), s is the distance AC in metres. You need to subtract it from 1200 m to find the distance CB.

Now try this

A car moves along a straight stretch of road AB. The car moves with initial speed $2\,\text{m s}^{-1}$ at point A. It accelerates constantly for 12 seconds, reaching a speed of $23\,\text{m s}^{-1}$ at point B. Find

(a) the acceleration of the car   **(2 marks)**

(b) the distance AB.   **(2 marks)**

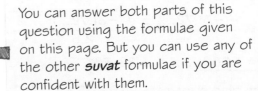

You can answer both parts of this question using the formulae given on this page. But you can use any of the other *suvat* formulae if you are confident with them.

Constant acceleration 2

Here are three more formulae you can use to solve problems involving constant acceleration in a STRAIGHT LINE. Together with the formulae on page 58, these are called the *SUVAT* formulae.

 1 $v^2 = u^2 + 2as$

2 $s = ut + \frac{1}{2}at^2$

 3 $s = vt - \frac{1}{2}at^2$

For a definition of what each letter represents, look at the diagram on page 58.

Worked example

A train moves along a straight track with constant acceleration. Three telegraph poles are set at equal intervals beside the track at points *A*, *B* and *C*, where $AB = 50$ m and $BC = 50$ m. The front of the train passes *A* with speed 22.5 m s^{-1}, and 2 s later it passes *B*.

Find

(a) the acceleration of the train   **(3 marks)**

$s = 50, u = 22.5, \cancel{v = ?}, a = ?, t = 2$

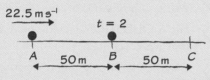

$s = ut + \frac{1}{2}at^2$

$50 = 22.5 \times 2 + \frac{1}{2} \times a \times 2^2$

$50 = 45 + 2a$

$a = 2.5 \text{ m s}^{-2}$

(b) the speed of the front of the train when it passes *C*
    (3 marks)

$s = 100, u = 22.5, v = ?, a = 2.5, \cancel{t = ?}$

$v^2 = u^2 + 2as$

$v^2 = 22.5^2 + 2 \times 2.5 \times 100$

$\quad = 1006.25$

$v = 31.72... = 31.7 \text{ m s}^{-1}$ (3 s.f.)

(c) the time that elapses from the instant the front of the train passes *B* to the instant it passes *C*.   **(4 marks)**

$s = 50, u = ?, v = 31.7214..., a = 2.5, t = ?$

$s = vt - \frac{1}{2}at^2$

$50 = 31.72... \times t - \frac{1}{2} \times 2.5 \times t^2$

$1.25t^2 - 31.72... t + 50 = 0$

$t = \dfrac{-(-31.72...) \pm \sqrt{(-31.72...)^2 - 4 \times 1.25 \times 50}}{2.5}$

$t = 1.688...$ or $\cancel{t = 23.688...}$

The time elapsed is 1.69 s. (3 s.f.)

Units

You need to make sure that your measurements are in the correct units.

☑ *t* (time) is measured in seconds

☑ *s* (displacement) is measured in metres

☑ *u, v* (velocity) is measured in m s^{-1}

m s^{-1} means m/s or 'metres per second'

☑ *a* (acceleration) is measured in m s^{-2}

m s^{-2} means m/s², 'metres per second squared', or 'metres per second per second'

(b) This formula involves v^2, so there are two possible values of *v*. You have been asked to find the **speed** of the front of the train. Speed is the **magnitude** of the velocity, so you need to give a positive answer.

(c) Don't use rounded answers in calculations. The exact answer to part (b) is $31.7214...$ or $\sqrt{1006.25}$, so use this in your calculation for part (c).

Now try this

A boat travels in a straight line with constant deceleration, between two buoys *A* and *B*, which are a distance 300 m apart. The boat passes buoy *A* with initial speed 16 m s^{-1}, and passes buoy *B* 30 seconds later. Find

(a) the deceleration of the boat
    (3 marks)

(b) the speed of the boat as it passes *B*   **(4 marks)**

(c) the distance from *B* at which the boat comes to rest.   **(4 marks)**

Motion under gravity

If you ignore AIR RESISTANCE, you can model an object moving freely under gravity as a particle with CONSTANT DOWNWARD ACCELERATION. This means you can use the constant acceleration formulae given on pages 58 and 59.

Up and down

Here are some useful facts about particles moving vertically under gravity.

If the particle is thrown upwards and takes t seconds to reach its MAXIMUM HEIGHT then it returns to its starting position after $2t$ seconds.

At its MAXIMUM HEIGHT, a vertically moving particle has ZERO velocity.

$0 \, \text{m s}^{-1}$

UP is the positive direction, so the acceleration due to gravity is NEGATIVE. It remains CONSTANT throughout. Show acceleration with a double arrow so you don't confuse it with velocity.

$-9.8 \, \text{m s}^{-2}$

You can choose which direction is positive in a question. You usually want UP to be the positive direction.

$u \, \text{m s}^{-1}$ $-u \, \text{m s}^{-1}$

When the particle returns to its initial position, it has the SAME VELOCITY as it started with but in the OPPOSITE DIRECTION.

Worked example

At time $t = 0$, a particle is projected vertically upwards with speed $u \, \text{m s}^{-1}$ from a point 10 m above the ground. At time T seconds, the particle hits the ground with speed $17.5 \, \text{m s}^{-1}$. Find

(a) the value of u **(3 marks)**

$s = -10$, $u = ?$, $v = -17.5$, $a = -9.8$, $\cancel{t = T}$

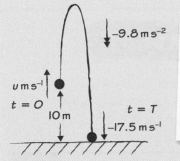

$-9.8 \, \text{m s}^{-2}$

$u \, \text{m s}^{-1}$
$t = 0$
$10 \, \text{m}$
$t = T$
$-17.5 \, \text{m s}^{-1}$

> The **positive** direction is **up**, so a and v are **negative**. The finishing position is 10 m **below** the starting position, so s is negative as well.

$v^2 = u^2 + 2as$

$(-17.5)^2 = u^2 + 2 \times (-9.8) \times (-10)$

$306.25 = u^2 + 196$

$u^2 = 110.25$

$u = 10.5 = 11 \, \text{m s}^{-1}$ (2 s.f.)

(b) the value of T.   **(4 marks)**

$\cancel{s = -10}$, $u = 10.5$, $v = -17.5$, $a = -9.8$, $t = T$

$v = u + at$

$-17.5 = 10.5 + (-9.8) \times T$

$9.8T = 28$

$T = 2.857... = 2.9 \, \text{s}$ (2 s.f.)

> Don't leave your answer as a fraction ($T = \frac{20}{7}$). You've used $g = 9.8 \, \text{m s}^{-2}$ so round to 2 s.f.

Accuracy and gravity

In your M1 exam, you should always use this value for the acceleration due to gravity:

$$g = 9.8 \, \text{m s}^{-2}$$

This value for g is correct to 2 SIGNIFICANT FIGURES. This means that if you use $g = 9.8 \, \text{m s}^{-2}$ in your calculation you should give your final answer correct to 2 significant figures.

Don't use rounded values in calculations. In the Worked example on the left, you can give the answer to part (a) as $11 \, \text{m s}^{-1}$, but you still need to use $u = 10.5$ in part (b).

Now try this

A diver projects herself upwards from a diving platform with a speed of $3.5 \, \text{m s}^{-1}$. The platform is 15 m above the water. Modelling the diver as a particle moving freely under gravity, find

(a) the greatest height above the water reached by the diver   **(4 marks)**

(b) the speed with which the diver hits the water   **(3 marks)**

(c) the total time from when the diver leaves the platform to when she hits the water.   **(3 marks)**

Speed–time graphs

You might need to sketch a speed–time graph in your M1 exam. Here is a speed–time graph for the motion of a train.

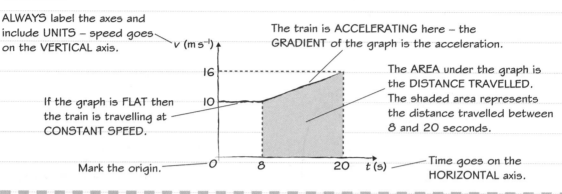

ALWAYS label the axes and include UNITS – speed goes on the VERTICAL axis.

The train is ACCELERATING here – the GRADIENT of the graph is the acceleration.

The AREA under the graph is the DISTANCE TRAVELLED. The shaded area represents the distance travelled between 8 and 20 seconds.

If the graph is FLAT then the train is travelling at CONSTANT SPEED.

Mark the origin.

Time goes on the HORIZONTAL axis.

Worked example

An athlete runs along a straight road. She starts from rest and moves with constant acceleration for 5 seconds, reaching a speed of 8 m s^{-1}. This speed is then maintained for T seconds. She then decelerates at a constant rate until she stops. She has run a total of 500 m in 75 s.

(a) Sketch a speed–time graph to illustrate the motion of the athlete. **(3 marks)**

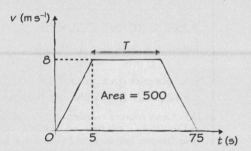

(b) Calculate the value of T. **(5 marks)**

Area under graph = 500

$500 = \frac{1}{2}(75 + T) \times 8$

$1000 = 600 + 8T$

$8T = 400$

$T = 50$

Golden rules

These are the two most important facts about speed–time graphs.

 Distance travelled = area under graph

In the example above, the train travels $\frac{1}{2}(10 + 16) \times 12 = 156 \text{ m}$ between 8 s and 20 s.

 Acceleration = gradient of graph

In the example above, between 8 s and 20 s the train is accelerating at $\frac{v}{t} = \frac{6}{12} = 0.5 \text{ m s}^{-2}$.

EXAM ALERT!

Make sure you label the axes on your speed–time graph and include units. Use dotted lines to show any values that you know.

> Students have struggled with this topic in recent exams – be prepared!

Remember the formula for the area of a trapezium: $A = \frac{1}{2}(a + b)h$. The area under the graph between $t = 0$ and $t = 75$ is the distance travelled by the athlete in that time.

Now try this

A truck is moving along a straight horizontal road. At time $t = 0$, the truck passes a point A with speed 18 m s^{-1}. The truck moves with constant speed 18 m s^{-1} until $t = 10 \text{ s}$. It then decelerates uniformly for 6 s. At time $t = 16 \text{ s}$, the speed of the truck is $V \text{ m s}^{-1}$, and this speed is maintained until the truck reaches the point B at time $t = 30 \text{ s}$.

(a) Sketch a speed–time graph to show the motion of the truck from A to B. **(3 marks)**

(b) Given that $AB = 455 \text{ m}$, find the value of V. **(5 marks)**

> If the truck **decelerates**, the graph will slope down.

Other motion graphs

You need to understand the key features of DISPLACEMENT–TIME and ACCELERATION–TIME graphs. These graphs are closely related to speed–time graphs, which are covered on page 61.

Displacement–time graphs

The gradient of a displacement–time graph tells you the VELOCITY of an object.

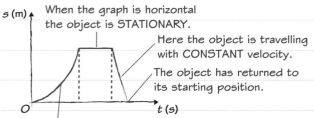

When the graph is horizontal the object is STATIONARY.

Here the object is travelling with CONSTANT velocity.

The object has returned to its starting position.

A curve shows the object is accelerating or decelerating. Here the gradient is increasing so the speed is INCREASING.

Acceleration–time graphs

In your M1 exam, acceleration–time graphs will usually consist of HORIZONTAL lines, showing periods of different constant acceleration.

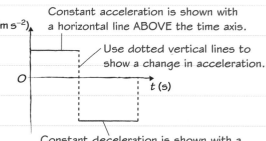

Constant acceleration is shown with a horizontal line ABOVE the time axis.

Use dotted vertical lines to show a change in acceleration.

Constant deceleration is shown with a horizontal line BELOW the time axis.

Worked example

The diagram shows a speed–time graph for the motion of a car.

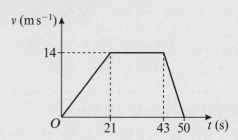

Sketch an acceleration–time graph for the motion of the car. **(5 marks)**

$$a_1 = \frac{14}{21} = \frac{2}{3}$$

$$a_2 = \frac{-14}{50 - 43} = \frac{-14}{7} = -2$$

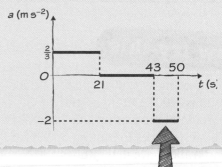

Between $t = 43$ and $t = 50$ the car is **decelerating**, so the acceleration is **negative**. Remember to draw **dotted** lines to show any jumps in acceleration, and to show the value of the deceleration on the vertical axis.

Before you can sketch the acceleration–time graph you need to work out the acceleration for each section of the car's journey. Work out the gradient of each section of the speed–time graph to find the acceleration.

The speed–time graph is flat between $t = 21$ and $t = 43$, so it has gradient 0. The car is not accelerating in this section of the journey, so draw a line at $a = 0$ on the acceleration–time graph. It's a good idea to draw this line a bit thicker so it shows up over the axis.

Convert all the times in minutes to seconds first. Remember that the distance travelled is the **area under** the speed–time graph.

Now try this

A train travels along a straight track, accelerating uniformly from rest for 30 seconds. It moves at constant speed $V\,\mathrm{m\,s^{-1}}$ for the next 2 minutes and then decelerates uniformly for 90 seconds until it comes to rest.

(a) For the motion of the train, sketch
   (i) a speed–time graph
   (ii) an acceleration–time graph. **(6 marks)**

(b) Given that the total distance moved by the train is 3270 m, find the value of V.

(4 marks)

Forces

A force acting on an object has DIRECTION and MAGNITUDE. The units of force are NEWTONS (N). 1 newton is the force needed to accelerate a 1 kg object at a rate of 1 m s^{-2}. Because of this, the units of force can be written as kg m s^{-2}.

$F = ma$

$F = ma$ is sometimes called the EQUATION OF MOTION. In words it is:

> force (N) = mass (kg) × acceleration (m s^{-2})

There are no formulae for M1 in the booklet. You need to remember $F = ma$.

This 4 kg block is resting on a smooth surface. If it is acted on by a force of 20 N it will accelerate at a rate of 5 m s^{-2}.

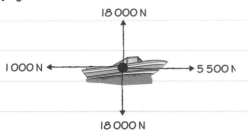

Resultant force

If there is more than one force acting on a particle you can find the RESULTANT in any given direction.

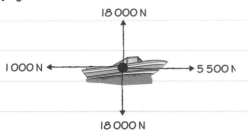

This boat is accelerating. The vertical forces have the same magnitude so their resultant is ZERO. The resultant force in the horizontal direction is 5500 − 1000 = 4500 N.

A car of mass 1000 kg is towing a caravan of mass 750 kg along a straight horizontal road.
The caravan is connected to the car by a tow-bar which is parallel to the direction of motion of the car and the caravan. The tow-bar is modelled as a light rod. The engine of the car provides a constant driving force of 3200 N. The resistances to the motion of the car and the caravan are modelled as constant forces of magnitude 800 newtons and R newtons respectively.

Given that the acceleration of the car and caravan is 0.88 m s^{-2}.

(a) show that $R = 860$ **(3 marks)**

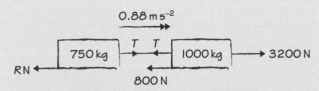

Using $F = ma$ for the whole system:
$$3200 - 800 - R = (750 + 1000) \times 0.88$$
$$2400 - R = 1540$$
$$R = 860$$

(b) find the tension in the tow-bar.   **(3 marks)**

Using $F = ma$ for the caravan only:
$$T - R = 750 \times 0.88$$
$$T - 860 = 660$$
$$T = 1520 \text{ N}$$

For part (b) you need to consider either the caravan or the car on its own.

Drawing a large, well-labelled diagram will help you see what is going on. For part (a) consider the caravan and the car as a **single system**. The resultant force acting on the system is $3200 - 800 - R$, and the combined mass is $750 + 1000$.

Tension and thrust

☑ TENSION is a force which will tend to STRETCH a rod, spring or string.

☑ THRUST is a force which will tend to COMPRESS a rod.

When a car accelerates it produces a tension in the tow-bar which in turn accelerates the caravan. If the car brakes, it produces a thrust in the tow-bar which decelerates the caravan.

A car of mass 1200 kg pulls a trailer of mass 400 kg along a straight horizontal road using a light tow-bar. The resistances to motion of the car and trailer have magnitudes 500 N and 200 N respectively. The engine of the car produces a constant driving force of magnitude 1500 N. Find

(a) the acceleration of the car and trailer   **(3 marks)**

(b) the magnitude of the tension in the tow-bar.   **(3 marks)**

Resolving forces

You can answer some questions by resolving forces into PERPENDICULAR COMPONENTS.

Using sin and cos

To resolve a force into components, imagine sketching a right-angled triangle, with the force as its hypotenuse. For example, a force of magnitude X acting at an angle θ to the horizontal can be resolved HORIZONTALLY and VERTICALLY:

$R(\rightarrow): X\cos\theta \qquad R(\uparrow): X\sin\theta$

You can use the notation $R(\rightarrow)$ and $R(\uparrow)$ to show which direction you are resolving. The arrow points in the POSITIVE direction.

This force has the same effect as a horizontal force of magnitude $X\cos\theta$ and a vertical force of magnitude $X\sin\theta$.

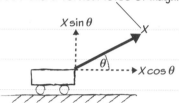

$X\cos\theta$ is ADJACENT to the angle, and $X\sin\theta$ is OPPOSITE the angle.

Worked example

A box of mass 5 kg is lying on a smooth plane which is inclined at an angle of 30° to the horizontal. The box is released from rest and accelerates at a m s^{-2} down the slope. Modelling the box as a particle, find

(a) the value of a **(3 marks)**

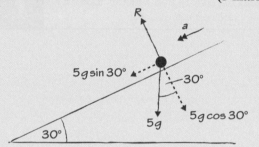

$R(\swarrow): 5g\sin 30° = 5a$

$\qquad 2.5g = 5a$

$\qquad\qquad a = 0.5g = 4.9$

(b) the magnitude of the normal reaction of the slope on the box. **(2 marks)**

$R(\nwarrow): R - 5g\cos 30° = 0$

$\qquad R = \dfrac{5\sqrt{3}}{2}g = 42\text{ N (2 s.f.)}$

Force of gravity

The force due to gravity is sometimes called the WEIGHT of an object. It is proportional to the MASS of an object, and acts DOWNWARDS.

$$F = mg$$

where F is the force in N, m is the mass in kg, and $g = 9.8$ m s^{-2}. If you use g in your calculations, remember to only give your answer correct to 2 significant figures.

Only the component of the force which acts **down the slope** contributes to the acceleration of the box. You need to resolve the **weight** of the box ($5g$ N) into components **parallel** and **perpendicular** to the slope. Use $R(\swarrow)$ to show that the positive direction is **down** the slope.

The **normal reaction** always acts **perpendicular** to the plane. It is **equal in magnitude** to the component of the weight that is perpendicular to the plane, and acts in the **opposite** direction.

Now try this

A truck is pulling a car using a light, inextensible tow-rope. The tow-rope is at an angle of 40° to the road. Together, the truck and car accelerate constantly at a rate of 2.5 m s^{-2}. The car has mass 800 kg and experiences a constant resistance to motion of magnitude 500 N. Find

(a) the tension in the tow-rope **(4 marks)**

(b) the normal reaction of the road on the car. **(2 marks)**

The car is being accelerated by the **horizontal** component of the tension in the tow-rope.

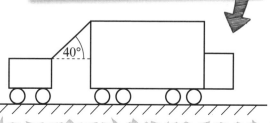

Friction

Friction is a force which acts in the OPPOSITE direction to the motion of a particle on a ROUGH surface.

Coefficient of friction

The coefficient of friction, μ, between an object and a surface is a measure of roughness. For a MOVING object the force of friction has magnitude

$$F = \mu R$$

where R is the magnitude of the NORMAL reaction between the object and the surface.

If $\mu = 0$ the surface is SMOOTH – there is NO friction. Any surface with $\mu > 0$ is called a ROUGH surface.

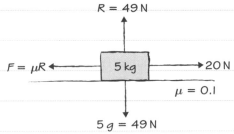

This box is accelerating along a rough surface. The coefficient of friction between the box and the surface is 0.1. The normal reaction is 49 N so

$F = \mu R = 0.1 \times 49 = 4.9\,\text{N}$

So the resultant force on the box is $20 - 4.9 = 15.1\,\text{N}$.

Worked example

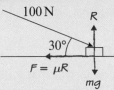

Everything in blue is part of the answer.

A small box is pushed along a floor. The floor is modelled as a rough horizontal plane and the box is modelled as a particle. The coefficient of friction between the box and the floor is $\frac{1}{2}$. The box is pushed by a force of magnitude 100 N which acts at an angle of 30° with the floor.

Given that the box moves with constant speed, find the mass of the box. **(7 marks)**

$R(\rightarrow)$: $100\cos 30° - F = 0$

$F = 50\sqrt{3}\,\text{N}$

$F = \mu R = \frac{1}{2}R$, so $R = 100\sqrt{3}\,\text{N}$

$R(\downarrow)$: $mg + 100\sin 30° - R = 0$

$m = \dfrac{100\sqrt{3} - 100\sin 30°}{g}$

$\quad = 12.571... = 13\,\text{kg}$ (2 s.f.)

EXAM ALERT!

Don't confuse **constant speed** with constant acceleration. Constant acceleration requires a resultant force. If an object is moving with constant speed, the resultant force on it is **zero**.

Students have struggled with this topic in recent exams – be prepared!

You need to resolve the 100 N force horizontally and vertically:

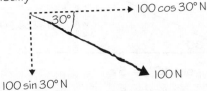

Use the **horizontal** component to work out the size of the frictional force, and then use this to work out the normal reaction, R.

Then use the **vertical** component to work out the mass of the box, m.

Remember that there are **two** forces acting vertically downwards on the block – its weight (mg) and the vertical component of the 100 N force.

Now try this

A block of mass 20 kg is being pulled along rough horizontal ground at a constant speed using a rope. The tension in the rope is P N and it makes an angle of 15° with the ground.
The coefficient of friction between the ground and the block is 0.5

Resolve vertically and horizontally to find two **simultaneous equations** in P and the normal reaction, R.

(a) Find the value of P. **(8 marks)**

The rope is cut.

(b) Explain whether the normal reaction between the ground and the block will increase or decrease. **(2 marks)**

Sloping planes

Questions involving FRICTION and sloping (or INCLINED) planes are really common. For a reminder about RESOLVING FORCES parallel and perpendicular to a sloping plane have a look at page 64.

An object moving freely on a rough plane inclined at an angle θ to the horizontal has THREE forces acting on it:

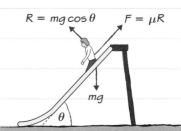

- WEIGHT $= mg$
- NORMAL REACTION, $R = mg\cos\theta$
- FRICTION, $F = \mu R$.

If the component of the weight that acts down the slope ($mg\sin\theta$) is greater than the friction, the object will ACCELERATE.

Worked example

A small brick of mass 0.5 kg is placed on a rough plane which is inclined to the horizontal at an angle θ, where $\tan\theta = \frac{4}{3}$, and released from rest. The coefficient of friction between the brick and the plane is $\frac{1}{3}$

Find the acceleration of the brick. **(9 marks)**

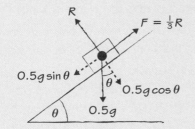

$R(\nwarrow):\ R - 0.5g\cos\theta = 0$

$\qquad\qquad R = 0.5g\cos\theta$

Using $\cos\theta = \dfrac{3}{5}:\quad R = 0.3g$

$R(\nearrow):\ 0.5g\sin\theta - F = 0.5a$

$\qquad 0.5g\sin\theta - \dfrac{1}{3}R = 0.5a$

Substituting the value of R into this equation:

$\qquad 0.5g\sin\theta - \dfrac{1}{3} \times 0.3g = 0.5a$

Using $\sin\theta = \dfrac{4}{5}:\quad 0.4g - 0.1g = 0.5a$

$\qquad\qquad\qquad\qquad 0.3g = 0.5a$

$a = \dfrac{3g}{5} = 5.9\,\text{ms}^{-2}$ (2 s.f.)

Trig ratios

If you are given one trigonometric ratio you can work out the values of the other two by sketching a triangle. Here are two examples.

1 $\tan\theta = \dfrac{4}{3}$ $\sqrt{3^2 + 4^2} = 5$ $\sin\theta = \dfrac{4}{5}$ $\cos\theta = \dfrac{3}{5}$

2 $\sin\alpha = \dfrac{3}{5}$ $\cos\alpha = \dfrac{4}{5}$ $\tan\alpha = \dfrac{3}{4}$ $\sqrt{5^2 - 3^2} = 4$

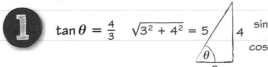
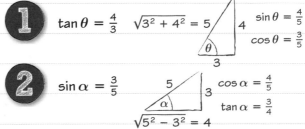

Ratios involving 3-4-5 triangles like these are common. They are designed to make the question EASIER to answer, so don't work out $\tan^{-1}\left(\frac{4}{3}\right)$ or $\sin^{-1}\left(\frac{3}{5}\right)$ to get the angle as a decimal.

Friction depends on the **normal reaction** so it's usually a good idea to resolve **perpendicular** to the plane first. This gives you the magnitude of the normal reaction, which you can use to find the frictional force.

Subtract the friction from the component of the weight that acts **down** the plane to find the resultant force down the plane acting on the brick. There is more about resultant forces and $F = ma$ on page 63.

Now try this

A box of mass 3 kg is pulled up a rough plane face by a force of magnitude 25 N acting parallel to the line of greatest slope of the plane. The plane is inclined at an angle of 40° to the horizontal. The coefficient of friction between the box and the plane is 0.2

By modelling the box as a particle, find

(a) the normal reaction of the plane on the box **(3 marks)**

(b) the acceleration of the box. **(5 marks)**

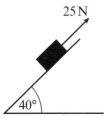

Pulleys

A pulley is used to connect two particles. The particles interact through the TENSION in the string.

Two particles A and B have masses 0.5 kg and 0.2 kg respectively. The particles are attached to the ends of a light inextensible string which passes over a smooth pulley. Both particles are held, with the string taut, at a height of 2 m above the floor. The particles are released from rest and in the subsequent motion B does not reach the pulley. Find

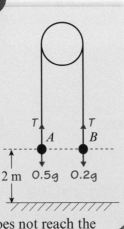

(a) the tension in the string immediately after the particles are released **(6 marks)**

$R(\downarrow)$: Using $F = ma$ for particle A:

$0.5g - T = 0.5a$ ①

$R(\uparrow)$: Using $F = ma$ for particle B:

$T - 0.2g = 0.2a$ ②

$2 \times$ ①: $g - 2T = a$

$-5 \times$ ②: $\underline{5T - g = a}$

$2g - 7T = 0$

$T = \dfrac{2g}{7} = 2.8\,N$

(b) the acceleration of A immediately after the particles are released **(2 marks)**

Substitute $T = 2.8\,N$ into ①:

$0.5g - 2.8 = 0.5a$ so $a = 4.2\,ms^{-2}$

(c) the speed of A when it hits the ground. **(3 marks)**

$s = 2, u = 0, v = ?, a = \dfrac{3g}{7}, \cancel{t = ?}$

$v^2 = u^2 + 2as$

$= 0^2 + 2 \times \dfrac{3g}{7} \times 2 = \dfrac{12g}{7}$

$v = 4.0987... = 4.1\,ms^{-1}$ (2 s.f.)

Using $F = ma$

When two particles are connected via a pulley, you will often have to write TWO EQUATIONS OF MOTION using $F = ma$. You can solve these SIMULTANEOUSLY to find any unknown values.

The tension in the string is the same at A as it is at B because the pulley is **smooth**. And both particles accelerate at the same rate, because the string is **inextensible**. There is more on **modelling assumptions** like this on page 81.

Follow these steps for parts (a) and (b).

1. Label your diagram with the tension in the string, and the weight of both particles.

2. Write an equation of motion for each particle. You can resolve up or down for each particle, but remember that the acceleration acts in the opposite direction for B as it does for A.

3. Solve your two equations of motion simultaneously to find T and a.

For part (c), you have to use the formulae for constant acceleration. Have a look at pages 58 and 59 for a reminder.

After the string is cut, particle B behaves as an object moving freely under gravity. Have a look at page 60 for more on this.

Two particles A and B have masses 4 kg and m kg respectively. They are connected by a light inextensible string which passes over a smooth light fixed pulley. The system is released from rest, and A descends with acceleration $0.2g$

(a) Find the tension in the string as A descends. **(3 marks)**

(b) Find the value of m. **(3 marks)**

After 1 s, the string is cut and particle B moves vertically under gravity.

(c) Find the time after the string is cut at which particle B returns to its initial position. **(9 marks)**

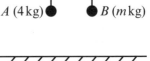

A (4 kg)●   ● B (m kg)

Connected particles 1

When two particles are connected via a pulley, one particle might be on a PLANE. If the plane is ROUGH, you'll have to consider FRICTION as well. Have a look at page 65 for a reminder.

Worked example

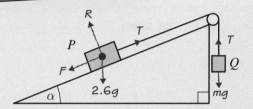

Two particles P and Q have masses 2.6 kg and m kg respectively. The particles are attached to the ends of a light inextensible string that passes over a smooth pulley which is fixed at the top of a rough plane. The plane is inclined to the horizontal at an angle α, where $\tan \alpha = \frac{5}{12}$. The coefficient of friction between P and the plane is 0.5. The particle P is held at rest on the inclined plane and the particle Q hangs freely below the pulley with the string taut. The system is released from rest and Q accelerates vertically downwards at 1.8 m s^{-2}. Find

(a) the magnitude of the normal reaction of the inclined plane on P **(2 marks)**

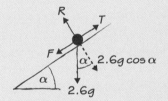

$R(\nwarrow): R - 2.6g \cos \alpha = 0$

Using $\cos \alpha = \frac{12}{13}$: $R = 2.6g \times \frac{12}{13}$

$\qquad\qquad\qquad = 24$ N (2 s.f.)

(b) the value of m. **(8 marks)**

$R(\nearrow):$ Using $F = ma$ for P to find T:

$\qquad T - F - 2.6g \sin \alpha = 2.6 \times 1.8$

Using $\sin \alpha = \frac{5}{13}$: $T - F = 14.48$ ①

$F = \mu R = 0.5 \times 24 = 12$

Substituting into ①: $T - 12 = 14.48$

$\qquad\qquad\qquad\qquad T = 26.48$

$R(\downarrow):$ Using $F = ma$ on Q:

$\qquad mg - T = 1.8m$

$9.8m - 26.48 = 1.8m$

$\qquad 8m = 26.48$

$\qquad\qquad m = 3.31 = 3.3$ kg (2 s.f.)

You have been given $\tan \alpha = \frac{5}{12}$. You can sketch a right-angled triangle to work out exact values of $\sin \alpha$ and $\cos \alpha$:

$\sqrt{12^2 + 5^2} = 13$

$\sin \alpha = \frac{5}{13}$

$\cos \alpha = \frac{12}{13}$

You might also be able to find these fractions on your calculator:

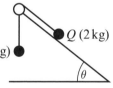

Resolve **parallel** to the plane to write an equation of motion for P, and resolve **vertically** to write an equation of motion for Q.

Now try this

Two particles P and Q of masses 4 kg and 2 kg respectively are attached to the ends of a light inextensible string, which runs over a smooth pulley. Q is held at rest on a rough plane inclined at an angle θ to the horizontal, where $\tan \theta = \frac{3}{4}$. The coefficient of friction between Q and the plane is $\frac{1}{4}$. The particles are released from rest and Q accelerates up the plane.

Q (2 kg)

P (4 kg)

θ

(a) Find the acceleration of Q. **(10 marks)**

After 0.6 s, particle P hits the floor and remains there. Particle Q continues up the slope, reaching its highest point after a further T s. In this motion Q does not reach the pulley.

(b) Find the value of T. **(6 marks)**

You need to use the **suvat** formulae for part (b). u will be the speed of Q after 0.6 s, and v will be 0. Have a look at pages 58 and 59 for a reminder.

Connected particles 2

When you're solving problems involving connected objects, you need to decide when to consider the WHOLE SYSTEM, and when to consider each object INDIVIDUALLY.

Worked example

One end of a light inextensible string is attached to a block A of mass $10\,kg$, which is at rest on a smooth plane inclined at

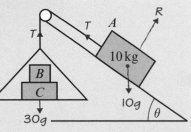

an angle θ to the horizontal, where $\sin\theta = \frac{3}{5}$. The other end of the string is attached via a pulley to a light scale pan which carries two blocks B and C. The mass of block B is $8\,kg$ and the mass of block C is $22\,kg$. The system is released from rest. Find

(a) (i) the acceleration of the scale pan

    (ii) the tension in the string   **(8 marks)**

(i) $R(\nwarrow)$: Using $F = ma$ on block A:

$$T - 10g\sin\theta = 10a$$

Using $\sin\theta = \frac{3}{5}$: $T - 6g = 10a$ ①

$R(\downarrow)$: Using $F = ma$ on blocks B and C combined:

$$30g - T = 30a \quad ②$$

① + ②: $24g = 40a$

$$a = 0.6g = 5.9\,ms^{-2}\ (2\ s.f.)$$

(ii) Substitute $a = 0.6g$ into ①:

$$T - 6g = 10 \times 0.6g$$

$$T = 12g = 120\,N\ (2\ s.f.)$$

(b) the magnitude of the force exerted on block B by block C.   **(3 marks)**

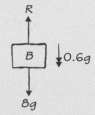

$R(\downarrow)$: Using $F = ma$ on block B:

$$8g - R = 8 \times 0.6g$$

$$R = 3.2g$$

So the force exerted on B by C is $31\,N$ (2 s.f.).

Pulley questions will always use $g = 9.8\,ms^{-2}$ so give your final answers correct to 2 significant figures.

Scale pans

If one block sits on top of another in a scale pan, you can find the FORCE EXERTED by one block on the other. This scale pan is accelerating at $2.2\,ms^{-2}$.

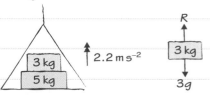

On its own, the green block has TWO forces acting on it: its weight, and the REACTION exerted on it by the orange block. An equation of motion for the green block (resolving in the upwards direction) is

$$R - 3g = 3 \times 2.2$$

So $R = 36\,N$. Because the two blocks are not moving relative to each other they exert EQUAL and OPPOSITE forces on each other, so the force exerted by the green block on the orange block is the same: $36\,N$.

The plane is **smooth** so you can ignore friction. For part (a), you need to consider blocks B and C as a single particle of mass $8 + 22 = 30\,kg$. For part (b), write an equation of motion for block B to find the force exerted on it by block C.

Now try this

A block R of mass $0.8\,kg$ is connected by means of a light inextensible string to a light scale pan, which carries two blocks P and Q. P and Q have masses $0.2\,kg$ and $m\,kg$ respectively. The system is released from rest and block R accelerates upwards at a rate of $1.5\,ms^{-2}$. Find

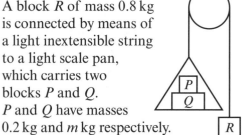

(a) the value of m **(6 marks)**

(b) the magnitude of the force exerted on block P by block Q.   **(3 marks)**

Collisions and momentum

If a question involves colliding particles, you need to use momentum to answer it.

Calculating momentum

The momentum of a particle of mass m kg travelling at v m s^{-1} is mv:

momentum = mass × velocity

Learn this formula – there are no M1 formulae in the booklet.

The UNITS of momentum are newton-seconds (N s) or kg m s^{-1}.

You need to choose a POSITIVE DIRECTION when you're working with momentum. Particles travelling in this direction will have POSITIVE momentum, and particles travelling in the opposite direction will have NEGATIVE momentum.

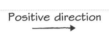

Positive direction →

12 m s^{-1} →
3 kg

4 m s^{-1} ←
15 kg

$mv = 12 \times 3$
$= 36$ N s

$mv = 15 \times (-4)$
$= -60$ N s

Conservation of momentum

In any collision, the TOTAL MOMENTUM in the system is CONSERVED. If you ADD UP the momentum of all the particles (remembering any NEGATIVE momentum) then it will be the same before and after the collision:

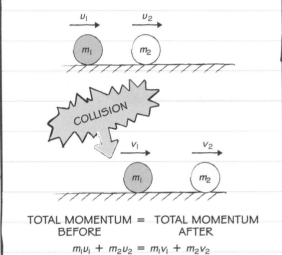

TOTAL MOMENTUM = TOTAL MOMENTUM
   BEFORE   AFTER

$m_1 u_1 + m_2 u_2 = m_1 v_1 + m_2 v_2$

Worked example

Two steel balls A and B of masses 0.4 kg and 0.2 kg respectively are moving towards each other on a smooth horizontal table. They collide directly. Immediately before the collision the speed of A is 6 m s^{-1} and the speed of B is 5 m s^{-1}. Immediately after the collision the direction of motion of A is unchanged and the speed of B is 3 times the speed of A.

Find the speed of A immediately after the collision. **(5 marks)**

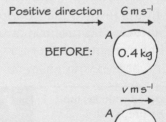

Positive direction →

BEFORE:
6 m s^{-1} → A 0.4 kg
5 m s^{-1} ← B 0.2 kg

AFTER:
v m s^{-1} → A 0.4 kg
$3v$ m s^{-1} → B 0.2 kg

$0.4 \times 6 + 0.2 \times (-5) = 0.4 \times v + 0.2 \times 3v$

$2.4 - 1 = v$

$v = 1.4$ m s^{-1}

This is the diagram you should sketch:

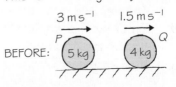

BEFORE:
3 m s^{-1} → P 5 kg
1.5 m s^{-1} → Q 4 kg

AFTER:
v m s^{-1} → R 9 kg

Sketch diagrams to show the motion of both balls before the collision and afterwards. Read the question carefully to work out which **direction** the balls are travelling in. Before the collision, ball B is travelling towards ball A, so taking **right** as the **positive direction**, ball B has **negative momentum**. Use the fact that the total momentum before the collision is equal to the total momentum after the collision to write an equation, and solve it to find v.

Now try this

Two particles P and Q of masses 5 kg and 4 kg respectively are moving in the same direction on a smooth horizontal table when they collide directly. Immediately before the collision the speeds of P and Q are 3 m s^{-1} and 1.5 m s^{-1} respectively. In the collision, the particles join to form a single particle R. Find the speed of R immediately after the collision. **(3 marks)**

Impulse

If a FORCE is applied to an object over a period of time, its MOMENTUM changes. This change in momentum is called IMPULSE.

Calculating impulse

If a force of F N acts on an object for time t s it exerts an impulse of Ft N s on the object:

$$\text{impulse} = \text{force} \times \text{time}$$

Impulse is ALSO the CHANGE IN MOMENTUM. If an object of mass m kg receives an impulse I N s which changes its velocity from u m s^{-1} to v m s^{-1}, then

$$I = mv - mu$$

Learn these – they're not in the formulae booklet.

Impulse in a collision

In a collision, each particle exerts an impulse on the other. You can work out the impulse exerted ON B BY A by considering the change in momentum of B.

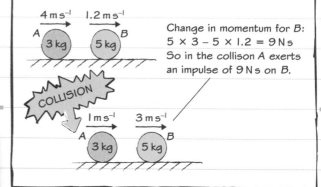

Change in momentum for B:
$5 \times 3 - 5 \times 1.2 = 9$ N s
So in the collison A exerts an impulse of 9 N s on B.

Worked example

A particle A of mass 2 kg is moving along a straight horizontal line with speed 12 m s^{-1}.

Another particle B of mass m kg is moving along the same straight line, in the opposite direction to A, with speed 8 m s^{-1}. The particles collide. The direction of motion of A is unchanged by the collision. Immediately after the collision, A is moving with speed 3 m s^{-1} and B is moving with speed 4 m s^{-1}. Find the magnitude of the impulse exerted by B on A in the collision.   **(2 marks)**

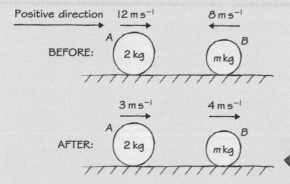

$I = mv - mu = 2 \times 3 - 2 \times 12$
$= 6 - 24 = -18$
The magnitude of the impulse is 18 N s.

Work out the change in momentum for particle A. Impulse can be negative as well as positive. Here the positive direction is to the **right**, and particle B exerts an impulse to the **left**, so the impulse is **negative**. The question asks for the **magnitude** of the impulse, so you need to **ignore** the negative sign and give a positive answer.

EXAM ALERT!

In your M1 exam, questions on momentum and impulse will always involve collisions on a **flat, horizontal surface**. This means that you don't need to consider gravity. Make sure you don't include g anywhere in your answers.

> Students have struggled with this topic in recent exams – be prepared!

Now try this

Two particles P and Q, of masses $3m$ kg and m kg respectively, are moving in opposite directions on a flat, horizontal surface. They collide directly. Immediately before the collision, the speeds of P and Q are 5 m s^{-1} and 4 m s^{-1} respectively. The direction of motion of P is unchanged by the collision.

Immediately after the collision, the speed of P is 1.4 m s^{-1}.

(a) Find the speed of Q after the collision.   **(3 marks)**

In the collision, the magnitude of the impulse exerted on Q by P is 8.1 N s.

(b) Find the value of m.   **(3 marks)**

> The impulse exerted on Q by P is equal to the change in momentum of Q.

Had a look ☐   Nearly there ☐   Nailed it! ☐

Static particles

A particle is in EQUILIBRIUM if the resultant of all the forces acting on it is ZERO. So the resultant in ANY DIRECTION will also be zero.

Finding unknown forces

You can resolve forces horizontally and vertically to find an unknown force. The particle on the right is in EQUILIBRIUM with three forces acting on it: 80 N, X N and Y N.

$R(\uparrow)$: $80 \sin 30° - X \sin 45° = 0$

$$X = \frac{80 \sin 30°}{\sin 45°}$$

$$= 40\sqrt{2}$$

$R(\rightarrow)$: $80 \cos 30° + 40\sqrt{2} \cos 45° - Y = 0$

$$Y = 109 \text{ (3 s.f.)}$$

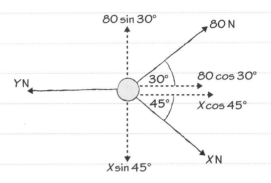

Worked example

A particle of mass 3 kg is attached at C to two identical light inextensible strings AC and BC, each inclined at 60° to the horizontal. The particle hangs in equilibrium. Find the tension in each string.

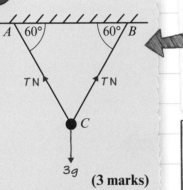

(3 marks)

$R(\uparrow)$: $2T \sin 60° - 3g = 0$

$$T = \frac{3g}{2 \sin 60°}$$

$$= g\sqrt{3}$$

$$= 17 \text{ N (2 s.f.)}$$

There are three forces acting on the particle: the tensions in the two strings (which will be identical) and the **weight** of the particle. Label all three forces on the diagram. Because the particle is in equilibrium, the resultant of the forces in the vertical direction will be **zero**.

Triangles of forces

If you are confident using vectors to represent forces, you could draw a TRIANGLE OF FORCES for this problem. You can use trigonometry to find the magnitude of T. There is more about writing forces as vectors on page 79.

Now try this

1.

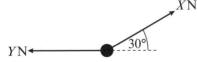

A particle of weight 5 kg is held in equilibrium by two light inextensible strings. One string is horizontal. The other string is inclined at an angle of 30° to the horizontal. The tension in the horizontal string is Y newtons and the tension in the other string is X newtons.
Find

(a) the value of X **(3 marks)**

(b) the value of Y. **(3 marks)**

2.

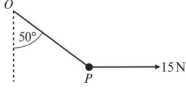

A particle P is attached to one end of a light inextensible string. The other end of the string is attached to a fixed point O. A horizontal force of magnitude 15 N is applied to P. The particle P is in equilibrium with the string taut and OP making an angle of 50° with the downward vertical. Find

(a) the tension in the string **(3 marks)**

(b) the weight of P. **(4 marks)**

Limiting equilibrium

If a particle on a ROUGH SURFACE is in limiting equilibrium (or ON THE POINT OF moving), then

- it is STATIC (so the resultant of all the forces acting on it is ZERO)

Have a look at page 72 for more on dealing with static particles.

- the frictional force is $F = \mu R$.

Look at pages 65 and 66 for a reminder about friction.

Add the weight of the ring, the normal reaction and the frictional force to the diagram. The ring is in **limiting equilibrium** so you know that

- the resultant force in any direction will be 0
- $F = \mu R$.

Resolve vertically to find the normal reaction, then resolve horizontally to find the value of μ.

Worked example

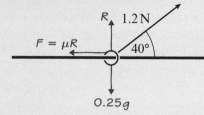

A small ring of mass 0.25 kg is threaded on a fixed rough horizontal rod. The ring is pulled upwards by a light string which makes an angle 40° with the horizontal, as shown. The string and the rod are in the same vertical plane. The tension in the string is 1.2 N and the coefficient of friction between the ring and the rod is μ.

Given that the ring is in limiting equilibrium, find

(a) the normal reaction between the ring and the rod   **(4 marks)**

$R(\uparrow)$: $\quad R + 1.2 \sin 40° - 0.25g = 0$

$\qquad R = 0.25g - 1.2 \sin 40°$

$\qquad\quad = 1.6786... = 1.7\,\text{N (2 s.f.)}$

(b) the value of μ.   **(6 marks)**

$R(\rightarrow)$: $\quad 1.2 \cos 40° - F = 0$

$\qquad \mu R = 1.2 \cos 40°$

$\qquad \mu = \dfrac{1.2 \cos 40°}{1.6786...}$

$\qquad\quad = 0.5476... = 0.55\,\text{(2 s.f.)}$

EXAM ALERT!

Remember to use **unrounded** values in later calculations. In this question, you could lose marks by using $R = 1.7$ N in part (b). Use the [Ans] button on your calculator to enter the exact value, or use at least 4 decimal places. You have used $g = 9.8\,\text{m s}^{-2}$ in this calculation, so you need to round any final answers to **2 significant figures**.

Students have struggled with this topic in recent exams – be prepared!

$F \leqslant \mu R$

If an object on a rough plane is NOT MOVING, the value of F is ONLY as large as it needs to be to resist motion. You sometimes write $F_{MAX} = \mu R$.

This block is resting on a sloping plane. The component of its weight acting down the slope is $3g \sin 30° = 14.7\,\text{N}$. This is less than $\mu R = 2.1g \cos 30° = 18\,\text{N}$, so the block does not move. It is in equilibrium, with $F = 14.7\,\text{N}$.

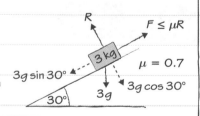

Now try this

Check whether the particle is on the point of moving **up** or **down** the slope. Here it is on the point of moving **up** the slope, so the frictional force will act **down** the slope.

A particle P of mass 5 kg is held at rest on a rough plane.
The plane is inclined to the horizontal at an angle α where $\cos \alpha = \frac{4}{5}$
The coefficient of friction between the particle and the plane is 0.5
The particle is held in place by a horizontal force of magnitude X N.
The particle is in equilibrium and on the point of moving up the plane.
Find the value of X.   **(7 marks)**

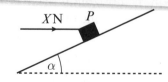

Moments 1

A moment is a measure of the TURNING EFFECT of a force on a body. You can use moments to answer questions about RODS in EQUILIBRIUM.

Taking moments

If a force of magnitude F N acts at a perpendicular distance x m from a point P, the MOMENT OF F ABOUT P is Fx:

moment = force × distance

The UNITS of a moment are newton-metres (N m). The turning effect of a moment can be either ANTICLOCKWISE or CLOCKWISE.

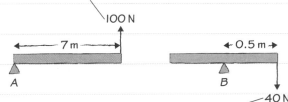

This force produces an ANTICLOCKWISE moment ABOUT A of $100 \times 7 = 700$ N m

This force produces a CLOCKWISE moment ABOUT B of $40 \times 0.5 = 20$ N m

---

Equilibrium

If a rod is HORIZONTAL and in equilibrium, then

$$\text{sum of clockwise moments} = \text{sum of anticlockwise moments}$$

$$\sum \circlearrowright = \sum \circlearrowleft$$

The rod on the right has weight 30 N and is held in place by a vertical force of 28 N. A particle of weight 6 N is on the end of the rod.

$\sum \circlearrowright$ moments about $P = 30 \times 2 + 6 \times 4$
$\qquad = 84$ N m
$\sum \circlearrowleft$ moments about $P = 28 \times 3 = 84$ N m

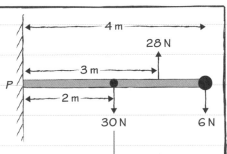

This rod is UNIFORM. That means that its full weight acts at the MIDPOINT of the rod. You can revise NON-UNIFORM rods on page 76.

Worked example

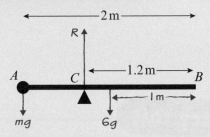

A uniform rod AB has length 2 m and mass 6 kg. A particle of mass m kg is attached to the rod at A. The rod is supported at C, where $CB = 1.2$ m, and the system is in equilibrium with AB horizontal. Find the value of m. **(4 marks)**

$\circlearrowleft$ moment about $C = 6g \times 0.2$
$\circlearrowright$ moment about $C = mg \times 0.8$
$\qquad \circlearrowleft$ moment $= \circlearrowright$ moment
$\qquad\qquad 1.2g = 0.8mg$
$\qquad\qquad\quad m = 1.5$

> If you take moments about C you can ignore the weight of the beam.

You can take moments about any point. Whichever point you choose, you can ignore any forces acting **at that point**. In this question there is a **normal reaction R** acting at C. The magnitude of this reaction will be $(mg + 6g)$ N, the total weight of the whole system. The easiest way to answer this question is to take moments about C. This means you can ignore the normal reaction R.

Now try this

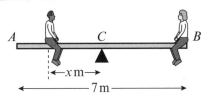

A seesaw consists of a beam AB of length 7 m supported by a smooth pivot at its centre C. Emma has mass 40 kg and sits on the end B. Paul has mass 50 kg and sits at a distance x m from C. The beam is modelled as a uniform rod.

Find the value of x for which the seesaw rests in horizontal equilibrium. **(3 marks)**

Moments 2

If a rod is hanging in EQUILIBRIUM, then the resultant force acting on it must be ZERO.
You sometimes need to RESOLVE VERTICALLY to find unknown forces in moments questions.

Worked example

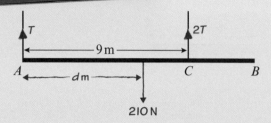

A steel girder AB has weight 210 N. It is held in equilibrium in a horizontal position by two vertical cables. One cable is attached to the end A. The other cable is attached to the point C on the girder, where $AC = 9$ m. The girder is modelled as a uniform rod, and the cables as light inextensible strings. Given that the tension in the cable at C is twice the tension in the cable at A

(a) find the tension in the cable at A **(2 marks)**

$R(\uparrow): T + 2T - 210 = 0$

$$T = 70\,N$$

(b) show that $AB = 12$ m. **(4 marks)**

Taking moments about A:

$\curvearrowright 210 \times d - 2T \times 9 \curvearrowleft$

$$210d = 1260$$

$$d = 6$$

$$AB = 2 \times d = 12\,m$$

A small load of weight W newtons is attached to the girder at B. The load is modelled as a particle. The girder remains in equilibrium in a horizontal position. The tension in the cable at C is now three times the tension in the cable at A.

(c) Find the value of W. **(7 marks)**

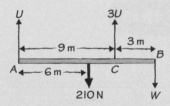

$R(\uparrow): U + 3U - 210 - W = 0$

$$4U - W = 210 \quad ①$$

Taking moments about B:

$\curvearrowright U \times 12 + 3U \times 3 = 210 \times 6 \curvearrowleft$

$$21U = 1260$$

$$U = 60$$

Substituting into ①: $4 \times 60 - W = 210$

$$W = 30$$

Tensions and reactions

There are two ways a rod can be supported in a moments question:

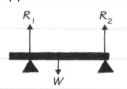 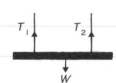

This rod is resting on supports, which produce a NORMAL REACTION on the rod.

This rod is supported by ropes or cables, which have a TENSION.

The calculations work in EXACTLY THE SAME WAY in both situations.

Start by labelling the diagram. The tension at C is twice the tension at A so label them T and $2T$.

(a) Resolve vertically for the **whole system** to work out the value of T.

(b) If you take moments about A you can ignore the tension in this cable. The rod is **uniform** so its weight acts at its midpoint. Find the distance from A to this point, then multiply by 2 to find the length of AD.

(c) This is a **new situation** so draw a new diagram showing the forces on the rod. The tensions will be different – choose a different letter from T to make sure you don't make a mistake.

Now try this

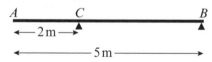

A uniform rod AB has mass 6 kg and length 5 m. The rod rests in horizontal equilibrium on two smooth supports. One support is at the end B. The other is at a point C on the beam, where $AC = 2$ m.

(a) Find the reaction on the beam at C.
(3 marks)

A particle of mass 18 kg is attached to the rod at a point D. The beam remains in equilibrium. The reactions on the beam at C and B are now equal.

(b) Find the distance AD. **(7 marks)**

Centres of mass

The centre of mass of an object is the point at which you can assume the WEIGHT of the object acts. In a UNIFORM rod, the centre of mass is the MIDPOINT of the rod. If a rod is NON-UNIFORM, the weight can act at a different point.

Golden rule

If a rod is NON-UNIFORM, DO NOT ASSUME the weight acts at its midpoint.

(a) Resolve vertically for the **whole system** to find X.

(b) The rod is **non-uniform** so its centre of mass G is not necessarily the midpoint of the rod. You need to assume that the weight of the rod acts at G, and use moments to find the length AG.

You could take moments at any point to solve this problem. For example:

Taking moments about P:

$$\circlearrowleft 4.5g \times PG = X \times 1.6 \circlearrowright$$
$$= 2.4g$$
$$PG = \frac{8}{15}\,\text{m}$$
$$AG = 0.8 + PG = \frac{4}{3}\,\text{m}$$

Worked example

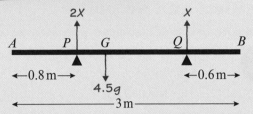

A non-uniform rod AB has length 3 m and mass 4.5 kg. The rod rests in equilibrium in a horizontal position, on two smooth supports at P and Q, where $AP = 0.8$ m and $QB = 0.6$ m. The centre of mass of the rod is at G. Given that the magnitude of the reaction of the support at P on the rod is twice the magnitude of the reaction of the support at Q on the rod, find

(a) the magnitude of the reaction of the support at Q on the rod   **(3 marks)**

$$R(\uparrow): 2X + X - 4.5g = 0$$
$$X = 1.5g = 15\,\text{N (2 s.f.)}$$

(b) the distance AG.   **(4 marks)**

Taking moments about A:

$$\circlearrowleft 4.5g \times AG = 2X \times 0.8 + X \times 2.4 \circlearrowright$$
$$= 4X$$
$$4.5g \times AG = 6g$$
$$AG = \frac{4}{3}\,\text{m}$$

On the point of tilting

If a rod is on the point of tilting, one of the reactions on the rod will be equal to ZERO.

This rod is being slid to the right. Initially it rests on two supports A and B. Just before it tips over to the right, it will be resting ONLY on B. The reaction at A will be zero.

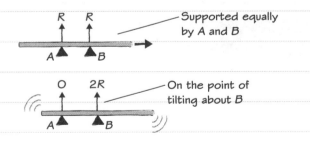

Now try this

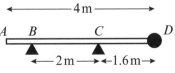

A plank AD weighs 20 kg and has length 4 m. The plank rests horizontally on two smooth supports at B and C, where $BC = 2$ m and $CD = 1.6$ m. A particle of mass m kg is attached to the plank at D. The plank is initally modelled as a uniform rod. With this model, the plank is on the point of tilting about C.

(a) The rod is on the point of tilting about C so the reaction at B will be zero.

(b) Assume that the weight of the plank acts at the centre of mass.

(a) Find the value of m.   **(6 marks)**

The plank is now modelled as a non-uniform rod. With the new model, the reaction at C is 75 N greater than the reaction at B.

(b) Find the distance of the centre of mass of the plank from D.   **(6 marks)**

Vectors

VELOCITY and DISPLACEMENT are both VECTOR QUANTITIES. This means they have MAGNITUDE and DIRECTION. You can use UNIT VECTORS **i** and **j** to describe the position or velocity of an object.

Position and velocity

Make sure you don't confuse position vectors and velocity vectors.

1 POSITION (or DISPLACEMENT) VECTORS tell you where an object is relative to a FIXED ORIGIN.

DISTANCE is the MAGNITUDE of a position vector.

If an object has position vector **r** = (a**i** + b**j**) m,

its distance from the origin is $|\mathbf{r}| = \sqrt{a^2 + b^2}$ m

2 VELOCITY VECTORS tell you what direction an object is moving in and how fast.

SPEED is the MAGNITUDE of a velocity vector.

If an object has velocity vector **v** = (p**i** + q**j**) m s⁻¹,

its speed is $|\mathbf{v}| = \sqrt{p^2 + q^2}$ m s⁻¹

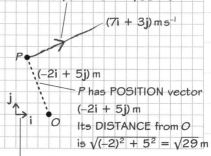

P moves with VELOCITY vector (7**i** + 3**j**) m s⁻¹

Its SPEED is $\sqrt{7^2 + 3^2} = \sqrt{58}$ m s⁻¹

(7**i** + 3**j**) m s⁻¹

(−2**i** + 5**j**) m

P has POSITION vector (−2**i** + 5**j**) m

Its DISTANCE from O is $\sqrt{(-2)^2 + 5^2} = \sqrt{29}$ m

i is the HORIZONTAL unit vector and **j** is the VERTICAL unit vector.

Velocity and time

If an object starts at a point with position vector **r₀** m and moves for time t seconds with velocity vector **v** then its new position vector **r** will be given by

$$\mathbf{r} = \mathbf{r_0} + \mathbf{v}t$$

In the diagram, Q starts with initial position vector **r₀** = (2**i** + 9**j**) m and moves with velocity vector **v** = (3**i** − 2**j**) m s⁻¹. After 3 seconds:

$\mathbf{r} = \mathbf{r_0} + \mathbf{v}t$
  = (2**i** + 9**j**) + 3(3**i** − 2**j**)
  = (2 + 3 × 3)**i** + (9 − 3 × 2)**j**
  = 11**i** + 3**j**

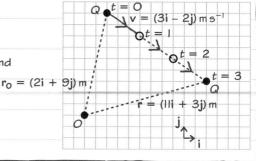

t = 0   **v** = (3**i** − 2**j**) m s⁻¹

t = 1

t = 2

r₀ = (2**i** + 9**j**) m

t = 3   Q

r = (11**i** + 3**j**) m

Worked example

A particle P is moving with constant velocity (−5**i** + 4**j**) m s⁻¹. At time $t = 9$ seconds, P is at the point with position vector (−12**i** − 2**j**) metres. Find the distance of P from the origin at time 5 s. **(5 marks)**

$\underline{r} = \underline{r_0} + \underline{v}t$

$(-12\underline{i} - 2\underline{j}) = \underline{r_0} + 4(-5\underline{i} + 4\underline{j})$

$\underline{r_0} = (-12\underline{i} - 2\underline{j}) - 4(-5\underline{i} + 4\underline{j})$

$\qquad = 8\underline{i} - 18\underline{j}$

$|\underline{r_0}| = \sqrt{8^2 + (-18)^2} = 19.7$ m (3 s.f.)

You know the position of P at $t = 9$ s and you want to know its position 4 seconds earlier. Let **r₀** be the position of P at 5 s, and use **r** = **r₀** + **v**t with $t = 4$, **v** = (−5**i** + 4**j**) m s⁻¹ and **r** = (−12**i** − 2**j**) m.

The **distance** from the origin is the **magnitude** of the vector $|\mathbf{r_0}| = \sqrt{a^2 + b^2}$.

Now try this

A ship S moves with constant velocity (−10**i** − 5**j**) km h⁻¹. It passes a buoy with position vector (12**i** + 25**j**) km at midday. Find

(a) the speed of the ship **(2 marks)**

(b) its position vector at 3 pm. **(3 marks)**

Velocity and position vectors have **units**. The units of velocity here are km h⁻¹ so measure time in hours.

Vectors and bearings

If you have to solve a vector problem involving bearings, **i** will be the unit vector DUE EAST and **j** will be the unit vector DUE NORTH.

Worked example

Two ships P and Q are moving with constant velocities. Ship P moves with velocity $(2\mathbf{i} - 3\mathbf{j})\,\mathrm{km\,h^{-1}}$ and ship Q moves with velocity $(3\mathbf{i} + 4\mathbf{j})\,\mathrm{km\,h^{-1}}$.

(a) Find, to the nearest degree, the bearing on which Q is moving. **(2 marks)**

$\tan\theta = \dfrac{3}{4}$ so $\theta = 36.86...°$

Bearing is 037° (nearest degree)

At 2 pm, ship P is at the point with position vector $(\mathbf{i} + \mathbf{j})$ km and ship Q is at the point with position vector $(-2\mathbf{j})$ km. At time t hours after 2 pm, the position vector of P is $\mathbf{p}$ km and the position vector of Q is $\mathbf{q}$ km.

(b) Write down expressions, in terms of t, for

  (i) $\mathbf{p}$

  (ii) $\mathbf{q}$

  (iii) $\overrightarrow{PQ}$. **(5 marks)**

(i) $\mathbf{p} = (\mathbf{i} + \mathbf{j}) + t(2\mathbf{i} - 3\mathbf{j})$

(ii) $\mathbf{q} = (-2\mathbf{j}) + t(3\mathbf{i} + 4\mathbf{j})$

(iii) $\mathbf{q} - \mathbf{p} = [(-2\mathbf{j}) + t(3\mathbf{i} + 4\mathbf{j})]$
$\qquad\qquad - [(\mathbf{i} + \mathbf{j}) + t(2\mathbf{i} - 3\mathbf{j})]$
$\qquad = (-\mathbf{i} - 3\mathbf{j}) + t(\mathbf{i} + 7\mathbf{j})$

(c) Find the time when

  (i) Q is due north of P

  (ii) Q is north-west of P. **(4 marks)**

$\overrightarrow{PQ} = (-\mathbf{i} - 3\mathbf{j}) + t(\mathbf{i} + 7\mathbf{j})$
$\qquad = (-1 + t)\mathbf{i} + (-3 + 7t)\mathbf{j}$

(i) **i** component $= 0$

$\qquad -1 + t = 0$

$\qquad t = 1$, so time is 3 pm

(ii) **i** component $= -\mathbf{j}$ component

$\qquad -1 + t = -(-3 + 7t)$

$\qquad 8t = 4$

$\qquad t = 0.5$, so time is 2.30 pm

In part (b), find expressions for the position vectors of A and B, $\mathbf{r}_A$ and $\mathbf{r}_B$ in terms of t. To show that A and B will **collide** you need to find a single value of t that makes the **i** components equal **and** the **j** components equal.

Finding a bearing

You can use trigonometry to find the bearing an object is moving on if you know its velocity vector. Remember that bearings are measured CLOCKWISE FROM NORTH and you should always give bearings to the NEAREST DEGREE.

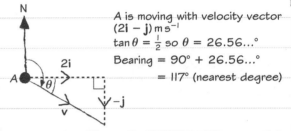

A is moving with velocity vector $(2\mathbf{i} - \mathbf{j})\,\mathrm{m\,s^{-1}}$

$\tan\theta = \frac{1}{2}$ so $\theta = 26.56...°$

Bearing $= 90° + 26.56...°$
$\qquad = 117°$ (nearest degree)

For part (b), use $\mathbf{r} = \mathbf{r_0} + \mathbf{v}t$ to write expressions for the position vectors of P and Q in terms of t.

For part (c), write the vector $\overrightarrow{PQ}$ in terms of its **i** component and its **j** component. When Q is due north of P the **i** component of $\overrightarrow{PQ}$ will be 0. When Q is north-west of P the **i** component of $\overrightarrow{PQ}$ will be **minus** the **j** component.

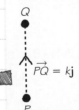

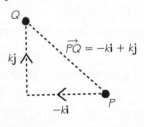

Now try this

A particle A moves with constant velocity $(-\mathbf{i} + 4\mathbf{j})\,\mathrm{m\,s^{-1}}$. At time $t = 0$, A is at the point with position vector $(3\mathbf{i} - 8\mathbf{j})$ m.

(a) Find the direction in which A is moving, giving your answer as a bearing. **(2 marks)**

At time $t = 0$, a second particle B is at the point with position vector $(-21\mathbf{i} + 16\mathbf{j})$ m, and is moving with velocity $(5\mathbf{i} - 2\mathbf{j})\,\mathrm{m\,s^{-1}}$.

(b) Show that A and B will collide at a point P and find the position vector of P. **(5 marks)**

Forces as vectors

FORCE and ACCELERATION are both vector quantities. You can describe them using **i** and **j** vectors.

Equation of motion

You can write equations of motion involving forces and accelerations written as vectors:

$$F = ma$$

F is the force vector in newtons

a is the acceleration vector in ms^{-2}

m is the mass in kg.

Mass is a SCALAR quantity. It has MAGNITUDE but NO DIRECTION. This means that the direction of the force is the same as the direction of the acceleration.

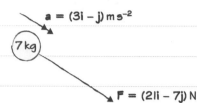

This particle is accelerating from rest at a rate of $a = (3i − j)\,ms^{-2}$. This acceleration is produced by a force of $F = 7(3i − j) = (21i − 7j)\,N$. After 5 seconds, it will have velocity given by $v = u + at = 0 + 5(3i − j) = (15i − 5j)\,ms^{-1}$

A particle P of mass 2 kg is moving under the action of a constant force F newtons. When $t = 0$, P has velocity $(3i + 2j)\,ms^{-1}$ and at time $t = 4\,s$, P has velocity $(15i − 4j)\,ms^{-1}$. Find

(a) the acceleration of P in terms of **i** and **j** (2 marks)

$$\underset{\sim}{v} = \underset{\sim}{u} + \underset{\sim}{a}t$$
$$(15\underset{\sim}{i} − 4\underset{\sim}{j}) = (3\underset{\sim}{i} + 2\underset{\sim}{j}) + 4\underset{\sim}{a}$$
$$4\underset{\sim}{a} = (12\underset{\sim}{i} − 6\underset{\sim}{j})$$
$$\underset{\sim}{a} = (3\underset{\sim}{i} − 1.5\underset{\sim}{j})\,ms^{-2}$$

(b) the magnitude of **F**   (4 marks)

$$\underset{\sim}{F} = m\underset{\sim}{a}$$
$$\underset{\sim}{F} = 2(3\underset{\sim}{i} − 1.5\underset{\sim}{i})$$
$$= (6\underset{\sim}{i} − 3\underset{\sim}{j})\,N$$

Magnitude of $\underset{\sim}{F}$: $|\underset{\sim}{F}| = \sqrt{6^2 + 3^2}$
$$= \sqrt{45} = 6.71\,N\ (3\ s.f.)$$

(c) the velocity of P at time $t = 8\,s$.   (3 marks)

$$\underset{\sim}{v} = \underset{\sim}{u} + \underset{\sim}{a}t$$
$$= (3\underset{\sim}{i} + 2\underset{\sim}{j}) + 8(3\underset{\sim}{i} − 1.5\underset{\sim}{j})$$
$$= (3 + 8 \times 3)\underset{\sim}{i} + (2 − 8 \times 1.5)\underset{\sim}{j}$$
$$= (27\underset{\sim}{i} − 10\underset{\sim}{j})\,ms^{-1}$$

Constant acceleration

If acceleration is constant, you can use this formula to connect initial velocity $u\,ms^{-1}$, final velocity $v\,ms^{-1}$, time $t\,s$ and acceleration $a\,ms^{-2}$:

$$v = u + at$$

u, **v** and **a** are all VECTORS and t is a SCALAR.

(a) P is moving under the action of a constant force, so it will have constant acceleration. You know the initial velocity (at $t = 0$) and the velocity at $t = 4\,s$, so you can use $v = u + at$ to find **a**.

(b) You are asked to find the **magnitude** of **F**. Find **F** in the form $ai + bj$ then use Pythagoras.

(c) Don't confuse **velocity** and **speed**. Here you are asked to find **velocity** so you need to leave your answer as a vector. Work out the **i** components and **j** components, then write your answer in the form $ai + bj$.

A particle Q of mass 2.5 kg is moving under the action of a constant force **F** newtons.
The velocity of Q is $(−4i + j)\,ms^{-1}$ at time $t = 0$, and $(6i − 5j)\,ms^{-1}$ at time $t = 5\,s$.
Find

(a) the speed of Q at $t = 0$ (2 marks)

(b) the vector **F** in the form $ai + bj$ (5 marks)

(c) the value of t when Q is moving parallel to **i**.   (4 marks)

Be careful with part (c). In vector questions, the particle doesn't have to be travelling in a straight line. The **direction** of the velocity is changing as well. The particle is travelling **parallel** to **i** when the **j** component of the velocity is **zero**.

$$\xrightarrow{\quad} v = (ki + 0j)\,ms^{-1}$$
$$\bullet Q$$

Vectors and resultants

You can use VECTOR ADDITION to find the resultant of forces given as vectors.

Finding resultants

To find the RESULTANT of forces given as vectors you ADD the vectors – add the **i** components and add the **j** components. The tension in the string produces two forces acting on this pulley.

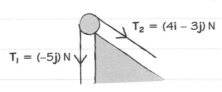

$T_2 = (4\mathbf{i} - 3\mathbf{j})$ N

$T_1 = (-5\mathbf{j})$ N

T_1 $T_R = T_1 + T_2$ T_2

The resultant force acting on this pulley is $T_R = T_1 + T_2 = (-5\mathbf{j}) + (4\mathbf{i} - 3\mathbf{j}) = (4\mathbf{i} - 8\mathbf{j})$ N

So it has magnitude $|T_R| = \sqrt{4^2 + 8^2} = 8.94$ N

Worked example

Three forces $\mathbf{F}_1$, $\mathbf{F}_2$ and $\mathbf{F}_3$ acting on a particle P are given by

$\mathbf{F}_1 = (7\mathbf{i} - 9\mathbf{j})$ N $\mathbf{F}_2 = (5\mathbf{i} + 6\mathbf{j})$ N $\mathbf{F}_3 = (p\mathbf{i} + q\mathbf{j})$ N

where p and q are constants.

Given that P is in equilibrium,

(a) find the value of p and the value of q.

(3 marks)

$\mathbf{F}_1 + \mathbf{F}_2 + \mathbf{F}_3 = 0$

$(7\mathbf{i} - 9\mathbf{j}) + (5\mathbf{i} + 6\mathbf{j}) + (p\mathbf{i} + q\mathbf{j}) = 0$

i components: $7 + 5 + p = 0$, so $p = -12$

j components: $-9 + 6 + q = 0$, so $q = 3$

The force $\mathbf{F}_3$ is now removed. The resultant of $\mathbf{F}_1$ and $\mathbf{F}_2$ is $\mathbf{R}$. Find

(b) the magnitude of $\mathbf{R}$ **(2 marks)**

$\mathbf{R} = \mathbf{F}_1 + \mathbf{F}_2$

$= (7\mathbf{i} - 9\mathbf{j}) + (5\mathbf{i} + 6\mathbf{j})$

$= (12\mathbf{i} - 3\mathbf{j})$ N

$|\mathbf{R}| = \sqrt{12^2 + (-3)^2} = 12.4$ N (3 s.f.)

(c) the angle, to the nearest degree, that the direction of $\mathbf{R}$ makes with **j**.   **(3 marks)**

$\mathbf{R} = (12\mathbf{i} - 3\mathbf{j})$ N

$\tan\theta = \dfrac{3}{12}$, so $\theta = 14°$ (nearest degree)

So the angle between **j** and $\mathbf{R}$ is

$90° + 14° = 104°$

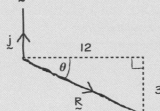

For part (c), draw a sketch to make sure you calculate the correct angle.

Equilibrium

If a particle is in equilibrium, the resultant force acting on it is ZERO.

F_3 F_1 F_2

The vectors of any forces acting on it will form a closed TRIANGLE.

For forces acting on a particle in equilibrium:

✓ the **i** components add up to zero

✓ the **j** components add up to zero.

EXAM ALERT!

Be careful with **accuracy** in vectors questions.

- Give **vectors** exactly in terms of **i** and **j**.
- Give **magnitudes** as surds, or to 3 s.f.
- Give **angles** correct to the **nearest degree**.

Students have struggled with this topic in recent exams – be prepared!

Now try this

A particle is acted upon by two forces $\mathbf{F}_1$ and $\mathbf{F}_2$, given by $\mathbf{F}_1 = (2\mathbf{i} - 6\mathbf{j})$ N, $\mathbf{F}_2 = (3\mathbf{i} + k\mathbf{j})$ N.

Given that the resultant $\mathbf{R}$ of the two forces acts in a direction parallel to the vector $(\mathbf{i} - \mathbf{j})$,

(a) find the value of k.   **(4 marks)**

A third force $\mathbf{F}_3$, given by $\mathbf{F}_3 = (p\mathbf{i} + q\mathbf{j})$ N is applied to the particle, so that it now lies in equilibrium.

(b) Find the value of p and the value of q.   **(3 marks)**

Modelling assumptions

In mechanics you MODEL real-life situations. The means that you make ASSUMPTIONS which simplify your calculations. You need to understand the effects of different modelling assumptions.

Rods and moments

✓ By modelling a plank or beam as a ROD you can ignore its WIDTH.

✓ If a rod is UNIFORM, the weight acts at the MIDPOINT of the rod.

✓ In a NON-UNIFORM rod, the weight does not necessarily act at the midpoint.

✓ You model objects on a rod as PARTICLES. This means you can assume their WEIGHTS act at a SINGLE POINT.

✓ Supports are SMOOTH, so the moments about that point are EQUAL if the rod is in equilibrium.

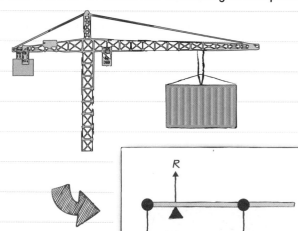

Worked example

The diagram shows a car pulling a caravan. The car is attached to the caravan by a light, inextensible tow-bar. The caravan and car accelerate together at $2.5 \, m \, s^{-2}$. State how you can use the assumption that the tow-bar is inextensible. **(1 mark)**

The caravan and car will have the same acceleration.

An **inextensible** tow-bar, string or rod only affects **acceleration**. Don't talk about the tension in the tow-bar in your answer.

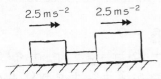

Motion under gravity

When an object moves freely under gravity, you ignore AIR RESISTANCE. This means the acceleration is CONSTANT. You also model objects as PARTICLES, so their weight acts at a single point. In MI questions, you are also assuming that the motion is VERTICAL.

Pulleys and strings

Learn these three modelling facts for questions involving pulleys.

1 The pulley is SMOOTH – the magnitude of the TENSION in the string will be the same on both sides of the pulley.

2 The string is INEXTENSIBLE – the magnitude of the ACCELERATION will be the same for both particles.

3 The string is LIGHT – you can IGNORE the WEIGHT of the string in any calculations.

Now try this

A block P of mass $0.8 \, kg$ is accelerating down a smooth plane inclined at an angle 30° to the horizontal. It is attached to a block Q of mass $0.1 \, kg$ by means of a light inextensible string running over a smooth pulley. P and Q are modelled as particles. State how you can use in your calculations the modelling assumptions that:

(a) the plane is smooth

(b) P and Q are modelled as particles

(c) the string is inextensible

(d) the string is light

(e) the pulley is smooth. **(5 marks)**

You are the examiner!

CHECKING YOUR WORK is one of the key skills you will need for your M1 exam. Each of these four students has made key mistakes in their working. Can you spot them all?

1

A stone is thrown vertically upwards with speed $16\,\mathrm{m\,s^{-1}}$ from a point h metres above the ground. The stone hits the ground 4 s later.

Find   (a) the value of h **(3 marks)**

      (b) the speed of the stone as it hits the ground.   **(3 marks)**

$s = h,\ u = 16,\ v = ?,\ a = 9.8,\ t = 4$

(a) $s = ut + \frac{1}{2}at^2$

$\qquad = 16 \times 4 + \frac{1}{2} \times 9.8 \times 4^2$

$\qquad = 142.4$

$\quad h = 140$ (2 s.f.)

(b) $v = u + at$

$\qquad = 16 + 9.8 \times 4$

$\qquad = 55$ (2 s.f.)

2

A small box of mass 15 kg rests on a rough horizontal plane. The coefficient of friction between the box and the plane is 0.2. A force of magnitude P newtons is applied to the box at 50° to the horizontal. The box is on the point of sliding along the plane. Find the value of P, giving your answer to 2 significant figures.   **(9 marks)**

$R(\rightarrow):\qquad P\cos 50° - F = 0$

$F = \mu R = 0.2R$ so

$\qquad\qquad P\cos 50° - 0.2R = 0 \qquad ①$

$R(\uparrow):\ R - 15g = 0$

$\qquad\qquad R = 15g$

Substitute into ①:

$P\cos 50° - 3g = 0$

$\qquad\qquad P = \dfrac{3g}{\cos 50°} = 46$ (2 s.f.)

3

A particle P moves with constant acceleration $(2\mathbf{i} - 5\mathbf{j})\,\mathrm{m\,s^{-2}}$. At time $t = 0$, P has speed $u\,\mathrm{m\,s^{-1}}$. At time $t = 3$ s, P has velocity $(-6\mathbf{i} + \mathbf{j})\,\mathrm{m\,s^{-1}}$.

Find the value of u.   **(5 marks)**

$\underset{\sim}{v} = \underset{\sim}{u} + \underset{\sim}{a}t$

$(-6\underset{\sim}{i} + \underset{\sim}{j}) = \underset{\sim}{u} + 3(2\underset{\sim}{i} - 5\underset{\sim}{j})$

$\qquad \underset{\sim}{u} = (-6\underset{\sim}{i} + \underset{\sim}{j}) - 3(2\underset{\sim}{i} - 5\underset{\sim}{j})$

$\qquad\quad = (-12\underset{\sim}{i} + 16\underset{\sim}{j})\,\mathrm{m\,s^{-1}}$

4

Two particles P and Q of masses 0.2 kg and 0.6 kg respectively are moving towards each other on a smooth horizontal table when they collide directly. Immediately before the collision, the speeds of P and Q are $8\,\mathrm{m\,s^{-1}}$ and $5\,\mathrm{m\,s^{-1}}$ respectively. In the collision, P and Q join to form a single particle R. Find the speed and direction of R immediately after the collision.   **(3 marks)**

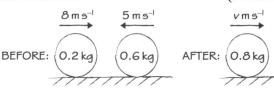

$8 \times 0.2 + 5 \times 0.6 = v \times 0.8$

$\qquad\qquad 0.8v = 4.6$

$\qquad\qquad\quad v = 5.75\,\mathrm{m\,s^{-1}}$

R is moving to the right with speed $5.75\,\mathrm{m\,s^{-1}}$.

Checking your work

If you have any time left at the end of your exam, you should check back through your working.

- ✓ Check you have answered EVERY PART and given all the information asked for.
- ✓ Check your ACCURACY. Give answers to 2 significant figures if you use $g = 9.8$ in your calculation, and 3 s.f. everywhere else.
- ✓ Draw LARGE, WELL-LABELED diagrams and make sure you show ALL THE FORCES acting on an object.
- ✓ If you've written working for a question somewhere else or on extra paper, make sure you say WHERE IT IS under the question.

Now try this

Find the mistakes in each student's answer on this page, and write out the correct working for each question. Turn over for the answers.

You are still the examiner!

BEFORE looking at this page, turn back to page 82 and try to spot the key mistake in each student's working. Use this page to CHECK your answers – the corrections are shown in red, and these answers are now 100% CORRECT.

1 A stone is thrown vertically upwards with speed $16\,\mathrm{m\,s^{-1}}$ from a point h metres above the ground. The stone hits the ground 4 s later.

Find (a) the value of h **(3 marks)**

(b) the speed of the stone as it hits the ground. **(3 marks)**

Taking upwards as the positive direction

$s = -h$, $u = 16$, $v = ?$, $a = -9.8$, $t = 4$

(a) $s = ut + \frac{1}{2}at^2 = 16 \times 4 - \frac{1}{2} \times 9.8 \times 4^2$

$= \underline{16 \times 4 + \frac{1}{2} \times 9.8 \times 4^2} = -14.4$

$= 142.4$ $h = 14$ (2 s.f.)

~~$h = 140$ (2 s.f.)~~

(b) $v = u + at$ $= 16 - 9.8 \times 4$

$= \underline{16 + 9.8 \times 4} = -23.2$

$= \underline{55.2\,\mathrm{m\,s^{-1}}}$ Speed $= 23\,\mathrm{m\,s^{-1}}$ (2 s.f.)

Top tip

Direction is important in **suvat** questions. If your positive direction is up, then s and a are **both negative**.

Revise motion under gravity on page 60.

Top tip

Don't forget to include **all** the forces when you're resolving. Learn more about this on pages 64 and 65.

2 A small box of mass 15 kg rests on a rough horizontal plane. The coefficient of friction between the box and the plane is 0.2. A force of magnitude P newtons is applied to the box at 50° to the horizontal. The box is on the point of sliding along the plane. Find the value of P, giving your answer to 2 significant figures. **(9 marks)**

$R(\rightarrow):$ $P\cos 50° - F = 0$

$F = \mu R = 0.2R$ so

$P\cos 50° - 0.2R = 0$ ①

$R(\uparrow):$ ~~$R = 15g = 0$~~ $P\sin 50° + R - 15g = 0$

~~$R = 15g$~~ $P\sin 50° + R = 15g$ ②

~~Substitute into ①:~~

~~$P\cos 50° - 3g = 0$~~

$$P = \frac{3g}{\cos 50°} = 46 \text{ (2 s.f.)}$$

$5 \times$ ① $5P\cos 50° - R = 0$

$+$ ② $\dfrac{P\sin 50° + R = 15g}{}$

$5P\cos 50° + P\sin 50° = 15g$

$P(5\cos 50° + \sin 50°) = 15g$

$P = 37$ (2 s.f.)

3 A particle P moves with constant acceleration $(2\mathbf{i} - 5\mathbf{j})\,\mathrm{m\,s^{-2}}$. At time $t = 0$, P has speed $u\,\mathrm{m\,s^{-1}}$. At time $t = 3\,\mathrm{s}$, P has velocity $(-6\mathbf{i} + \mathbf{j})\,\mathrm{m\,s^{-1}}$.

Find the value of u. **(5 marks)**

$\underset{\sim}{v} = \underset{\sim}{u} + \underset{\sim}{a}t$

$(-6\underset{\sim}{i} + \underset{\sim}{j}) = \underset{\sim}{u} + 3(2\underset{\sim}{i} - 5\underset{\sim}{j})$

$\underset{\sim}{u} = (-6\underset{\sim}{i} + \underset{\sim}{j}) - 3(2\underset{\sim}{i} - 5\underset{\sim}{j})$

$= (-12\underset{\sim}{i} + 16\underset{\sim}{j})\,\mathrm{m\,s^{-1}}$

$u = \sqrt{(-12)^2 + 16^2} = 20\,\mathrm{m\,s^{-1}}$

Top tip

Check whether you are asked for the **velocity** or the **speed**. Speed is the **magnitude** of the velocity vector.

Acceleration and speed vectors are covered on pages 77 and 79.

Top tip

Momentum and impulse have **direction** as well as magnitude. Choose a **positive** direction and stick to it.

Revise colliding particles on page 70.

4 Two particles P and Q of masses 0.2 kg and 0.6 kg respectively are moving towards each other on a smooth horizontal table when they collide directly. Immediately before the collision, the speeds of P and Q are $8\,\mathrm{m\,s^{-1}}$ and $5\,\mathrm{m\,s^{-1}}$ respectively. In the collision, P and Q join to form a single particle R. Find the speed and direction of R immediately after the collision. **(3 marks)**

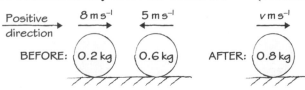

$8 \times 0.2 + 5 \times (-0.6) = v \times 0.8$

$0.8v = \underline{4.6} \; -1.4$

$v = \underline{5.75\,\mathrm{m\,s^{-1}}} \; -1.75\,\mathrm{m\,s^{-1}}$

R is moving to the <u>right</u> with speed <u>5.75</u>$\,\mathrm{m\,s^{-1}}$.

            left   1.75

Mean

The mean is a measure of CENTRAL TENDENCY. The mean is sometimes written as $\bar{x}$. You might have to calculate an ESTIMATE of the mean of GROUPED data given in a FREQUENCY TABLE.

Formulae for the mean

Learn these two formulae for the mean – they're not given in the formulae booklet.

 For n discrete data values, the mean is:

$$\bar{x} = \frac{\sum x}{n}$$

— The SUM of the data values
— The NUMBER of data values

 For data given in a frequency table:

$$\bar{x} = \frac{\sum fx}{\sum f}$$

— The SUM of (frequency × data value) or (frequency × midpoint)
— The TOTAL frequency

Grouped data

You can use formula 2 on the left with a GROUPED FREQUENCY DISTRIBUTION. The value of x for each group is the MIDPOINT of that group.

Height, h (cm)	Midpoint	
$0 \leqslant t < 5$	2.5	$\frac{0+5}{2} = 2.5$
$5 \leqslant t < 7$	6	$\frac{5+7}{2} = 6$
$7 \leqslant t < 10$	8.5	

Using summarised data

You might be given SUMMARY STATISTICS for the data. These can save you time in your calculations. You can use either $\sum x$ or $\sum fx$ together with the TOTAL NUMBER OF DATA VALUES (n or $\sum f$) to calculate the mean.

Worked example

As part of a study, a researcher recorded the heights, in cm, of 600 four-year olds in a grouped frequency table. The midpoint of each class was represented by x and the corresponding frequency by f, giving

$$\sum fx = 58\,250$$

Estimate the mean of this distribution.

(1 mark)

$$\frac{58\,250}{600} = 97.1\,\text{cm (1 d.p.)}$$

Use $\bar{x} = \dfrac{\sum fx}{\sum f}$ to calculate the mean. $\sum f$ is the total frequency, which is 600 in this case.

Worked example

A teacher asked her class of 30 students how long, to the nearest hour, they spent on a homework project.

Hours	1–3	4–7	8–10	11–20
Frequency	7	12	8	3
Midpoint	2	5.5	9	15.5

(a) Find the midpoints of the 4–7 hour and 8–10 hour groups.   **(2 marks)**

$$\frac{4+7}{2} = 5.5 \qquad \frac{8+10}{2} = 9$$

(b) Estimate the mean of the time spent on the project.   **(2 marks)**

$$\bar{x} = \frac{\sum fx}{\sum f} = \frac{7 \times 2 + 12 \times 5.5 + 8 \times 9 + 3 \times 15.5}{30}$$

$$= \frac{198.5}{30} = 6.6\,\text{hours (1 d.p.)}$$

Work out (frequency × midpoint) for each group, then add them together to find $\sum fx$. Write down all your working, and round your answer to 1 decimal place.

Now try this

Jamie recorded the temperature at his school at midday, $x\,°C$, each day for 15 days. He summarised his results: $\sum x = 251$
Paul recorded the temperature in °C on the next 5 days.
Here are his results: 19   22   15   21   16

You know the sum of the first 15 values. Add the next 5 values then divide by the total number of values, 20.

(a) Calculate the mean temperature during the whole 20 days.   **(2 marks)**

On the next day, the midday temperature was 16 °C.

(b) State, giving a reason, the effect this will have on the mean for the whole 21 days.   **(1 mark)**

Median and quartiles

The MEDIAN (Q_2), the
LOWER QUARTILE (Q_1),
the UPPER QUARTILE (Q_3)
and the PERCENTILES are
all measures of LOCATION.

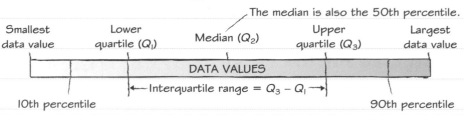

The median is also the 50th percentile.

Smallest data value | Lower quartile (Q_1) | Median (Q_2) | Upper quartile (Q_3) | Largest data value

DATA VALUES

← Interquartile range = $Q_3 - Q_1$ →

10th percentile   90th percentile

Discrete data

Follow these steps to work out the median and quartiles for *n* DISCRETE data values.

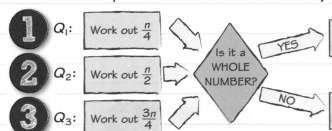

1 Q_1: Work out $\frac{n}{4}$

2 Q_2: Work out $\frac{n}{2}$

3 Q_3: Work out $\frac{3n}{4}$

Is it a WHOLE NUMBER?

YES → Use the value HALF WAY between this data value and the NEXT one.

NO → Round up to the next WHOLE NUMBER and use this data value.

You can revise how to find the median and quartiles for GROUPED CONTINUOUS DATA on page 86.

Worked example

This stem and leaf diagram shows the marks obtained by 26 people who took the driving theory test.

Mark		Totals
1	8	(1)
2	0 3 3 7 8 ⑨	(6)
3	1 1 1 1 2 ③ ④ 5 5 6 8	(11)
4	0 0 2 ③ 3 3 4 5	(8)

Key | 2 | 7 means 27

(a) Write down the modal mark. **(1 mark)**

31

(b) Find the values of the lower quartile, the median and the upper quartile.

(3 marks)

$\frac{n}{4} = 6.5$, $Q_1 = 29$

$\frac{n}{2} = 13$, $Q_2 = \frac{33 + 34}{2} = 33.5$

$\frac{3n}{4} = 19.5$, $Q_3 = 40$

In your S1 exam, discrete data will often be given in a **stem and leaf** diagram. The numbers in brackets show the total frequency for each row. You can use these totals to save time in your calculations.

The **modal** mark is the most frequently occurring mark. 31 appears 4 times, so this is the modal mark.

$\frac{n}{4} = 6.5$. This is **not** a whole number, so round up. The lower quartile (Q_1) is the 7th data value.

$\frac{n}{2} = 13$. This is a whole number, so the median (Q_2) is **half way** between the 13th and 14th data values.

$\frac{3n}{4} = 19.5$. This is not a whole number, so round up. The upper quartile (Q_3) is the 20th data value.

Now try this

Here are the ages in years of the passengers on a coach.

(a) Write down the modal age.
(1 mark)

(b) Find the values of the lower quartile, the median and the upper quartile. **(3 marks)**

Age		Totals
1	3 6 9 9	(4)
2	1 1 2 3 3 4 5 5 5 5 5 6 8 8 9	(16)
3	0 0 1 2 3 3 4 4 5 7 8 8 9	(13)
4	0 1 1 2 3 3 5 7 9	(9)
5	2 2 4 6 7 7 9	(7)
6		(0)
7	2	(1)

Key
2 | 9 means 29

Linear interpolation

You can use linear interpolation to estimate the MEDIAN and QUARTILES of GROUPED CONTINUOUS data. You don't know the exact data values, so you assume the data values are EVENLY DISTRIBUTED within each group.

Using proportion

In the Worked example on the right, the median is in the 101–130 group. To use interpolation, you assume that the heights in this group are EVENLY DISTRIBUTED between the LOWER and UPPER CLASS BOUNDARIES.

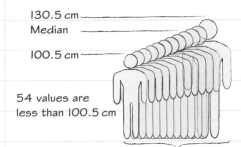

130.5 cm
Median
100.5 cm

54 values are less than 100.5 cm

There are 125 students in the 101–130 group, so each student is worth $30 \div 125 = 0.24$ cm

There are 54 values below 100.5 cm so the median is $145 - 54 = 91$ values into the group. Each value is worth 0.24 cm, so the median is $100.5 + 91 \times 0.24 = 122.34$ cm.

Worked example

This table shows the heights, to the nearest cm, of 290 students in a school.

Height (cm)	Number of students
71–100	54
101–130	125
131–160	87
161–190	24

Use interpolation to estimate the median height. **(2 marks)**

$$\frac{290}{2} = 145$$

$$100.5 + (145 - 54) \times \frac{30}{125} = 122.34 \text{ cm}$$

Work out $\frac{n}{2}$ to find the position of the median.

Choosing class boundaries

You need to be careful when you are working out lower and upper class boundaries.

Time (mins)
1–5
6–8
9–12
13–20

These data have been rounded to the nearest minute and there are GAPS between the groups. The lower boundary for this group is 8.5 minutes, and the upper boundary is 12.5 minutes.

Distance, x (cm)
$100 \leqslant x < 150$
$150 \leqslant x < 250$
$250 \leqslant x < 350$
$350 \leqslant x < 500$

There are NO GAPS between the groups here. The lower boundary for this group is 100 m and the upper boundary is 150 m.

Now try this

This table summarises the hand spans, to the nearest cm, of a group of 178 people.

Hand span (cm)	Frequency
10–14	29
15–17	64
18–19	55
20–22	21
23–30	9

Use interpolation to estimate the median Q_2, the lower quartile Q_1 and the upper quartile Q_3 of these data. **(4 marks)**

You can use interpolation to estimate the quartiles in exactly the same way as you estimate the median.

$\frac{n}{4} = 44.5$, so Q_1 is $44.5 - 29 = 15.5$ values into the 15–17 group. This group is $17.5 - 14.5 = 3$ cm wide, so each value is worth $\frac{3}{64}$ cm. The estimate for Q_1 is

$$14.5 + (44.5 - 29) \times \frac{3}{64}$$

Round your answers to 2 decimal places.

Standard deviation 1

Standard deviation and VARIANCE are both measures of SPREAD (or DISPERSION). Standard deviation is used more frequently because it has the SAME UNITS as the data.

Discrete data

For n discrete data values:

$$\text{Variance} = \frac{\sum x^2}{n} - \left(\frac{\sum x}{n}\right)^2$$

Standard deviation = SD = $\sqrt{\text{Variance}}$

You can revise how to find the variance and standard deviation for GROUPED CONTINUOUS DATA on page 86.

Notation

You need to be familiar with the notations used in statistics formulae.

✓ $\sum x^2$ means the sum of the squares of the data values.

✓ σ is sometimes used for the standard deviation.

✓ σ^2 is sometimes used for the variance.

Worked example

Here are the ages in years of the passengers on a coach.

		Key	$2\,|\,9$ means 29

Age		Totals
1	3 6 9 9	(4)
2	1 1 2 3 3 4 5 5 5 5 5 6 8 8 9	(16)
3	0 0 1 2 3 3 4 4 5 7 8 8 9	(13)
4	0 1 1 2 3 3 5 7 9	(9)
5	2 2 4 6 7 7 9	(7)
6		(0)
7	2	(1)

Given that $\sum x = 1756$ and $\sum x^2 = 69\,942$, find the standard deviation of the ages. **(2 marks)**

$n = 4 + 16 + 13 + 9 + 7 + 0 + 1 = 50$

$\text{Variance} = \dfrac{69942}{50} - \left(\dfrac{1756}{50}\right)^2 = 165.4256$

$\text{SD} = \sqrt{165.4256} = 12.9 \text{ (3 s.f.)}$

If you need to calculate the standard deviation of discrete data, you will usually be given the values of $\sum x$, $\sum x^2$ or both. Follow these steps to find the standard deviation.

1. Work out n by adding together the totals for each row.

2. Substitute $\sum x^2$, $\sum x$ and n into the formula for variance.

3. Square root your answer to find the standard deviation.

Watch out!

You need to LEARN the formula for variance at the top of the page. It is NOT given in the formulae booklet. DO NOT use the formula in the booklet for the variance of a DISCRETE RANDOM VARIABLE. This is a different topic, and you can revise it on page 104.

Now try this

This stem and leaf diagram shows the marks obtained by 26 people who took the driving theory test.

Mark		Totals
1	8	(1)
2	0 3 3 7 8 9	(6)
3	1 1 1 1 2 3 4 5 5 6 8	(11)
4	0 0 2 3 3 3 4 5	(8)

Key	$2\,|\,7$ means 27

Given that $\sum x^2 = 30\,911$, find the standard deviation of the marks obtained by these students. **(2 marks)**

You have not been given $\sum x$. Work it out by adding together all the data values. Do not work out the square root of $\sum x^2$. $\sum x^2$ is not the same thing as $(\sum x)^2$.

Standard deviation 2

You can ESTIMATE the variance and standard deviation of GROUPED CONTINUOUS DATA given in a frequency table using the MIDPOINTS, x, of each group.

Grouped continuous data

For data given in a frequency table:

$$\text{Variance} = \frac{\sum fx^2}{\sum f} - \left(\frac{\sum fx}{\sum f}\right)^2 = \frac{\sum fx^2}{n} - (\bar{x})^2$$

Standard deviation $= SD = \sqrt{\text{Variance}}$

Learn these formulae – they are NOT in the booklet.

Notation

$\sum fx^2$ is the SUM of (frequency × midpoint^2). This is NOT the same as $\left(\sum fx\right)^2$.

For a reminder about the other notation used in the formula for variance, have a look at pages 84 and 87.

Worked example

This table shows the times a random sample of 150 people took to complete a puzzle.

Time, t (min)	Number of people	Midpoint
$0 \leqslant t < 5$	23	2.5
$5 \leqslant t < 7$	82	6
$7 \leqslant t < 10$	36	8.5
$10 \leqslant t < 15$	9	12.5

Estimate the standard deviation of these data. **(5 marks)**

$\sum f = 150$

$\sum fx = 23 \times 2.5 + 82 \times 6 + 36 \times 8.5 + 9 \times 12.5$
$\quad\quad = 968$

$\sum fx^2 = 23 \times 2.5^2 + 82 \times 6^2 + 36 \times 8.5^2 + 9 \times 12.5^2$
$\quad\quad = 7103$

$\text{Variance} = \dfrac{7103}{150} - \left(\dfrac{968}{150}\right)^2 = 5.7078\ldots$

$SD = \sqrt{5.7078\ldots} = 2.39$ (3 s.f.)

You have not been given $\sum fx$ or $\sum fx^2$ so you need to work them out. Start by finding the **midpoints** of each group, and write them in the table.

You are told that there were 150 people in the sample, so $\sum f = 150$.

Work out $\sum fx$ and $\sum fx^2$ using your calculator. Remember that x is the **midpoint** for each row.

Finally substitute into the formula for variance, and don't forget to take the square root to find the standard deviation.

You don't need to give units with your answer, but you do need to round to a suitable degree of accuracy, like 3 s.f.

Now try this

A researcher timed how long, to the nearest minute, a group of shoppers spent in a supermarket checkout queue.

Minutes	1–3	4–6	7–10	11–20
Frequency	48	31	15	6
Midpoint		5	8.5	

(You may use $\sum fx^2 = 3492.25$)

(a) Find the midpoints of the 1–3 hour and 11–20 hour groups. **(2 marks)**

(b) Estimate the standard deviation for these data. **(3 marks)**

(a) The midpoint of the 1–3 group is $\dfrac{1+3}{2}$

(b) You have been given $\sum fx^2$ but you need to calculate $\sum fx$ and $\sum f$. Remember that $\sum fx$ is not the square root of $\sum fx^2$. You need to calculate it separately using the midpoints.

Box plots and outliers

A box plot shows the MAXIMUM and MINIMUM values and the QUARTILES of a distribution. It is usually drawn on graph paper with a scale.

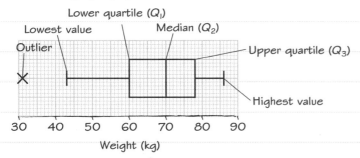

Half the weights were between 60 kg and 78 kg. 25% of the weights were less than 60 kg.

Outliers

A value which doesn't fall within the main body of the data is called an outlier. You can use the QUARTILES and the interquartile range (IQR) to define outliers. The most common definition is:

✓ values less than $Q_1 - 1.5 \times IQR$

✓ values greater than $Q_3 + 1.5 \times IQR$

On the diagram on the left, the IQR is $78 - 60 = 18$. The data value 31 is an outlier because it is less than $60 - 1.5 \times 18 = 33$.

Outliers can be defined in different ways. If you need to use outliers in your S1 exam you will be told how they are defined in that case.

Worked example

Here is a table showing information about the test scores for all the students in a school.

Two lowest values	2, 5
Lower quartile	10
Median	15
Upper quartile	26
Two highest values	40, 47

An outlier is a value that is greater than Q_3 plus 1.0 times the interquartile range or less than Q_1 minus 1.0 times the interquartile range.

Draw a box plot to represent these data, indicating clearly any outliers. **(5 marks)**

$IQR = 26 - 10 = 16$

$Q_1 - 1.0 \times IQR = -6$ $Q_3 + 1.0 \times IQR = 42$

Read the question carefully – any rule used to specify outliers will **always** be given in the question. You need to work out the lower and upper boundaries for the outliers before deciding which data values (if any) are outliers. 47 is greater than $Q_3 + 1.0 \times IQR$ so using this definition it is an outlier – you need to mark it on your box plot with a cross.

Always use a ruler and a sharp pencil when you are drawing graphs or box plots in your exam.

Whiskers and outliers

When there is an outlier, you can use either of these as your 'highest' or 'lowest' value:

1 the highest or lowest data value which is NOT an outlier

This is shown in the Worked example on the left.

2 the boundary of the normal data values that are not outliers.

In the Worked example, you could also draw the right-hand whisker up to 42.

Now try this

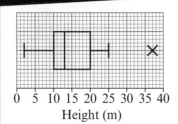

The box plot shows a summary of the heights, in metres, of the trees in a park.

(a) (i) Write down the height that 75% of the trees are shorter than.

(ii) State the name given to this value. **(2 marks)**

In (b), write down the name, what it means **and** one way of determining it.

(b) Explain what you understand by the (×) on the box plot. **(2 marks)**

Histograms

Histograms are usually used to represent GROUPED CONTINUOUS DATA. You probably won't be asked to draw a histogram in your S1 exam, but you might have to INTERPRET one, or make calculations about WIDTHS and HEIGHTS of bars.

Worked example

The histogram shows the finishing times, to the nearest minute, of 40 runners in a 1500 m race.

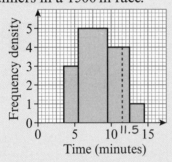

(a) Complete the table. **(2 marks)**

Finishing time (min)	Frequency
4–5	6
6–9	20
10–12	12
13–14	2

(b) Estimate the number of runners who finished the race in between 5.5 and 11.5 minutes. **(2 marks)**

$$20 + \frac{2}{3} \times 12 = 28$$

Your answer is only an estimate because you don't know how the data are distributed within each class.

Histogram facts

✓ No gaps between the bars.

✓ AREA of each bar is proportional to frequency.

✓ Vertical axis is labelled 'Frequency density'.

✓ Bars can be different widths.

✓ Frequency density = $\dfrac{\text{frequency}}{\text{class width}}$

✓ Bars are drawn between CLASS BOUNDARIES.

Have a look at page 86 for a reminder about upper and lower class boundaries.

The 6–9 bar is plotted from 5.5 to 9.5, so it has width 4. Its frequency density is 5.

Frequency = frequency density × class width
$$= 5 \times 4 = 20$$

You can work out the frequency in the 10–12 class using the total number of runners (40 − 20 − 6 − 2 = 12), or using the formula for frequency density.

EXAM ALERT!

Be careful – 11.5 isn't one of the class boundaries. Frequency is proportional to **area** in a histogram. $\frac{2}{3}$ of the 10–12 bar is below 11.5, so you should include $\frac{2}{3}$ of these runners.

Students have struggled with this topic in recent exams – be prepared!

Now try this

Alison weighed 50 apples, to the nearest gram. This table shows her results.

Weight (g)	55–57	58–63	64–68
Frequency	12	30	8

A histogram was drawn and the bar representing the 58–63 class was 4 cm wide and 6 cm high. For the 55–57 class, find

(a) the width   **(1 mark)**

(b) the height   **(2 marks)**

of the bar representing this class.

(a) When calculating the width, remember that the data has been rounded, so the class boundaries are half a unit above or below the values given in the table. The bar for the 58–63 class would be drawn from 57.5 to 63.5.

(b) Use the fact that the **area** of each bar is **proportional** to the frequency.

Skewness

Skewness is a way of describing the shape of a distribution. You need to be able to determine skewness by looking at a HISTOGRAM or a BOX PLOT, or using the QUARTILES, or using the MEAN, MEDIAN and MODE. There are THREE types of skewness.

 No skew (symmetric)

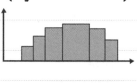

$Q_2 - Q_1 = Q_3 - Q_2$
Mode = Median = Mean

 Positive skew

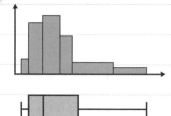

$Q_2 - Q_1 < Q_3 - Q_2$
Mode < Median < Mean

 Negative skew

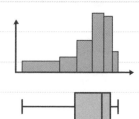

$Q_2 - Q_1 > Q_3 - Q_2$
Mean < Median < Mode

Worked example

This box plot summarises the distribution of the lengths, in cm, of all the snakes in a zoo.

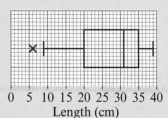

0 5 10 15 20 25 30 35 40
Length (cm)

Describe the skewness of the distribution. Justify your answer.

(2 marks)

$Q_2 - Q_1 = 31 - 20 = 11$
$Q_3 - Q_2 = 35 - 31 = 4$
So $Q_2 - Q_1 > Q_3 - Q_2$
Negative skew.

> You can see from the shape of the box plot that most of the data values are grouped at the upper end of the distribution. This means it is **negatively** skewed.
>
> Make sure you choose the right evidence to **justify** your answer. You can't tell the mean or the mode from a box plot, so the safest way is to use the quartiles.

Worked example

A researcher recorded the reaction times, in milliseconds, of 2000 individuals. He estimated the median and quartiles as follows:

$Q_1 = 18.6, Q_2 = 20.9, Q_3 = 26.5$

One measure of skewness is found using

$$\frac{Q_1 - 2Q_2 + Q_3}{Q_3 - Q_1}$$

Evaluate this measure and describe the skewness of these data. **(3 marks)**

$$\frac{18.6 - 2 \times 20.9 + 26.5}{26.5 - 18.6} = 0.418 \ (3 \text{ s.f.})$$

The skew is positive.

> If you have to calculate a **measure** or **coefficient** of skewness in the exam, it will be defined in the question.

Now try this

A group of 12 sprinters measured their 100 m times, in seconds.

12.5 10.7 11.3 11.6 10.5 11.8 13.5 15.2 14.1 11.9 10.3 12.8

Describe the skewness of this data. Justify your answer.

(4 marks)

> You will need to calculate either the **mean** and the **median**, or the **quartiles**, to justify your answer.

Comparing distributions

If you need to compare two distributions, you can use THREE things.

 1 Measures of LOCATION like the mean, median, mode and quartiles
Revise these on pages 84–86.

 2 Measures of SPREAD, like the range, interquartile range, variance, or standard deviation
Revise these on pages 85, 87 and 88.

 3 SKEWNESS
Revise this on page 91.

Worked example

This box plot shows the distribution of the prices of cars at Garage A.

At Garage B, the cheapest car was £1200 and the most expensive was £8400. The three quartiles were 3000, 6000 and 7400 respectively.

(a) On the same axes, draw a box plot to represent the data from Garage B. **(3 marks)**

(b) Compare and contrast the two box plots. **(4 marks)**

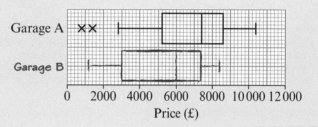

Median for Garage A (£7400) > Median for Garage B (£6000)

IQR for Garage B (£4400) > IQR for Garage A (£3400)

Both garages show negative skew $(Q_2 - Q_1 > Q_3 - Q_2)$.

At Garage A 50% of the cars cost less than £7400, but at Garage B 75% of the cars cost less than £7400.

Try to make four different observations for part (b).

1. Compare one measure of **location**, such as the median.

2. Compare a measure of **spread**, such as the interquartile range.

3. Compare **skewness**. Remember you can say that the distributions are similar as well as different. You can usually see the skewness of a distribution from a box plot so you don't need to do any calculations.

4. Describe the distributions in the **context** given in the question.

Now try this

The heights, in cm, of the members of two basketball teams are shown in this back-to-back stem and leaf diagram.

Key	7 | 18 | 2 means 187 cm in Team A and 182 cm in Team B

	Team A	Height (cm)	Team B	
(1)	7	18	2 3 5 5 9	(5)
(6)	8 8 5 4 2 0	19	0 1 3 4 4 5 5 7 7	(9)
(9)	9 6 6 5 3 2 2 1 0	20	0 2 5 6	(4)
(2)	6 3	21		

In part (c), make sure you compare one measure of **location**, one measure of **spread** and the **skewness** of the distributions.

For Team A

(a) find the values of the lower quartile, the median and the upper quartile **(3 marks)**

(b) (i) find the mean, $\bar{x}$, of the heights

  (ii) given that $\sum x^2 = 727\,823$, find the standard deviation of the heights. **(4 marks)**

For Team B, the mean is 193.5, $Q_1 = 189$, $Q_2 = 194$, $Q_3 = 197$ and the standard deviation is 7.1

(c) Compare the height distributions of the members of the two basketball teams. **(3 marks)**

Drawing Venn diagrams

You can use a Venn diagram to represent different EVENTS in a SAMPLE SPACE.

This Venn diagram shows the results when 50 people were surveyed about whether they owned a dog (D) or a cat (C). The rectangle represents the whole sample space (S), and each event is represented by an oval.

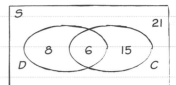

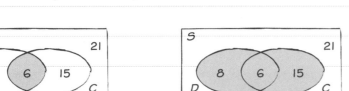

6 people owned a dog AND a cat. You can write this event as $D \cap C$. ∩ means AND or INTERSECTION.

8 + 6 + 15 = 29 people owned a dog OR a cat. You can write this event as $D \cup C$. ∪ means OR or UNION.

15 + 21 = 36 people DID NOT own a dog. You can write this event as D'. D' means NOT D or the COMPLEMENT of D.

Worked example

200 students were surveyed about whether they are taking history, German or physics A-Level:

87 take history

30 take German

49 take physics

12 take history and German

26 take history and physics

8 take German and physics

2 take all three subjects.

Draw a Venn diagram to represent this information.   **(5 marks)**

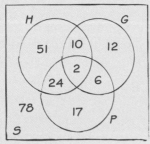

$H \cap G \cap P$
You can fill in the centre of the Venn diagram first. 2 students take all three subjects.

$H \cap G \cap P'$
The 12 students who take history and German **include** the 2 students who take all three subjects. So 12 − 2 = 10 students take history and German but **not** physics.

$H \cap G' \cap P'$
The 87 students who take history **include** the 10 + 2 + 24 = 36 students who take at least one other subject. So 87 − 36 = 51 take **only** history.

$H' \cap G' \cap P'$
51 + 12 + 17 + 10 + 24 + 6 + 2 = 122 students take at least one subject. So 200 − 122 = 78 take **none** of the three subjects.

Now try this

An Indian restaurant recorded the bread choices at 100 tables. 56 tables ordered naan, 22 tables ordered roti and 40 ordered paratha. There were 8 tables that ordered naan and roti, 19 that ordered naan and paratha, and 15 that ordered roti and paratha. 6 tables ordered all three types of bread.

Represent these data on a Venn diagram.   **(5 marks)**

Make sure you label the whole sample space S, and draw three closed, intersecting circles or ovals to represent the three events. Label them N, R and P.

Using Venn diagrams

You can use Venn diagrams to help you answer PROBABILITY questions. Find the region in the Venn diagram which SATISFIES THE CONDITIONS in the question, add up the total number of SUCCESSFUL OUTCOMES and divide by the total number of possible outcomes.

Worked example

This Venn diagram shows the numbers of students in a class who play tennis, football and hockey.

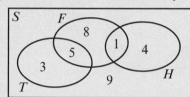

One of these students is selected at random.

(a) Show that the probability that the student plays more than one of the sports is $\frac{1}{5}$ **(2 marks)**

$3 + 5 + 8 + 9 + 1 + 4 = 30$

$\frac{5 + 1}{30} = \frac{6}{30} = \frac{1}{5}$

(b) Find the probability that the student plays either football or tennis, or both. **(2 marks)**

$\frac{3 + 8 + 1 + 5}{30} = \frac{17}{30}$

(c) Write down the probability that the student plays
   (i) tennis but not football
   (ii) all three sports. **(2 marks)**

(i) $\frac{3}{30} = \frac{1}{10}$ (ii) 0

EXAM ALERT!

Make sure you add up the outcomes for **all** the regions you are interested in:

(a)   (b)   (c) (i)

For part (c) (ii), there is no region where all three sports overlap, so no students played all three sports.

> Students have struggled with this topic in recent exams – be prepared!

Worked example

For the events A and B, $P(A \cap B') = 0.27$, $P(A' \cap B) = 0.14$ and $P(A \cup B) = 0.72$

(a) Draw a Venn diagram to illustrate the complete sample space for events A and B. **(3 marks)**

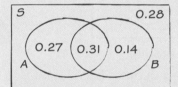

> The total of all the probabilities must add up to 1.

(b) Write down the value of $P(A)$ and the value of $P(B)$. **(3 marks)**

$P(A) = 0.27 + 0.31 = 0.58$

$P(B) = 0.31 + 0.14 = 0.45$

Now try this

A survey showed that 80% of students in a school own a laptop, and 22% of students own a tablet. 15% of students own neither a laptop nor a tablet.

(a) Draw a Venn diagram to represent this information.
   (4 marks)

A student is chosen at random.

(b) Write down the probability that this student owns a laptop but not a tablet. **(1 mark)**

> You can write probabilities as percentages on a Venn diagram. Remember that the percentages in the whole sample space need to add up to 100%.

Conditional probability

If one event HAS ALREADY OCCURRED, the probability of other events occurring might CHANGE. This is called conditional probability. The probability that an event X occurs GIVEN THAT an event Y has ALREADY occurred is written as $P(X \mid Y)$.

Using Venn diagrams

You can solve some conditional probability problems using a Venn diagram. If an event has already occurred, then the sample space for the other events is RESTRICTED. These Venn diagrams show the outcomes of two events, A and B.

Complete sample space

$P(A) = \dfrac{8 + 3}{8 + 3 + 4 + 5}$

$= \dfrac{11}{20}$

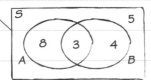

Event B occurs

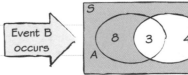

Restricted sample space GIVEN THAT event B has occurred

$P(A \mid B) = \dfrac{3}{3 + 4} = \dfrac{3}{7}$

Worked example

This Venn diagram shows the burger toppings chosen by a group of 50 diners at a restaurant. The choices are avocado, bacon and cheese.

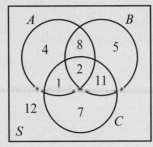

A diner is chosen at random.

(a) Given that the diner chooses bacon, find the probability that she also chooses avocado. **(2 marks)**

$$\frac{8 + 2}{8 + 2 + 11 + 5} = \frac{10}{26} = \frac{5}{13}$$

A second diner is chosen at random.

(b) Given that the diner chooses at least one of the three toppings, find the probability that she chooses all three. **(3 marks)**

$$\frac{2}{4 + 8 + 5 + 1 + 2 + 11 + 7} = \frac{2}{38} = \frac{1}{19}$$

(a) Look at this restricted sample space:

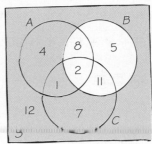

Of the $8 + 2 + 11 + 5 = 26$ diners who chose bacon, $8 + 2 = 10$ also chose avocado.

(b) Look at this restricted sample space:

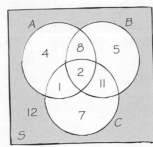

Look at this restricted sample space:

Now try this

Look at the Venn diagram in the Worked example. A third diner is chosen at random. Given that the diner chooses either avocado or bacon, work out the probability that she chooses cheese.

(3 marks)

Probability formulae

These two probability formulae are given in the formulae booklet. If a probability problem involves SET NOTATION (∪ and ∩) and it does not ask you to draw a Venn diagram, it might be easier to solve it using these formulae.

Probability

$$P(A \cup B) = P(A) + P(B) - P(A \cap B)$$
$$P(A \cap B) = P(A)\,P(B|A)$$

This is sometimes called the ADDITION RULE.

This is the CONDITIONAL PROBABILITY RULE.
Look at the restricted sample space AFTER event A has occurred:

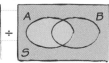

$$P(B \mid A) = \frac{P(A \cap B)}{P(A)}$$

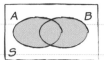 = 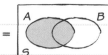 + 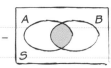 −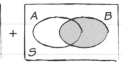

Worked example

Two events A and B are such that
$P(A \cap B') = 0.15$, $P(B) = 0.3$ and $P(A \mid B) = 0.2$
Find the value of

(a) $P(A \cap B)$ **(2 marks)**

$P(A \cap B) = P(B) \times P(A \mid B)$
$= 0.3 \times 0.2$
$= 0.06$

(b) $P(A \cup B)$ **(1 mark)**

$0.15 + 0.3 = 0.45$

(c) $P(A)$ **(2 marks)**

$P(A \cup B) = P(A) + P(B) - P(A \cap B)$
$0.45 = P(A) + 0.3 - 0.06$
$P(A) = 0.21$

(a) This is the conditional probability rule.

(b) Use the fact that
$$P(A \cup B) = P(A \cap B') + P(B)$$
You can see this from this Venn diagram, but it is a useful formula to learn.

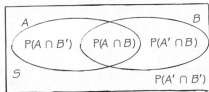

(c) This is the addition rule. You could also use the fact that
$$P(A) = P(A \cap B') + P(A \cap B)$$
$$= 0.15 + 0.06$$

Now try this

In a survey of a group of students $\frac{2}{3}$ played competitive sports and $\frac{2}{5}$ played video games. Of those who played competitive sports, $\frac{7}{25}$ also played video games.

Find the probability that a randomly selected member of the group

(a) plays competitive sports and video games **(2 marks)**

(b) plays neither competitive sports nor video games. **(4 marks)**

You might need to define your own events. For the randomly selected student, there are two events:

C = plays competitive sports
V = plays video games.

You can rewrite the information given as
$P(C) = \frac{2}{3}$, $P(V) = \frac{2}{5}$ and $P(V \mid C) = \frac{7}{25}$

(a) You want to find $P(C \cap V)$. You can use the formula $P(C \cap V) = P(C) \times P(V \mid C)$

(b) You want to find $P(C' \cap V')$.
Use your result to part (a), and the addition rule.

Then use the fact that
$P(C' \cap V') = 1 - P(C \cup V)$

Independent events

Two events are statistically independent if the outcome of one has NO EFFECT on the probability of the other.

Determining independence

If two events A and B are independent then:

 $P(A \mid B) = P(A)$ So $P(A \mid B') = P(A)$

 $P(B \mid A) = P(B)$ So $P(B \mid A') = P(B)$

 $P(A \cap B) = P(A) \times P(B)$

You only need to show that ONE of these conditions is true to show that A and B are independent.
If any ONE of these is NOT TRUE then the two events are NOT INDEPENDENT.

You need to remember these conditions for independence – they are not given in the formulae booklet.

You could also use conditional probability:

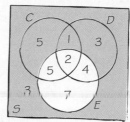

There is more on this on page 95.

$P(D \mid E) = \dfrac{2 + 4}{5 + 2 + 4 + 7} = \dfrac{6}{18} = \dfrac{1}{3} = P(D)$

This Venn diagram shows the numbers of students in a class of 30 who watched Coronation Street (C), Doctor Who (D) or EastEnders (E).

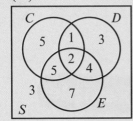

Determine whether watching EastEnders and watching Doctor Who are statistically independent. **(3 marks)**

$P(D) = \dfrac{1 + 3 + 2 + 4}{30} = \dfrac{10}{30} = \dfrac{1}{3}$

$P(E) = \dfrac{5 + 2 + 4 + 7}{30} = \dfrac{18}{30} = \dfrac{3}{5}$

$P(D \cap E) = \dfrac{2 + 4}{30} = \dfrac{6}{30} = \dfrac{1}{5}$

$P(D) \times P(E) = \dfrac{1}{3} \times \dfrac{3}{5} = \dfrac{1}{5} = P(D \cap E)$

So D and E are statistically independent.

Mutually exclusive events

Two events are mutually exclusive if they CANNOT BOTH occur.
On the Venn diagram on the right, the events A and B are mutually exclusive because they DO NOT OVERLAP.

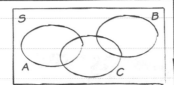

For two mutually exclusive events A and B: $P(A \cap B) = 0$ so $P(A \cup B) = P(A) + P(B)$

This is a version of the addition formula in the booklet. There is more about this on page 96.

The events A and B are independent.
$P(A) = \frac{2}{5}$ and $P(A \cup B) = \frac{3}{4}$
Find

(a) $P(B)$ **(4 marks)**

(b) $P(A' \cap B)$ **(2 marks)**

(c) $P(B' \mid A)$.   **(2 marks)**

For part (a) you will need to use the formula
$P(A \cup B) = P(A) + P(B) - P(A \cap B)$
A and B are independent so you know that
$P(A \cap B) = P(A) \times P(B)$
Use this condition to write $P(A \cap B)$ in terms of $P(B)$, and then solve an equation to find the value of $P(B)$.

Tree diagrams

Tree diagrams can be used to solve some probability problems. In your S1 exam, it's usually only a good idea to draw a tree diagram when you are told to do so in the question.

Worked example

A computer virus is known to infect 7% of all computers. A software company writes a virus checker to determine whether or not a computer is infected. If a computer is infected, the test is positive with probability 0.95

If a computer is not infected, the test is positive with probability 0.1

(a) Draw a tree diagram to represent this information. **(3 marks)**

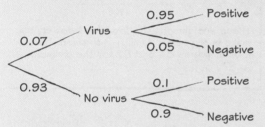

A computer is selected at random and tested.

(b) Find the probability that the test is positive. **(3 marks)**

P(Positive) = 0.07 × 0.95 + 0.93 × 0.1
 = 0.1595

A second computer is selected at random and tests positive for the virus.

(c) Find the probability that this computer does not have the virus. **(2 marks)**

$$P(\text{No virus} \mid \text{Positive}) = \frac{P(\text{No virus} \cap \text{Positive})}{P(\text{Positive})}$$

$$= \frac{0.93 \times 0.1}{0.1595}$$

$$= 0.583 \text{ (3 s.f.)}$$

Tree diagram checklist

Make sure that you:

✓ write a probability on EVERY branch

✓ write an outcome at the END of every branch.

In your S1 exam you DON'T need to:

✗ draw a tree diagram unless it's asked for in the question

✗ work out the probabilities of ALL the final outcomes – you will be asked for specific probabilities later in the question.

On each pair of branches the probabilities need to **add up to 1**.
So P(No virus) = 1 − 0.07 = 0.93

On a tree diagram you:

P(Virus ∩ Positive) = 0.07 × 0.95
P(No virus ∩ Positive) = 0.93 × 0.1
Add these together to find P(Positive).

This is a conditional probability question. You need to use the formula
$$P(B) = P(A)\,P(B \mid A) \text{ or } P(B \mid A) = \frac{P(A \cap B)}{P(A)}$$
The probability that the computer does **not** have the virus is high even if it tests positive, so this test is not very effective.

Now try this

In a board game, Amy picks a question card. She can pick an easy, medium or hard question, with probabilities 0.54, 0.31 and 0.15 respectively.

The probabilities that she answers each type of question correctly are 0.8, 0.5 and 0.1 respectively.

(a) Draw a tree diagram to represent this information. **(3 marks)**

(b) Amy picks a card at random and answers the question. Work out the probability that she answers the question correctly. **(4 marks)**

(c) Given that Amy answers the question correctly, find the probability that it was not a hard question. **(4 marks)**

Correlation

Correlation tells you about the relationship between two variables. The PRODUCT MOMENT CORRELATION COEFFICIENT (PMCC) is an important measure of correlation. Revise how to CALCULATE it on this page, and how to INTERPRET it on page 100.

Calculating the PMCC

The letter r is usually used for the PMCC.
Use this formula to calculate it:

$$r = \frac{S_{xy}}{\sqrt{S_{xx}S_{yy}}}$$

It is always a value between -1 and 1.

This formula is given in the booklet. There are other versions of this formula in the booklet as well, but this one is the most useful.

Summary statistics

The values S_{xy}, S_{xx} and S_{yy} in the formula for the PMCC are summary statistics. You might be given these, or you might have to calculate them yourself.

$$S_{xx} = \sum x^2 - \frac{(\sum x)^2}{n}$$

$$S_{yy} = \sum y^2 - \frac{(\sum y)^2}{n}$$

$$S_{xy} = \sum xy - \frac{(\sum x)(\sum y)}{n}$$

These are given in the formulae booklet, but make sure you are familiar with them. Have a look at pages 84 and 87 for the definitions of $\sum x$ and $\sum x^2$.

Worked example

The ages h years and w years of a group of 8 husbands and wives are shown in the table below.

h	36	72	37	36	51	50	47	50
w	35	67	33	35	50	46	47	42

$\left[\sum h^2 = 18\,955,\ \sum w^2 = 16\,617,\ \sum hw = 17\,724\right]$

(a) Calculate S_{hh}, S_{ww} and S_{hw}. **(6 marks)**

$\sum h = 379$ $\sum w = 355$

$S_{hh} = 18955 - \dfrac{379^2}{8} = 999.875$

$S_{ww} = 16617 - \dfrac{355^2}{8} = 863.875$

$S_{hw} = 17724 - \dfrac{379 \times 355}{8} = 905.875$

(b) Calculate the value of the product moment correlation coefficient between h and w. **(3 marks)**

$r = \dfrac{S_{hw}}{\sqrt{S_{hh}S_{ww}}} = \dfrac{905.875}{\sqrt{999.875 \times 863.875}}$

$= 0.97469\ldots = 0.975$ (3 s.f.)

You have been given $\sum h^2$, $\sum w^2$ and $\sum hw$. You also need to know $\sum h$ and $\sum w$.

$\sum h = 36 + 72 + 37 + 36 +$
$\qquad 50 + 47 + 50$
$\quad = 379$

$\sum w = 35 + 67 + 33 + 35 + 50 +$
$\qquad 46 + 47 + 42$
$\quad = 355$

Calculator caution

If your calculator can work out the PMCC automatically, you should only use this to CHECK your answer. Use the formulae given on this page, and always WRITE DOWN the calculations you are using to show your working.

Now try this

A biologist recorded the length, l cm, and the weight, w kg, of 50 rabbits.
The following summary statistics were calculated from his data.

$\sum l = 2015$ $\sum l^2 = 81\,938.5$ $\sum w = 176.5$ $\sum lw = 7332.5$ $S_{ww} = 72.25$

(a) Find S_{ll} and S_{lw}. **(3 marks)**

(b) Calculate, to 3 significant figures, the product moment correlation coefficient between l and w. **(2 marks)**

Understanding the PMCC

The PRODUCT MOMENT CORRELATION COEFFICIENT (PMCC) tells you the STRENGTH of the LINEAR CORRELATION between two variables.

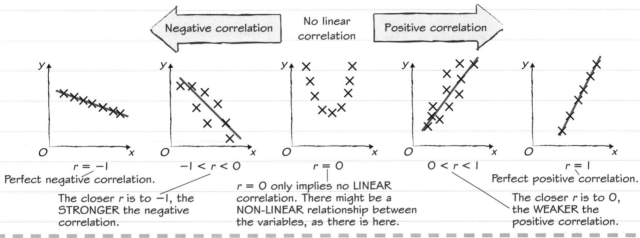

Negative correlation   No linear correlation   Positive correlation

$r = -1$
Perfect negative correlation.

$-1 < r < 0$
The closer r is to -1, the STRONGER the negative correlation.

$r = 0$
$r = 0$ only implies no LINEAR correlation. There might be a NON-LINEAR relationship between the variables, as there is here.

$0 < r < 1$
The closer r is to 0, the WEAKER the positive correlation.

$r = 1$
Perfect positive correlation.

Worked example

A biologist recorded the gestation period, d days, and average litter size, x, of 15 mammals.

These data are summarised below.

$S_{dd} = 301\,700$ $S_{xx} = 25.28$ $S_{dx} = -1233$

(a) Calculate, to 3 significant figures, the product moment correlation coefficient for these data. **(2 marks)**

$$r = \frac{-1233}{\sqrt{301700 \times 25.28}} = -0.446 \text{ (3 s.f.)}$$

(b) Give an interpretation of your coefficient. **(1 mark)**

As the gestation period of the mammals increases, the average litter size decreases.

Correlation and real life

Just because two variables show correlation, they are NOT NECESSARILY connected. If you recorded mobile phone ownership and house values over the last 20 years you would see strong positive correlation, as both have increased. But common sense tells you that these variables are probably not connected.

EXAM ALERT!

Interpret means you need to refer to the **context** of the question. **Do not** just write 'negative correlation'. You need to write a sentence about gestation periods and litter sizes for these data.

Students have struggled with this topic in recent exams – be prepared!

Now try this

A student drew scatter diagrams for three sets of data.

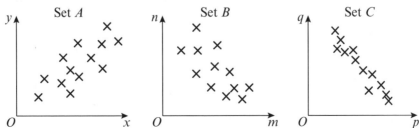

Set *A*   Set *B*   Set *C*

The student calculated the value of the product moment correlation coefficient for each of the sets of data. The values were -0.48, -0.93 and 0.72

Write down, with a reason, which value corresponds to which set of data. **(6 marks)**

Regression lines

A regression line on a SCATTER DIAGRAM is a type of LINE OF BEST FIT. It can be used as a LINEAR MODEL for the relationship between the two variables.

Finding the regression line

The equation of the regression line (or LEAST SQUARES regression line) of y on x is

$$y = a + bx$$

where $b = \dfrac{S_{xy}}{S_{xx}}$ and $a = \bar{y} - b\bar{x}$ ——— Mean of the y values
——— Mean of the x values

b is called the REGRESSION COEFFICIENT.

These formulae are given in the booklet. For a reminder about calculating S_{xy} and S_{xx} look at page 99.

Order is important

The formula on the left gives you the regression line of Y ON X. The ORDER of the variables IS important – the regression line of x on y will have a DIFFERENT EQUATION.

In the regression model $y = a + bx$, x is the INDEPENDENT (or EXPLANATORY) variable, and y is the DEPENDENT (or RESPONSE) variable. In an experiment, x would be the variable you changed, and y would be the variable you recorded. You always plot the explanatory variable on the HORIZONTAL axis.

Worked example

An internet provider advertises an internet connection speed of 12 Mbps. Dhevan records the speed of 8 internet connections, v Mbps, at different distances, d km, from the phone exchange.

d	9.2	13.6	7.5	4.2	5.9	5.3	22.1	0.8
v	8.3	7.8	8.5	11.4	10.3	9.5	6.2	10.9

[You may use $S_{dd} = 307.2$, $S_{vv} = 21.23$ and $S_{dv} = -74.19$]

(a) Find the equation of the regression line of v on d in the form $v = a + bd$ **(5 marks)**

$$b = \frac{S_{dv}}{S_{dd}} = \frac{-74.19}{307.2} = -0.24150\ldots$$

$$\bar{d} = \frac{9.2 + 13.6 + 7.5 + 4.2 + 5.9 + 5.3 + 22.1 + 0.8}{8}$$
$$= 8.575$$

$$\bar{v} = \frac{8.3 + 7.8 + 8.5 + 11.4 + 10.3 + 9.5 + 6.2 + 10.9}{8}$$
$$= 9.1125$$

$$a = \bar{v} - b\bar{d} = 9.1125 - (-0.2415\ldots) \times 8.575$$
$$= 11.1833\ldots$$

$$v = 11.18 - 0.2415d$$

You need to calculate the values of $\bar{d}$ and $\bar{v}$ before you can calculate the equation of the regression line. Always **calculate the value of b first**, because you need to use it in your calculation for a. Be really careful when you are substituting b into the formulae. b is **negative** here (because the correlation is negative), so your final equation will have a minus sign in it.

Validity

The value of the PRODUCT MOMENT CORRELATION COEFFICIENT tells you how accurately a LINEAR model represents the data. The closer it is to -1 or 1, the more accurate the model.

(b) State, with a reason, which variable is the explanatory variable. **(2 marks)**

Distance, d, because this variable can be controlled.

The product moment correlation coefficient for these data is -0.919

(c) Explain why a regression model of the form $v = a + bd$ is supported for these data. **(1 mark)**

r is close to -1, so the data show strong negative linear correlation.

Now try this

The body weight, x kg, and the brain weight, y grams, of 10 small mammals was recorded. The data are summarised below.

$S_{xx} = 205.09$ $\quad \sum xy = 2972.76$
$\sum x = 42.01$ $\quad \sum y = 338.72$

(a) Find S_{xy}. **(2 marks)**

(b) Calculate the equation of the regression line of y on x in the form $y = a + bx$ **(3 marks)**

Using regression lines

If you know a value of the INDEPENDENT variable, you can use a regression line (or its equation) to ESTIMATE the corresponding value of the DEPENDENT VARIABLE. This scatter diagram shows the mileage in miles per gallon of 9 cars, and their engine capacities.

To estimate the mileage of a car with a 3 litre engine, read up from 3 on the horizontal axis to the regression line, then across to the vertical axis. The estimate is 18 mpg. You could also use the equation of the regression line:
$y = 42.7 - 8.21 \times 3 = 18.07$

✗ $x = 1$ is OUTSIDE THE RANGE of the data. This is called EXTRAPOLATION and it produces an UNRELIABLE ESTIMATE.

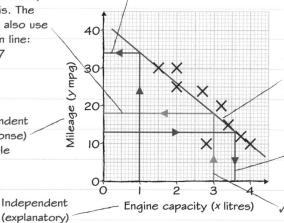

Dependent (response) variable

Independent (explanatory) variable

Engine capacity (x litres)

The equation of the regression line of y on x is $y = 42.7 - 8.21x$.

✗ You can only estimate a value of the DEPENDENT variable. You can't use the regression line of y on x to estimate a value of x given a value of y.

✓ $x = 3$ is WITHIN the range of the data. This is called INTERPOLATION and it produces a RELIABLE ESTIMATE.

Worked example

The age, x years, and shell size, y mm, of 8 Dungeness crabs were recorded.

y	151.8	150.4	140.3	133.4	155.9	153.3	141.6	127.7
x	3.3	3.0	2.4	2.3	3.3	3.0	2.7	2.2

$[S_{yy} = 726.68 \quad S_{xx} = 1.355 \quad S_{xy} = 29.85$
$\bar{y} = 144.3 \quad \bar{x} = 2.775]$

(a) Find the equation of the regression line of y on x in the form $y = a + bx$ **(4 marks)**

$b = \dfrac{S_{xy}}{S_{xx}} = \dfrac{29.85}{1.355} = 22.029...$

$a = 144.3 - 22.029... \times 2.775 = 83.168...$

$y = 83.17 + 22.03x$

(b) Give a practical interpretation of the slope, b. **(1 mark)**

A typical crab shell will grow about 22 mm per year.

(c) Use your regression line to estimate the shell size of a Dungeness crab which is 1.6 years old. **(2 marks)**

$y = 83.17 + 22.03 \times 1.6 = 118.418$ so a 1.6-year-old crab will have a shell size of approximately 118 mm.

(d) Comment on the reliability of your estimate, giving a reason for your answer. **(2 marks)**

This estimate is not reliable because it is an extrapolation. The age of this crab falls outside the range of ages in the data.

Interpreting the slope

The value of b in the regression model is the SLOPE or GRADIENT of the line. This tells you roughly how much the DEPENDENT variable increases when the INDEPENDENT variable increases by 1.

In (d), **interpolation** is more reliable than **extrapolation**. $x = 1.6$ is outside the range of the data, so this is not a reliable estimate.

Now try this

(a) Use the regression model in the Worked example to estimate the shell size of a Dungeness crab which is 2.9 years old. **(2 marks)**

(b) Comment on the reliability of your estimate, giving a reason for your answer. **(2 marks)**

(c) Calculate the product moment correlation coefficient for these data. **(2 marks)**

(d) Is a linear regression model a suitable model for these data? Give a reason for your answer. **(1 mark)**

Coding

Coding is a way of making statistics calculations easier. Each data value is CODED to make a new set of data values. It is especially useful when you are dealing with LARGE DATA VALUES.

Transforming data

You can use this formula to transform a data value x into a new data value y:

$$y = \frac{x - a}{b}$$

a and b are numbers chosen to make the calculations as simple as possible. In your S1 exam, you will be told which values of a and b are being used.

Effects of coding

If data is coded, some statistics will change and some will not.

	Before	After
Data values	x	$\frac{x - a}{b}$
Mean	$\bar{x}$	$\frac{\bar{x} - a}{b}$
Median	m	$\frac{m - a}{b}$
Standard deviation	s	$\frac{s}{b}$
PMCC	r	r
S_{xx}	S_{xx}	$\frac{S_{xx}}{b^2}$

Worked example

A farmer collected data on the annual rainfall, x cm, and the annual yield of peas, p tonnes per acre. The data for annual rainfall was coded using $v = \frac{x - 5}{10}$ and the following statistics were found.

$$S_{vv} = 5.753 \quad S_{pv} = 1.688 \quad S_{pp} = 1.168$$
$$\bar{p} = 3.22 \quad \bar{v} = 4.42$$

(a) Find the equation of the regression line of p on v in the form $p = a + bv$ **(4 marks)**

$$b = \frac{S_{pv}}{S_{vv}} = \frac{1.688}{5.753} = 0.2934\ldots$$

$$a = 3.22 - 4.42 \times 0.2934\ldots = 1.9231\ldots$$

$$p = 1.92 + 0.293v$$

(b) Using your regression line, estimate the annual yield of peas per acre when the annual rainfall is 85 cm.   **(2 marks)**

$$x = 85 \text{ so } v = \frac{85 - 5}{10} = 8$$

$$p = 1.92 + 0.293 \times 8 = 4.264$$

Be careful when you are asked to predict values from a regression equation using coded data. You have been given the **real-life** value, but the regression equation uses the **coded** values. Convert $x = 85$ into the coded value **before** substituting it into the regression equation.

You could also substitute $v = \frac{x - 5}{10}$ to find the regression line of p on x:

$$p = 1.92 + 0.293 \left(\frac{x - 5}{10}\right)$$

$$= 1.7735 + 0.0293x$$

Now try this

A group of 10 students took computer-marked tests in maths and ICT. Their maths marks, x, and ICT marks, y, are summarised below.

$$\sum x = 668 \quad \sum x^2 = 47\,870 \quad S_{xx} = 3247.6 \quad S_{yy} = 3204.9 \quad S_{xy} = 2485.8$$

(a) Calculate the mean, $\bar{x}$, and standard deviation of the maths marks.   **(3 marks)**

(b) Find the product moment correlation coefficient of these data.   **(2 marks)**

An instructor discovered that a computer error had caused the first question to be marked correct on all the students' maths tests. He reduced each student's mark by 8, and then increased it by 10%.

(c) Find the mean and standard deviation of the adjusted maths marks.   **(4 marks)**

(d) Write down the value of the correlation coefficient between the adjusted maths marks and the ICT marks.   **(1 mark)**

Random variables

A DISCRETE RANDOM VARIABLE can take a range of discrete NUMERICAL VALUES. To define a random variable you need to know the range of values it can take (its SAMPLE SPACE) and the probability that it takes each one. The probability that the random variable takes a certain value is given by its PROBABILITY FUNCTION.

The sum of probabilities

The most important fact you will use about random variables in your S1 exam is that the probabilities of ALL THE POSSIBLE VALUES of any random variable, X, always ADD UP TO 1. Another way of saying this is:

$$\sum_{\text{all } x} P(X = x) = 1$$

You always use UPPER CASE letters for random variables, and LOWER CASE letters for the values they can take. $P(X = x)$ means 'the probability that the random variable X takes the value x'.

Probability distributions

You can write the outcome from this spinner as a random variable X.

You can write its PROBABILITY DISTRIBUTION in a table.

This is the SAMPLE SPACE for this random variable. X can only take these values.

x	3	5	7
$P(X = x)$	$\frac{1}{6}$	$\frac{1}{3}$	$\frac{1}{2}$

$\frac{1}{6} + \frac{1}{3} + \frac{1}{2} = 1$

Its probability distribution could also be given using a PROBABILITY FUNCTION:

$$P(X = x) = \frac{x - 1}{12} \quad x = 3, 5, 7$$

For example $P(X = 5) = \frac{5 - 1}{12} = \frac{4}{12} = \frac{1}{3}$

Worked example

The random variable X has probability function

$$P(X = x) = \begin{cases} kx^2, & x = 1, 2, 3 \\ 2kx, & x = 4, 5 \end{cases}$$

where k is a constant.

(a) Find the value of k.   **(2 marks)**

$k + 4k + 9k + 8k + 10k = 1$

$32k = 1$

$k = \frac{1}{32}$

(b) Find $P(X > 2)$.   **(2 marks)**

$P(X > 2) = P(X = 3) + P(X = 4) + P(X = 5)$

$= \frac{9}{32} + \frac{8}{32} + \frac{10}{32} = \frac{27}{32}$

The curly bracket means that the probability function is different for different values of x. For $x = 1$, 2 and 3 you use $P(X = x) = kx^2$ and for $x = 4$ and 5 you use $P(X = x) = 2kx$.

For part (a), write an expression for the sum of the probabilities in terms of k. $\sum P(X = x) = 1$, so you can write an equation and solve it to find k.

For part (b), add up the probabilities for the values of X which make the inequality true.

Now try this

For part (b), solve the inequality first.

1. The random variable Y has probability function

$$P(Y = y) = \frac{(y - 1)^2}{30} \quad y = 2, 3, 4, 5$$

(a) Construct a table giving the probability distribution of Y.   **(3 marks)**

(b) Find $P(Y > 3)$.   **(2 marks)**

2. The discrete random variable X has probability distribution given by

x	-2	-1	0	1	2
$P(X = x)$	0.1	a	0.15	$2a$	0.15

where a is a constant.

(a) Find the value of a.   **(2 marks)**

(b) Find $P(3X + 1 \leqslant 6)$.   **(2 marks)**

Cumulative distribution

The CUMULATIVE DISTRIBUTION FUNCTION $F(x)$ of a random variable is defined as

$$F(x) = P(X \leqslant x)$$

You can think of it as the RUNNING TOTAL of the probabilities.

This row shows the cumulative distribution function of X.

Here is the probability distribution of a random variable with probability function $P(X = x) = 0.05x, \quad x = 1, 3, 6, 10$

x	1	3	6	10
$P(X = x)$	0.05	0.15	0.3	0.5
$F(x)$	0.05	0.2	0.5	1

$F(6) = P(X \leqslant 6)$
$= P(X = 1) + P(X = 3) + P(X = 6)$
$= 0.05 + 0.15 + 0.3 = 0.5$

Worked example

The discrete random variable Y can only take the values 1, 2 or 3. For these values the cumulative distribution function is defined by

$$F(y) = \frac{(y + k)^2}{49}, \quad y = 1, 2, 3$$

where k is a positive integer.

(a) Find k. **(2 marks)**

$F(3) = 1$

$\dfrac{(3 + k)^2}{49} = 1$

$(3 + k)^2 = 49$

$3 + k = \pm 7$

$\underline{k = 4}$ or $k = -10$

(b) Find the probability distribution of Y.

(3 marks)

$F(1) = \dfrac{(1 + 4)^2}{49} = \dfrac{25}{49}$

$F(2) = \dfrac{(2 + 4)^2}{49} = \dfrac{36}{49}$

y	1	2	3
$P(Y = y)$	$\dfrac{25}{49}$	$\dfrac{11}{49}$	$\dfrac{13}{49}$

Key facts for F(x)

Remember these key facts about the cumulative distribution function of a random variable X.

✓ It is always written with an UPPER CASE F.

✓ It is always INCREASING.

✓ $F(x)$ is only defined if x is in the SAMPLE SPACE of X.

✓ For the SMALLEST value of x, $F(x) = P(X = x)$.

✓ For the LARGEST value of x, $F(x) = 1$.

The largest possible value of the random variable is 3, so $F(3) = 1$. Use this fact to write an equation and solve it to find k.
$F(y)$ is the **cumulative** distribution function, so:

$P(X = 1) = F(1) = \dfrac{25}{49}$

$P(X = 2) = F(2) - F(1) = \dfrac{36}{49} - \dfrac{25}{49} = \dfrac{11}{49}$

$P(X = 3) = F(3) - F(2) = 1 - \dfrac{36}{49} = \dfrac{13}{49}$

Now try this

The discrete random variable X can only take the values 1, 2, 3 or 4. It has probability distribution

x	1	2	3	4
$P(X = x)$	a	0.4	b	c

where a, b and c are constants.

The cumulative distribution function $F(x)$ of X is given in the following table

x	1	2	3	4
$F(x)$	0.2	d	0.7	e

where d and e are constants.

(a) Compare the probability distribution and the **cumulative** distribution to work out the missing values. Remember that $F(4) = 1$.

(b) Solve the inequality first:
$P(2X - 1 > 4)$ so $P(X > 2.5)$

(a) Find the values of a, b, c, d and e.

(6 marks)

(b) Find $P(2X - 1 > 4)$. **(2 marks)**

Expectation and variance

You can calculate the expectation and the variance of a DISCRETE RANDOM VARIABLE.

Expectation

The EXPECTATION of a random variable X is sometimes called the MEAN of X. It is written as $E(X)$ or μ. Use this formula to work it out:

$$E(X) = \sum_{\text{all } x} x P(X = x)$$

Multiply each value for x by its probability, then add them all together.

Variance

The VARIANCE of a random variable X is written as $\text{Var}(X)$ or σ^2. Work it out using this formula:

$$\text{Var}(X) = E(X^2) - [E(X)]^2$$

These formulae are in the booklet, but they look more complicated. It's simpler to memorise these straightforward versions.

Worked example

Multiply each x-value by its probability, then add them all together. It's easiest to find $E(X)$ when the frequency distribution is written out in a table.

The discrete random variable X has the probability distribution

x	1	2	3	4
$P(X = x)$	0.6	0.05	0.1	0.25

(a) Find $E(X)$ **(2 marks)**

$E(X) = \sum x P(X = x)$

$= (1 \times 0.6) + (2 \times 0.05) + (3 \times 0.1) + (4 \times 0.25) = 2.0$

(b) Find $\text{Var}(X)$ **(3 marks)**

$E(X^2) = (1^2 \times 0.6) + (2^2 \times 0.05) + (3^2 \times 0.1) + (4^2 \times 0.25)$

$= 5.7$

$\text{Var}(X) = E(X^2) - [E(X)]^2 \ 5.7 - 2^2 = 1.7$

Finding $E(X^2)$

Before you can calculate the VARIANCE you need to know $E(X)$ and $E(X^2)$. To find $E(X^2)$ you multiply the SQUARE of each value for x by its probability, then add them all together.

Discrete uniform distribution

If all the probabilities of a random variable X are the same, then it has a DISCRETE UNIFORM DISTRIBUTION.

If $x = 1, 2, 3, \dots, n$ and $P(X = x) = \frac{1}{n}$ then

$$E(X) = \frac{n+1}{2} \qquad \text{Var}(X) = \frac{(n+1)(n-1)}{12}$$

You could work these out, but if you learn them you might save some time in the exam.

The random variable Y has the discrete uniform distribution $P(Y = y) = \frac{1}{6}, \ y = 1, 2, 3, 4, 5, 6$

y	1	2	3	4	5	6
$P(Y = y)$	$\frac{1}{6}$	$\frac{1}{6}$	$\frac{1}{6}$	$\frac{1}{6}$	$\frac{1}{6}$	$\frac{1}{6}$

$E(X) = \frac{6+1}{2} = \frac{7}{2}$ $\text{Var}(X) = \frac{(6+1)(6-1)}{12} = \frac{35}{12}$

Now try this

The sum of the probabilities must add up to 1, so $0.25 + 0.1 + a + b = 1$.

1. The discrete random variable X has the probability function
$$P(X = x) = \frac{(3x - 2)}{22} \text{ for } x = 1, 2, 3, 4$$
(a) Construct a table giving the probability distribution of X. **(3 marks)**
(b) Find the exact value of $E(X)$. **(2 marks)**
(c) Show that $\text{Var}(X) = 0.785$ to 3 significant figures. **(4 marks)**

2. The discrete random variable X has the probability distribution

x	0	1	2	3
$P(X = x)$	0.25	0.1	a	b

(a) Given that $E(X) = 1.5$, write down two equations involving a and b. **(3 marks)**
(b) Find the value of a and the value of b. **(3 marks)**

Functions of random variables

If you know the EXPECTATION and the VARIANCE of a discrete random variable, then you can find the expectation and variance of a FUNCTION of the random variable using these rules.

 $E(aX + b) = aE(X) + b$

 $Var(aX + b) = a^2 Var(X)$

Neither of these rules is given in the formulae booklet so make sure you LEARN them.

Worked example

The discrete random variable X has the probability distribution

x	1	2	3	4
$P(X = x)$	0.2	0.2	0.3	0.3

Given that $E(X) = 2.7$ and $Var(X) = 1.21$, find

(a) $E(3X - 1)$ **(2 marks)**

$E(3X - 1) = 3E(X) - 1$
      $= 3 \times 2.7 - 1$
      $= 7.1$

(b) $Var(2X + 4)$ **(2 marks)**

$Var(2X + 4) = 2^2 \times Var(X)$
          $= 4 \times 1.21$
          $= 4.84$

This is the probability distribution for the random variable $Y = 3X - 1$.

y	2	5	8	11
$P(Y = y)$	0.2	0.2	0.3	0.3

The values of x are transformed, but the **probabilities stay the same**. You could work out $E(Y)$ directly from the table:

$E(Y) = (2 \times 0.2) + (5 \times 0.2) + (8 \times 0.3)$
        $+ (11 \times 0.3)$
      $= 0.4 + 1 + 2.4 + 3.3$
      $= 7.1$ ✓

Be careful – the value of b (the '+ 4' in this part) has **no effect** on the variance.

Worked example

The random variable X has the discrete uniform distribution

$$P(X = x) = \frac{1}{4} \quad x = 1, 2, 3, 4$$

(a) Write down the value of $E(X)$ and show that $Var(X) = \frac{5}{4}$ **(3 marks)**

$E(X) = \dfrac{n + 1}{2} = \dfrac{5}{2}$

$Var(X) = \dfrac{(n - 1)(n + 1)}{12} = \dfrac{(4 - 1)(4 + 1)}{12}$

        $= \dfrac{15}{12} = \dfrac{5}{4}$

(b) Find $E(3X - 1)$ **(2 marks)**

$E(3X - 1) = 3E(X) - 1$
        $= 3 \times \dfrac{5}{2} - 1 = \dfrac{13}{2}$

(c) Find $Var(6 - 2X)$ **(2 marks)**

$Var(6 - 2X) = (-2)^2 \times Var(X)$

        $= 4 \times \dfrac{5}{4} = 5$

EXAM ALERT!

The question says 'write down' so you can save time by quoting the formulae for the expectation and variance of a **discrete uniform distribution** directly. For a reminder about these, look at page 106.

Students have struggled with this topic in recent exams – be prepared!

Now try this

1. For a discrete random variable X, $E(X) = -0.4$ and $Var(X) = 5.8$, find
   (a) $E(1 - 3X)$ **(2 marks)**
   (b) $Var(3X - 10)$.   **(2 marks)**

2. The random variable Y has probability function
   $$P(Y = y) = \frac{\sqrt{y}}{10} \quad y = 1, 4, 9, 16$$
   (a) Find $E(2Y + 1)$ **(3 marks)**
   (b) Find $Var(5 - Y)$ **(4 marks)**

Normal distribution 1

The normal distribution is a good model for lots of CONTINUOUS distributions in real life. A normal distribution is defined by its MEAN, μ, and its STANDARD DEVIATION, σ. You write $N(\mu, \sigma^2)$.

This is the STANDARD normal distribution curve, Z. It has MEAN (μ) = 0 and STANDARD DEVIATION (σ) = 1.

This means 'Z is distributed with a normal distribution with $\mu = 0$ and $\sigma = 1$'.

The shaded AREA is the PROBABILITY that $Z < a$ (or $Z \le a$). The total area under the standard normal distribution curve is 1.

$Z \sim N(0, 1^2)$ $P(Z < a)$ is given by the function $\Phi(z)$. Φ is the Greek capital letter phi. You can find $\Phi(z)$ using the TABLES in the FORMULAE BOOKLET.

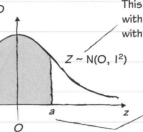

Golden rule

The normal distribution tables in the formula booklet use STANDARDISED (z) values. You need to STANDARDISE any x-values BEFORE using the tables.

$$z = \frac{x - \mu}{\sigma}$$

Using tables

Here is a small extract from the NORMAL DISTRIBUTION table in the formulae booklet.

z	$\Phi(z)$
1.00	0.8413
1.01	0.8438
1.02	0.8461
1.03	0.8485

Using the table, $\Phi(1.02) = 0.8461$

$P(Z < 1.02) = 0.8461$
This is the shaded area in the diagram.

$Z \sim N(0, 1^2)$

Worked example

The lifetimes of fuses produced in a certain factory are normally distributed with mean 1400 hours and standard deviation 250 hours.

(a) Find the probability that a fuse produced by the factory has a lifetime of less than 1655 hours. **(2 marks)**

$$z = \frac{x - \mu}{\sigma} = \frac{1655 - 1400}{250} = 1.02$$

$P(X < 1655) = P(Z < 1.02) = 0.8461$

(b) In a batch of 2000 fuses, find the expected number having a lifetime of less than 1655 hours. **(2 marks)**

$0.8461 \times 2000 = 1690$ (3 s.f.)

From tables, $\Phi(1.02) = 0.8461$

Now try this

Remember to **standardise** the x-value before looking at the tables in the formulae booklet.
$$P(X < 3.2) = P\left(Z < \frac{3.2 - 3}{0.5}\right) = \Phi(0.4)$$

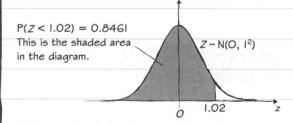

1. X is a random variable distributed with $X \sim N(3, 0.5^2)$
   Find $P(X < 3.2)$. **(2 marks)**

2. The numbers of matches in a box are found to be normally distributed with $\mu = 70$ and $\sigma = 6$

   (a) Find the probability that a randomly chosen match box contains fewer than 80 matches. **(2 marks)**

   Two matchboxes are chosen at random.

   (b) Find the probability that both matchboxes contain fewer than 80 matches. **(2 marks)**

Normal distribution 2

The NORMAL DISTRIBUTION TABLES in the formulae booklet only give values of $\Phi(z)$ for $z > 0$. You can use SYMMETRY to solve problems where $z < 0$, or to find $P(z > a)$. Here are three useful examples.

 P(z > a)

 z < 0

 P(c < z < d)

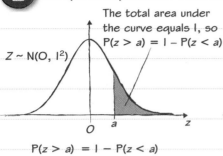

$P(z > a) = 1 - P(z < a)$
$= 1 - \Phi(a)$

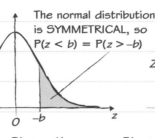

$P(z < b) = P(z > -b)$
$= 1 - P(z < -b)$
$= 1 - \Phi(-b)$

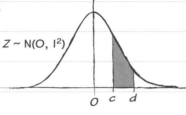

$P(c < z < d) = P(z < d) - P(z < c)$
$= \Phi(d) - \Phi(c)$

Using a calculator

Some calculators can work out $P(a < z < b)$ or $P(z > a)$ directly. If you are using one of these calculators in your S1 exam, make sure that you:

- ☑ know how YOUR calculator works
- ☑ STANDARDISE the x-value to show that you understand the process
- ☑ WRITE DOWN the probability you are calculating, like $P(z > 2.5)$
- ☑ give any answers to AT LEAST 3 significant figures.

Worked example

The weights of bags of compost filled by a machine are distributed normally with mean 21 kg and standard deviation 0.4 kg. The bags are advertised as containing 20 kg of compost, and the company must refill any bags weighing less than this.

Work out the probability that a bag must be refilled. **(3 marks)**

$z = \dfrac{20 - 21}{0.4} = -2.5$

$P(Z < -2.5) = P(Z > 2.5)$
$\qquad\qquad = 1 - P(Z < 2.5)$
$\qquad\qquad = 1 - 0.9938 = 0.0062$

Worked example

R is a normal random variable with mean 36 and standard deviation 8.5

(a) Find $P(R > 40)$. **(3 marks)**

$P(R > 40) = P\left(Z > \dfrac{40 - 36}{8.5}\right)$

$\qquad\qquad = 1 - P(Z < 0.47)$
$\qquad\qquad = 1 - 0.6808 = 0.3192$

(b) Find $P(32 \leqslant R \leqslant 37)$. **(4 marks)**

$P(32 \leqslant R \leqslant 37)$
$= P\left(\dfrac{32 - 36}{8.5} \leqslant Z \leqslant \dfrac{37 - 36}{8.5}\right)$
$= P(-0.47 \leqslant Z \leqslant 1.18)$
$= P(Z \leqslant 1.18) - P(Z \leqslant -0.47)$
$= P(Z \leqslant 1.18) - [1 - P(Z \leqslant 0.47)]$
$= 0.8810 - [1 - 0.6808]$
$= 0.5618$

 When you are working with a normal distribution you can treat $<$ and $\leqslant$ the same, because the variable is **continuous**.

Now try this

The heights of a group of dogs, x mm, are modelled by the random variable $X \sim N(410, 125^2)$

Find

(a) $P(X > 500)$ **(3 marks)**

(b) $P(X < 350)$ **(3 marks)**

(c) $P(380 < X < 420)$. **(4 marks)**

Finding unknown values

You might need to find a MISSING Z-VALUE or X-VALUE in a NORMAL DISTRIBUTION if you know the PROBABILITY. You can look up values of $\Phi(z)$ in the tables in the formulae booklet to find the corresponding value of z.

Worked example

A random variable X is normally distributed with mean 100 and standard deviation 12. Find a such that $P(X < a) = 0.409$ **(4 marks)**

$P(X < a) = P\left(Z < \dfrac{a - 100}{12}\right) = 0.409$

$1 - 0.409 = 0.591$

$P(Z < 0.23) = 0.591$

So $\dfrac{a - 100}{12} = -0.23$

$a = 97.24$

> The probability is less than 0.5 so you need to use $1 - 0.409 = 0.591$
> This probability isn't in the percentage points table, so use the larger table of values in reverse. From the table, $\Phi(0.23) = 0.591$, so $\Phi(-0.23) = 0.409$

Using the formulae booklet

You can use the PERCENTAGE POINTS TABLE in the formulae booklet to look up the values of z for certain probabilities.

p	z
0.0500	1.6449
0.0250	1.9600
0.0100	2.3263

This row tells you that $P(Z > 1.96) = 0.025$

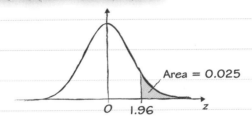

Area = 0.025

Be careful. This table gives areas to the RIGHT of a z-value, and not all the probabilities are listed.

Worked example

The lengths of the films released in one year, L minutes, are normally distributed with $L \sim N(128, 15^2)$

(a) Write down the median length of film. **(1 mark)**

128 minutes

(b) Find the upper quartile, Q_3, of L. **(3 marks)**

$P(L < Q_3) = P\left(Z < \dfrac{Q_3 - 128}{15}\right) = 0.75$

$\dfrac{Q_3 - 128}{15} = 0.67$

$Q_3 = 138$ (3 s.f.)

(c) Write down the lower quartile, Q_1, of L. **(1 mark)**

$Q_1 = 128 - (138 - 128) = 118$

(a) A normal distribution is **symmetric** so mean = median.

(b) 75% of the values are below the upper quartile, so $P(L < Q_3) = 0.75$. This extract from the **normal distribution** table in the formulae booklet shows that if $\Phi(z) = 0.75$ then z is between 0.67 and 0.68. $z = 0.67$ gives a **closer** value to 0.75 so choose this.

0.66	0.7454
0.67	0.7486
0.68	0.7517
0.69	0.7549

(c) L is symmetric so $Q_3 - 128 = 128 - Q_1$

There is more about symmetry and skewness on page 91.

Now try this

The weights of some courgettes, W grams, were modelled by $W \sim N(450, 100^2)$

(a) Find w such that $P(432 < W < w) = 0.3$ **(4 marks)**

There are two successful outcomes:
1. First courgette ✓   Second courgette ✗
2. First courgette ✗   Second courgette ✓

Two courgettes are chosen at random.

(b) Find the probability that only one weighs between 432 grams and w grams. **(3 marks)**

Finding μ and σ

You might need to use information about a normal distribution to find its MEAN (μ) and its STANDARD DEVIATION (σ).

Worked example

The times taken for a search engine to complete a web search are normally distributed with mean 0.63 seconds. The company states that 97.5% of searches are completed in less than 1 second.

Find the standard deviation of the times taken to complete a web search. **(4 marks)**

$$P(X < 1) = P\left(Z < \frac{1 - 0.63}{\sigma}\right) = 0.975$$

$$\frac{1 - 0.63}{\sigma} = 1.96$$

$$0.37 = 1.96\sigma$$

$$\sigma = 0.189 \text{ (3 s.f.)}$$

If you need to find μ or σ in your S1 exam, you will often be able to use the **percentage points table** in the booklet. Have a look at page 110 for a reminder on how this table works.

$P(X < 1) = 0.975$ so
$P(X > 1) = 1 - 0.975 = 0.025$

The percentage points table tells you that this occurs at $z = 1.96$

So $z = \dfrac{1 - 0.63}{\sigma} = 1.96$

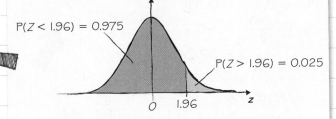

$P(Z < 1.96) = 0.975$

$P(Z > 1.96) = 0.025$

Worked example

X is a normally distributed random variable with mean μ and standard deviation σ.
$P(X > 8.6) = 0.3$ and $P(X < 7.7) = 0.05$
(a) Show that $\mu = 7.7 + 1.6449\sigma$

(3 marks)

$$P(X < 7.7) = P\left(Z < \frac{7.7 - \mu}{\sigma}\right) = 0.05$$

$$\frac{7.7 - \mu}{\sigma} = -1.6449$$

$$\mu = 7.7 + 1.6449\sigma$$

(b) Obtain a second equation and hence find the value of μ and the value of σ.

(4 marks)

$$P(X > 8.6) = P\left(Z > \frac{8.6 - \mu}{\sigma}\right) = 0.3$$

$$\frac{8.6 - \mu}{\sigma} = 0.5244$$

$$\mu = 8.6 - 0.5244\sigma$$

So $7.7 + 1.6449\sigma = 8.6 - 0.5244\sigma$

$$2.1693\sigma = 0.9$$

$$\sigma = 0.4149...$$

$$= 0.415 \text{ (3 s.f.)}$$

$$\mu = 8.6 - 0.5244 \times 0.4149...$$

$$= 8.3824...$$

$$= 8.38 \text{ (3 s.f.)}$$

You can show this information on a sketch. This can help you visualise the problem.

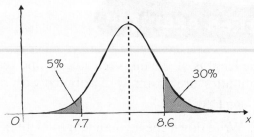

5%   30%

O 7.7   8.6 x

The sketch makes it clear that $x = 7.7$ will give a **negative** z-value, that $x = 8.6$ will give a **positive** z-value, and that μ is between 7.7 and 8.6

If you don't know μ **or** σ, and you are given two probability facts, then you will have to solve a pair of **simultaneous equations** to find μ and σ.

Now try this

The weights of the oranges in a crate are normally distributed with mean μ grams and standard deviation σ grams. 20% of the oranges are lighter than 175 grams and 10% are heavier than 230 grams.

Find the value of μ and the value of σ.

(6 marks)

You are the examiner!

CHECKING YOUR WORK is one of the key skills you will need for your S1 exam. Each of these three students has made key mistakes in BOTH PARTS of their working. Can you spot them all?

1 The discrete random variable X can take only the values 1, 2 and 3
For these values the cumulative distribution function is defined by

$$F(x) = \frac{x^3 + k}{60} \qquad x = 1, 2, 3$$

(a) Find the value of k. **(2 marks)**

Given that $\text{Var}(X) = \dfrac{197}{240}$

(b) find the exact value of $\text{Var}(6X + 3)$
(2 marks)

(a) $F(1) + F(2) + F(3) = 1$

$\dfrac{1+k}{60} + \dfrac{8+k}{60} + \dfrac{27+k}{60} = 1$

$36 + 3k = 60$

$k = 8$

(b) $\text{Var}(6X + 3) = 6\text{Var}(X) + 3$

$= 6 \times \dfrac{197}{240} + 3$

$= \dfrac{317}{40}$

2 In a survey a random sample of 130 teenagers were asked how many hours, to the nearest hour, they spent online in the last week. The results are summarised in the table.

Number of hours	Frequency
0–5	17
6–7	18
8–10	40
11–20	55

A histogram was drawn and the group (8–10) was represented by a rectangle that was 3 cm wide and 4 cm high.

(a) Calculate the width and height of the rectangle representing the group (6–7). **(3 marks)**

(b) Use linear interpolation to estimate the median. **(4 marks)**

(a) $7.5 - 5.5 = 2$

Frequency density $= \dfrac{18}{2} = 9$

2 cm wide and 9 cm high.

(b) Median $= 130 \div 2 = $ 65th value

$17 + 18 = 35$ data values in first two groups

$8 + (65 - 35) \times \dfrac{2}{40} = 9.5$

3 A council collected data on the daily mass of rubbish collected on the streets, m kg, and the number of hours of sunshine, h. The data for rubbish was coded using $x = \dfrac{m - 200}{10}$ and the following statistics were found.

$S_{xx} = 228.9$, $S_{xh} = 115.1$, $S_{hh} = 60.9$, $\bar{x} = 3.1$, $\bar{h} = 4.9$

(a) Show that the equation of the regression line of x on h is $x = -6.16 + 1.89h$ **(4 marks)**

(b) Using your regression line estimate the mass of rubbish collected on a day when there were 7 hours of sunshine. **(2 marks)**

(a) $b = \dfrac{115.1}{228.9} = 0.5028\ldots$

$a = 3.1 - 4.9 \times 0.5028\ldots = 0.6360\ldots$

$x = 0.636 + 0.503h$

(b) $x = -6.16 + 1.89h$

$= -6.16 + 1.89 \times 7$

$= 7.07$

Checking your work

If you have any time left at the end of your exam, you should check back through your working.

☑ Check you have answered EVERY PART and given all the information asked for.

☑ Check that you have given your answer to at least 3 SIGNIFICANT FIGURES.

☑ Double-check any calculations, especially for the STANDARD DEVIATION and S_{xx}, S_{yy} and S_{xy}.

☑ Make sure everything is EASY TO READ.

☑ Cross out any incorrect working with a SINGLE NEAT LINE and UNDERLINE the correct answer.

Now try this

Find the mistakes in each student's answer on this page, and write out the correct working for each question. Turn over for the answers.

You are still the examiner!

BEFORE looking at this page, turn back to page 112 and try to spot the key mistakes in each student's working. Use this page to CHECK your answers – the corrections are shown in red, and these answers are now 100% CORRECT.

1

The discrete random variable X can take only the values 1, 2 and 3. For these values the cumulative distribution function is defined by

$$F(x) = \frac{x^3 + k}{60} \qquad x = 1, 2, 3$$

(a) Find the value of k. **(2 marks)**

Given that $\text{Var}(X) = \dfrac{197}{240}$

(b) find the exact value of $\text{Var}(6X + 3)$ **(2 marks)**

(a) ~~F(1) + F(2) + F(3) = 1~~   F(3) = 1

$$\frac{1 + k}{60} + \frac{8 + k}{60} + \frac{27 + k}{60} = 1 \qquad \frac{27 + k}{60} = 1$$

$$36 + 3k = 60 \qquad 27 + k = 60$$

$$~~k = 8~~ \qquad k = 33$$

(b) $\text{Var}(6X + 3) = 6^2 \text{Var}(X) ~~+ 3~~$

$$= ~~6~~ \times \frac{197}{240} ~~+ 3~~ \quad 36 \times \frac{197}{240}$$

$$= \frac{~~317~~}{~~40~~} \quad \frac{591}{20}$$

Top tip

(a) Make sure you know the difference between the **probability function** $P(X = x)$ and the **cumulative distribution function** $F(x)$. Have a look at page 105.

(b) Learn the rules for the expectation and variance of **functions** of random variables. Check out page 107 for more.

2

In a survey a random sample of 130 teenagers were asked how many hours, to the nearest hour, they spent online in the last week. The results are summarised in the table.

A histogram was drawn and the group (8–10) was

Number of hours	Frequency
0–5	17
6–7	18
8–10	40
11–20	55

represented by a rectangle that was 3 cm wide and 4 cm high.

(a) Calculate the width and height of the rectangle representing the group (6–7). **(3 marks)**

(b) Use linear interpolation to estimate the median. **(4 marks)**

(a) $7.5 - 5.5 = 2$ Width = 2 cm

$$~~\text{Frequency density} = \frac{18}{2} = 9~~$$

~~2 cm wide and 9 cm high.~~

$$\frac{2h}{18} = \frac{3 \times 4}{40} \qquad \text{so} \quad h = 2.7$$

(b) Median = $130 \div 2 = 65$th value

$17 + 18 = 35$ data values in first two groups

$$~~8~~ + (65 - 35) \times \frac{\overset{3}{\cancel{2}}}{40} = \overset{9.75}{\cancel{9.5}}$$

7.5

Top tip

(a) In a histogram the area is **proportional** to the frequency, not necessarily **equal** to it. Use proportion to work out the height.
Histograms are on page 90.

(b) Be really careful with **class boundaries**. The (8–10) group starts at 7.5, and has class width $10.5 - 7.5 = 3$
See page 86.

3

A council collected data on the daily mass of rubbish collected on the streets, m kg, and the number of hours of sunshine, h. The data for rubbish was coded using $x = \dfrac{m - 200}{10}$ and the following statistics were found.

$S_{xx} = 228.9$, $S_{xh} = 115.1$, $S_{hh} = 60.9$, $\bar{x} = 3.1$, $\bar{h} = 4.9$

(a) Show that the equation of the regression line of x on h is $x = -6.16 + 1.89h$ **(4 marks)**

(b) Using your regression line estimate the mass of rubbish collected on a day when there were 7 hours of sunshine. **(2 marks)**

(a) $b = \dfrac{115.1}{\overset{60.9}{\cancel{228.9}}} = ~~0.5028\ldots~~ \quad 1.8899\ldots$

$a = 3.1 - 4.9 \times \underset{1.8899\ldots}{~~0.5028\ldots~~} = \underset{-6.1609\ldots}{~~0.6360\ldots~~}$

$x = ~~0.636 + 0.503h~~$
$\quad -6.16 + 1.89h$

(b) $x = -6.16 + 1.89h$

$= -6.16 + 1.89 \times 7$

$= 7.07 \quad \dfrac{m - 200}{10} = 7.07$ so $m = 271$ (3 s.f.)

Top tip

(a) The **order** of the variables is important in a regression line. For x on h you need to divide by S_{hh} not S_{xx} when working out b.
There's more on page 101.

(b) The x-value is correct but the data is **coded** so you haven't finished. Reverse the coding to find m.
Coding is covered on page 103.

Flow charts

A flow chart is a simple way of describing an ALGORITHM. There are three types of box in a flow diagram.

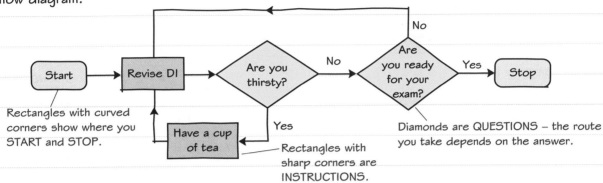

Rectangles with curved corners show where you START and STOP.

Rectangles with sharp corners are INSTRUCTIONS.

Diamonds are QUESTIONS – the route you take depends on the answer.

Worked example

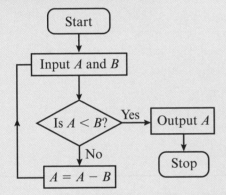

The flow chart describes an algorithm.

(a) Use the flow chart with $A = 18$ and $B = 7$ to complete the table.

(4 marks)

A	B	A < B?	Output
18	7	No	
11	7	No	
4	7	Yes	4

(b) Explain what is achieved by this flow chart. **(2 marks)**

The flow chart determines the remainder when A is divided by B.

(c) Given that $A = kB$ for some positive integer k, write down the output of the flow chart. **(1 mark)**

0

The value of A changes each time you go through the loop in the flow chart, so use the table to keep track of your working. There is no output for the first two rows of the table, so leave this column blank.

Now try this

In part (b), if you can't see what the flow chart achieves, try a few more values of X: 99, 17 and 41 would be good. Can you explain why the flow chart stops when $N^2 > X$?

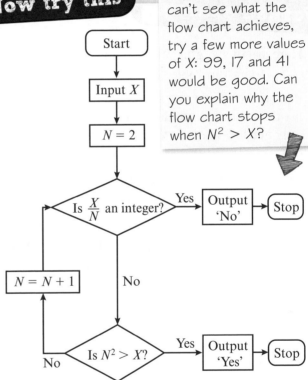

(a) Use the flow chart with $X = 13$ to complete the table. **(4 marks)**

X	N	$\frac{X}{N}$ an integer?	$N^2 > X$?	Output

(b) What does the flow chart tell you about X? **(2 marks)**

(c) Write down the output from the flow chart when

(i) $X = 101$ (ii) $X = 4718$ **(2 marks)**

Bubble sort

Bubble sort is an algorithm for arranging an unordered list into ASCENDING or DESCENDING order.

1 COMPARE the first pair of elements in the list and SWAP them if they are in the wrong order.

To put the list 7 4 2 9 3 in ASCENDING order, start by comparing 7 and 4. They're in the wrong order, so SWAP the first pair.

2 Then compare the second and third elements, then the third and fourth, and so on. When you reach the end you have completed the FIRST PASS.

7 and 9 are in the correct order so leave them where they are.

3 Carry on making passes, starting each time from the beginning of the NEW list. When there are NO SWAPS in a pass then the list is in order.

This list is in order after the third pass.

7	4	2	9	3	SWAP
4	7	2	9	3	SWAP
4	2	7	9	3	NO SWAP
4	2	7	3	9	SWAP

First pass

After second pass ——— 2 4 3 7 9

After third pass ——— 2 3 4 7 9

Worked example

Here are the lengths of some films in minutes.

92 103 120 88 96 109 115 90 88

Perform a bubble sort on the numbers in the list to sort them into **descending** order. You only need to write down the final result of each pass. **(4 marks)**

92	103	120	88	96	109	115	90	88
103	120	92	96	109	115	90	88	88
120	103	96	109	115	92	90	88	88
120	103	109	115	96	92	90	88	88
120	109	115	103	96	92	90	88	88
120	115	109	103	96	92	90	88	88

The list is sorted.

Read the question carefully. You only need to show each comparison if you are told to. Here you are told to show the **final result** of each pass. Make sure you write down that the list is sorted, or show a final pass with no changes.

Check it!
Make sure you have included all the numbers from the original list in your ordered list.

Bubble sort checklist

- ✓ Work in the same direction for each pass.
- ✓ Show the list after each complete pass.
- ✓ State that the list is sorted.
- ✓ Double-check against the original list.

Playing snooker

You can think of each pass in the Worked example like a snooker shot. In each pass, the first element jumps up the list until it 'hits' a smaller element. When it does, it stays where it is, and 'knocks' the smaller element on.

Original list 92 103 120 88 96 109 115 90 88

After first pass 103 120 92 96 109 115 90 88 88

Now try this

Here are the masses of some eggs in grams.

71 65 80 75 79 65 63 85 82 69 70

Perform a bubble sort on the numbers in the list to sort them into **ascending** order. You only need to write down the final result of each pass. **(4 marks)**

Always check whether you are sorting into **ascending** or **descending** order. On the first pass, the 'snooker balls' that move are 71, 80 and 85.

Quick sort

You can use the quick sort algorithm to arrange a list into ALPHABETICAL or NUMERICAL order.

1 Find the MIDDLE element in the list (rounding UP if necessary) and circle it. This is called the PIVOT.

8   7   2   ③   6   5   1

The first pivot is 3

2 Write down any elements less than the pivot to its LEFT, and any elements greater to its RIGHT. Keep the elements in the SAME ORDER as in the original list.

2   ①   ③   8   7   ⑥   5

Ignore any previous pivots.

The pivot for this sublist is 6.

3 IGNORE the previous pivot, and apply steps 1 and 2 to BOTH of the new smaller SUBLISTS you've created.

①   ②   ③   ⑤   ⑥   8   ⑦

Circle any elements on their own.

This sublist has two elements.

4 Once all the elements are circled, the list is sorted.

①   ②   ③   ⑤   ⑥   ⑦   ⑧

Every element has been selected as a pivot, so the list is in order.

Worked example

Ellie Kath Will Yaniv James Andy Lara Bi

Use a quick sort to produce a list of these names in ascending alphabetical order. You must make your pivots clear. **(5 marks)**

E   K   W   Y   Ⓙ   A   L   B
E   Ⓐ   B   Ⓙ   K   W   Ⓨ   L
Ⓐ   E   Ⓑ   Ⓙ   K   Ⓦ   L   Ⓨ
Ⓐ   Ⓑ   Ⓔ   Ⓙ   K   Ⓛ   Ⓦ   Ⓨ
Ⓐ   Ⓑ   Ⓔ   Ⓙ   Ⓚ   Ⓛ   Ⓦ   Ⓨ

Use the **initial letter** of each name to save time, and make sure you know the order of the alphabet! There are eight elements in the list, so in the first row the fifth element (J) is the pivot.

In the second row, the two sublists are EAB and KWYL. Make sure you write the elements in the sublists in **the same order** as they appeared in the original list. You ignore the pivot from the previous row (J) so shade it in, or draw it in a box.

EXAM ALERT!

Always use the **algorithm** to decide when the list is sorted. In the fourth row, the list is in order, but you haven't finished. There is still one sublist with two elements (K L). You need to **show** the pivot for this list (L) and then write the list in order with all the pivots shown.

Students have struggled with this topic in recent exams – be prepared!

Quick sort checklist

☑ Show ALL your PIVOTS by circling or underlining them.

☑ Make it clear that you are selecting MORE THAN ONE pivot in a single pass.

☑ Keep going if there are any sublists with TWO OR MORE elements.

For large lists, the quick sort algorithm will usually order a list MORE QUICKLY than the bubble sort algorithm because the number of pivots can DOUBLE with each pass.

Now try this

23   25   17   12   22   20   19   26   29   21   13

The list of numbers above is to be sorted into **ascending** order. Use quick sort to obtain the ordered list. You must make your pivots clear. **(5 marks)**

If there are n elements in a list, the middle element is the $\left(\dfrac{n+1}{2}\right)$th element (rounding up if necessary).

Binary search

Computers often need to search for an item in a large list. A binary search is a very quick way of finding an item in an ORDERED list.

1 Check that the list is IN ORDER.

2 Find the MIDDLE element in the list (rounding UP if necessary) and circle it. This is the PIVOT.

3 If the item you need to find comes BEFORE the pivot then REJECT the pivot and everything AFTER it. If it comes after, then reject the pivot and everything that comes BEFORE.

4 Go back to step 2 with your REDUCED list.

5 Stop when the pivot is the item you are looking for, and state that you have found it.

If a list is long, use $\frac{n+1}{2}$ to find the pivot, rounding up if necessary. There are 10 items in the original list: $\frac{10+1}{2} = 5.5$ so the pivot is **6** (Norfolk). Essex comes **before** Norfolk so reject Norfolk and all the entries after it in the list. Make sure you write down the pivot and the part of the list you are rejecting. It's a good idea to **write out** the new list after each iteration. Don't stop when you reach one item. You still need to **select it as a pivot**, then **state** that it has been found.

Worked example

Here is a list of some UK counties in alphabetical order.

1. Antrim   6. Norfolk
2. Cornwall   7. Powys
3. Dorset   8. Suffolk
4. Essex   9. Wiltshire
5. Kent   10. Yorkshire

Use the binary search algorithm to locate the county Essex in the list.   **(4 marks)**

First pivot = Norfolk → Reject N to Y
Second pivot = Dorset → Reject A to D
Third pivot = Kent → Reject K
Fourth pivot = Essex → Essex found

Iterations

Each pass of an algorithm is called an ITERATION. You can find the MAXIMUM number of iterations for a binary search by working out the maximum number of elements left after each pass.

If there are 10 elements, the maximum number of iterations is 4.

Before...	1st pass	2nd pass	3rd pass	4th pass
Max. no. of items	10	5	2	1

Binary search checklist

☑ Can only be applied to an ORDERED list.

You might have to use bubble sort or quick sort to order the list first in your exam.

☑ If the pivot is not the item you are looking for, you always reject it.

☑ State which part of the list you are rejecting.

☑ State when you have found the item.

Now try this

Here is a list of insects in alphabetical order.

Ant   Beetle   Cicada   Earwig   Housefly   Ladybird   Mite   Sandfly   Termite   Wasp

Use the binary search algorithm on this list to locate the insect Sandfly.   **(4 marks)**

Bin packing 1

Here are two decision maths problems which are mathematically similar.

1 A group of people of different weights have to travel in a lift which can only carry 600 kg.
How many rides are needed on the lift?

MAX LOAD 600 KG

2 A carpenter wants to cut specific lengths of wood from 8 m planks.
How many planks does he need?

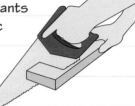

You can use the FIRST-FIT bin-packing algorithm to answer decision maths problems like these.

First-fit bin-packing algorithm

1 Use the ORDER GIVEN in the question.

2 Place each item into the FIRST AVAILABLE BIN it will fit in, starting from bin 1.

👍 Simple and quick.

👎 Unlikely to give OPTIMAL solution.

Lower bound

To find a lower bound for the number of bins needed, you divide the sum of all the items by the size of each bin, then ROUND UP to the next whole number.

There is NO GUARANTEE that it is possible to find a way to pack the items into this number of bins.

Worked example

A decorator wants to cut the following lengths, in metres, of wallpaper.

  2.4 1.8 0.8 3.5 1.6 1.2 3.1 2.5 0.7

The wallpaper is sold in 4 m rolls.

(a) Obtain a lower bound for the number of 4 m rolls of wallpaper needed. **(2 marks)**

$2.4 + 1.8 + 0.8 + 3.5 + 1.6 + 1.2 + 3.1 + 2.5 + 0.7 = 17.6$

$17.6 \div 4 = 4.4$ so lower bound = 5 rolls

(b) Use the first-fit bin-packing algorithm to determine the number of 4 m rolls of wallpaper needed. **(4 marks)**

Roll 1: 2.4 0.8 0.7

Roll 2: 1.8 1.6

Roll 3: 3.5

Roll 4: 1.2 2.5

Roll 5: 3.1

(a) Add up all the lengths then divide by 4. The answer is 4.4, so round up to 5 to find the **lower bound.**

(b) Each roll of wallpaper is a 'bin'. Write a heading for each bin – you know you will need at least 5. At the start all the bins are empty.

Item 1: 2.4 will fit in bin 1.

Item 2: 2.4 + 1.8 = 4.2 > 4 so 1.8 will **not** fit in bin 1. Place it in bin 2.

Item 3: 2.4 + 0.8 = 3.2 < 4, so 0.8 **will** fit in bin 1. Place it in bin 1 …

… and so on.

Make sure you write out exactly which items end up in which bins. In part (a) you worked out that 5 was the lower bound for the number of bins, so you know that this packing is **optimal**. There may be more than one optimal packing for any given bin-packing problem.

Now try this

For part (c), multiply the number of tapes needed by 90 to work out the total amount of space, then subtract the total length of all the interviews.

Here are the lengths, in minutes, of some interviews.

  47 71 39 19 22 27 6 80 55 32 28 32 41 50

The interviews are to be recorded onto tapes of length 90 minutes.

(a) Obtain a lower bound for the number of 90 min tapes needed. **(2 marks)**

(b) Use the first-fit bin-packing algorithm to determine the number of 90 min tapes needed. **(4 marks)**

(c) How much wasted space is there on these tapes? **(1 mark)**

Bin packing 2

As well as the FIRST-FIT algorithm covered on page 118, there are two more bin-packing algorithms that you need to learn for your D1 exam.

First-fit decreasing algorithm

1 Arrange the items in DESCENDING ORDER.

2 Apply the FIRST-FIT algorithm to the ORDERED list.

👍 Fairly quick and often gives a good solution.

👎 Might not provide OPTIMAL solution.

Full bins algorithm

1 Find any combinations that will FILL a bin.

2 Pack any remaining items using the FIRST-FIT algorithm.

👍 Most likely to give optimal solution.

👎 Hard to do, especially with large lists.

Worked example

80 72 65 60 28 27 21 16 11 9

The above list of numbers is arranged in **descending** order.

(a) Use the first-fit decreasing bin-packing algorithm to determine how the numbers listed above can be packed into bins of size 100 **(3 marks)**

Bin 1: 80 16
Bin 2: 72 28
Bin 3: 65 27
Bin 4: 60 21 11
Bin 5: 9

(b) Use full bins to obtain an optimal solution that uses the minimum number of bins, and explain why your solution is optimal. **(4 marks)**

Full bin 1: 72 28
Full bin 2: 80 11 9
Bin 3: 65 27
Bin 4: 60 21 16
Total of all 10 numbers = 389
389 ÷ 100 = 3.89 so optimal solution is 4 bins.

Sort then pack

In order to use the FIRST-FIT DECREASING bin-sorting algorithm, the list needs to be arranged in DESCENDING order. In your D1 exam, you will often be asked to order the list first using BUBBLE SORT or QUICK SORT.

Have a look at pages 115 and 116 for a reminder about using these algorithms.

(b) Look for groups of numbers that add up to 100, then fill the other bins using the **first-fit** algorithm.

EXAM ALERT!

You might have used bar charts to represent bin-packing problems in your D1 course. Don't waste time drawing bar charts in your exam – it's easier and quicker just to write the bin numbers and the items, and use your calculator to work out whether an item will fit.

Students have struggled with this topic in recent exams – be prepared!

Now try this

A builder is asked to replace the guttering on a house. The lengths needed, in metres, are

0.6, 4.0, 2.5, 3.2, 1.0, 2.6, 0.4, 0.3, 4.0 and 0.5

Guttering is sold in 4 m lengths.

(a) Carry out a quick sort to produce a list of the lengths needed in **descending** order. You should show the result of each pass and identify your pivots clearly. **(5 marks)**

(b) Apply the first-fit decreasing bin-packing algorithm to your ordered list to determine the total number of 4 m lengths needed. **(4 marks)**

(c) Does the answer to part (b) use the minimum number of 4 m lengths? You must justify your answer. **(2 marks)**

Graphs

In decision maths, a graph is a set of points (called VERTICES or NODES) that are connected by lines (called EDGES or ARCS). Here are three examples.

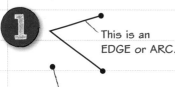

1 This is an EDGE or ARC.

This is a VERTEX or NODE – it doesn't have to be connected to any edges.

2 This vertex has DEGREE or VALENCY 3 because it is connected to 3 edges. Because 3 is an odd number, this is an ODD VERTEX.

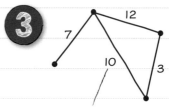

3 This graph is WEIGHTED because each edge has a number (or WEIGHT). A weighted graph is sometimes called a NETWORK.

Paths and connectedness

A PATH is a route through a graph from one vertex to another. It must travel along the edges of the graph, and no vertex can be repeated. If a path exists between two vertices, they are CONNECTED.

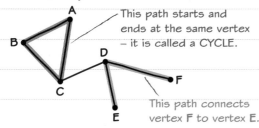

This path starts and ends at the same vertex – it is called a CYCLE.

This path connects vertex F to vertex E.

A graph is CONNECTED if every vertex is connected to every other vertex. Graph 2 at the top of the page is connected but graph 1 is not.

Subgraphs and trees

A subset of the vertices and edges of a graph is called a SUBGRAPH.

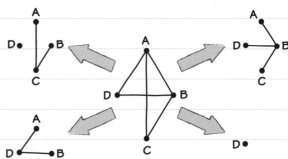

If a graph is CONNECTED and contains NO CYCLES then it is called a TREE. A subgraph of a graph which contains ALL VERTICES of the graph and is also a tree is called a SPANNING TREE. The top-right subgraph above is a spanning tree – none of the others are.

Worked example

Explain the terms

(a) tree **(2 marks)**

A connected graph containing no cycles.

(b) spanning tree. **(2 marks)**

A subgraph of a graph which includes all the vertices and is also a tree.

Complete graphs

A graph is complete if it contains an edge between EVERY PAIR of vertices.

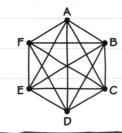

Now try this

The diagram shows a graph.

(a) Write down the valency of vertex **A**. **(1 mark)**

(b) Identify (i) a path from **B** to **D**
        (ii) a cycle. **(2 marks)**

(c) Sketch
    (i) a spanning tree for this graph
    (ii) a complete subgraph of this graph. **(3 marks)**

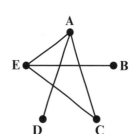

Drawing networks

You can draw a network (or a WEIGHTED GRAPH) from a TABLE or MATRIX. The row and column headings are the VERTICES, and the entries in the table tell you the WEIGHT of each EDGE.

For a reminder about the terminology used for graphs, have a look at page 120.

	A	B	C	D	E
A	–	21	–	82	37
B	21	–	15	–	28
C	–	15	–	–	41
D	82	–	–	–	–
E	37	28	41	–	–

This table describes this network

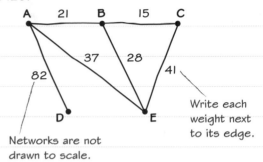

There is no edge connecting vertex **D** to vertex **E**.

Networks are not drawn to scale.

Write each weight next to its edge.

Worked example

	A	B	C	D	E	F
A	–	10	–	7	14	–
B	10	–	4	–	12	13
C	–	4	–	–	8	11
D	7	–	–	–	9	–
E	14	12	8	9	–	5
F	–	13	11	–	5	–

The table shows the distances, in km, of a network of roads between six towns, **A**, **B**, **C**, **D**, **E** and **F**. Complete the drawing of the network below by adding the necessary arcs from vertex **B** together with their weights. **(2 marks)**

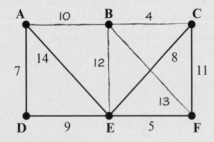

If you have to draw a network in your DI exam, you will usually be given the **vertices** in the answer booklet. You might also have to complete a **partially drawn** network like this. Be careful if there are two edges which cross on your network. You need to label each edge with its weight in an **unambiguous** way. If you put your label close to the point where the edges cross, it won't be clear which weight belongs to which edge.

Weight

PATHS and SUBGRAPHS can have different weights. To find the weight of a path in a network, add up the weights of all of its edges. Here is a spanning tree of the network shown in the Worked example.

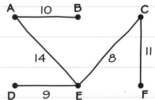

The total weight of this spanning tree is
10 + 14 + 9 + 8 + 11 = 52 km

The definition of a spanning tree is on page 120.

Now try this

The table shows the distances, in metres, between four vertices, **A**, **B**, **C** and **D**, in a network.

(a) Draw the weighted network diagram for this table. **(3 marks)**

(b) Sketch a spanning tree for this network. **(2 marks)**

(c) Write down the weight of your spanning tree. **(1 mark)**

	A	B	C	D
A	–	22	14	12
B	22	–	19	25
C	14	19	–	16
D	12	25	16	–

Kruskal's algorithm

You can use Kruskal's algorithm to find a MINIMUM SPANNING TREE in a NETWORK.

1 Sort all the edges into ASCENDING order of weight.

2 Choose the first edge in your list and INCLUDE it in your minimum spanning tree.

3 Look at the next edge in your list.
- If it forms a CYCLE with the edges you've already chosen, then REJECT it.
- Otherwise, include it in your minimum spanning tree.
The definition of a cycle is on page 120.

4 Repeat step 3 until you have connected all the vertices in your network.

Minimum spanning tree

Graphs can have more than one spanning tree. The spanning tree with the least TOTAL WEIGHT is called the minimum spanning tree or MINIMUM CONNECTOR. Here are three spanning trees for a simple network.

Weight = 8 Weight = 7 Weight = 9

This is the minimum spanning tree.

Spanning trees are covered on page 120, and there is more about weight on page 121.

Worked example

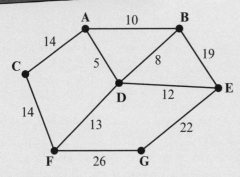

(a) Use Kruskal's algorithm to find a minimum spanning tree for the network shown above. You should list the arcs in the order in which you consider them. In each case, state whether you are adding that arc to your minimum spanning tree.
(3 marks)

AD (5)✓, DB (8)✓, AB (10)✗, DE (12)✓, DF (13)✓, AC (14)✓, CF (14)✗, BE (19)✗, EG (22)✓.
All vertices connected.

(b) Draw the minimum spanning tree using the vertices given below. **(1 mark)**

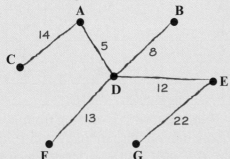

(c) Write down the total weight of the minimum spanning tree. **(1 mark)**

5 + 8 + 12 + 13 + 14 + 22 = 74

It's a good idea to sketch the spanning tree as you add edges (arcs), or mark the included edges on your diagram. This makes it easier to identify **cycles**. Be careful though – don't just show ticks and crosses on a diagram. You need to show the edges you include and the edges you reject **in the right order**. Write them down as a list, using ticks and crosses to show whether they are included or rejected, and always refer to the edges by their **end vertices**, not just by their lengths.

The first edge you **reject** is **AB**, because it would form a cycle with the two edges already included. If two edges have the **same weight**, consider them **one at a time** in any order.

Now try this

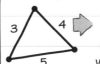 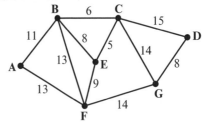

Use Kruskal's algorithm to find a minimum connector for the network shown above.
(3 marks)

Minimum **connector** is another name for a minimum spanning tree.

Prim's algorithm

Prim's algorithm is a method for finding a MINIMUM SPANNING TREE in a NETWORK.

1 Choose ANY VERTEX as a starting point.
The starting vertex will usually be GIVEN in the question.

2 Include the arc with the LEAST WEIGHT attached to that vertex.

3 Choose the arc of LEAST WEIGHT that joins a NEW VERTEX to the tree.
You don't need to worry about CYCLES because you have to add a NEW vertex each time.

4 Repeat step 3 until you have connected all the vertices in your network.

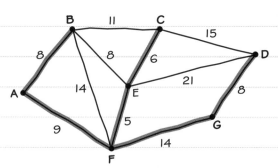

Applying Prim's algorithm starting at vertex A, the arcs are added in this order:
AB, AF, EF, EC, FG, GD

Worked example

	1		2	3	4
	A	B	C	D	E
A	—	12	7	10	21
B	12	—	14	⑪	15
C	⑦	14	—	9	10
D	10	11	⑨	—	14
E	21	15	⑩	14	—

The table shows the lengths, in km, of fibre optic connections between five telephone exchanges.

Use Prim's algorithm, starting from **A**, to find a minimum spanning tree for this table. You must list the **arcs** that form your tree **in the order that they are selected**.   **(3 marks)**

AC, CD, CE, BD

You can apply Prim's algorithm directly to a network given in **table** or **matrix** form. Follow these steps.

1. Cross off row **A** and write '1' over column **A**.
2. Choose the least entry in that column (7).
3. Write down your first arc (**AC**).
4. Cross off the row associated with this entry, and number its column '2'.
5. Choose the least undeleted entry in any numbered column (9).
6. Write down your second arc (**CD**) …
… and so on, until every row is crossed off.

If you are applying Prim's algorithm to a table or a network diagram, you need to **write down** the arcs you include in the **correct order**.

Prim's vs Kruskal's

Prim's algorithm and Kruskal's algorithm both find a minimum spanning tree. Here are some of the key DIFFERENCES between them.

✓ Prim's starts at any VERTEX and adds VERTICES, whereas Kruskal's starts with the EDGE of least weight and adds EDGES.

✓ You have to check for CYCLES when using Kruskal's algorithm.

✓ With Prim's, the tree stays CONNECTED as it grows.

✓ You can apply Prim's algorithm directly to a network given in TABLE form.

Now try this

	A	B	C	D	E
A	–	52	91	28	35
B	52	–	75	32	29
C	91	75	–	57	10
D	28	32	57	–	40
E	35	29	10	40	–

(a) Use Prim's algorithm, starting from **A**, to find a minimum spanning tree for this table. You must list the order in which you selected the **edges** of your tree.   **(3 marks)**

(b) Draw your tree and write down its total weight.   **(2 marks)**

Dijkstra's algorithm

Dijkstra's algorithm is a way of finding the SHORTEST PATH between two vertices in a network.

1 NUMBER your starting vertex 1 and assign it FINAL VALUE 0. This vertex is now ACTIVE.
Call the active vertex X.

2 For each UNNUMBERED vertex, Y, that is DIRECTLY CONNECTED to X:

$$\frac{\text{WORKING}}{\text{VALUE AT } Y} = \frac{\text{FINAL}}{\text{VALUE AT } X} + \frac{\text{LENGTH}}{\text{OF ARC } XY}$$

If this is LESS than the current working value at vertex Y, then REPLACE IT.

3 Look at EVERY unnumbered vertex. Number the one with the SMALLEST working value, and write this as its FINAL VALUE.
The final value is the length of the shortest route from vertex 1 to this vertex.

4 Go back to step 2 using this vertex as your new active vertex, X. Continue until the end vertex has a final value.

5 Trace the path backwards. Include an arc if:

$$\frac{\text{ARC}}{\text{WEIGHT}} = \frac{\text{DIFFERENCE IN FINAL}}{\text{VALUES OF END VERTICES}}$$

Keeping track

In your exam, you can use the diagram in the answer booklet to keep track of your working.

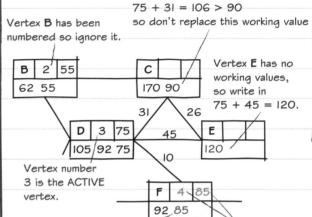

Vertex B has been numbered so ignore it.

75 + 31 = 106 > 90 so don't replace this working value

Vertex E has no working values, so write in 75 + 45 = 120.

Vertex number 3 is the ACTIVE vertex.

75 + 10 = 85 < 92 so replace the working value – write the new working value at the END on the BOTTOM ROW.

Vertex F now has the SMALLEST working value (85) so NUMBER it with the next number, 4, and write 85 as its FINAL VALUE.

Worked example

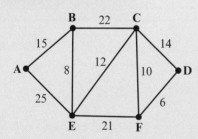

The diagram shows a network of footpaths. The number on each arc gives the length of that path, in km.

Use Dijkstra's algorithm to find the shortest route from **A** to **D**. State your shortest route and its length. **(5 marks)**

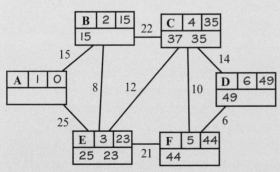

Shortest route = ABECD, of length 49 km

You need to list the working values **in the correct order** to show that you understand how the algorithm works. It's safest not to cross any values out – just write the new working value next to the old one.

To work out the route, you trace backwards through your network.

Final value (D) – Final value (F) = 49 – 44 = 5 but **DF** = 6 so **don't** include DF.

Final value (D) – Final value (C) = 49 – 35 = 14 and **CD** = 14 so **do** include CD.

Now try this

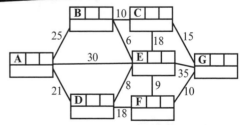

(a) Use Dijkstra's algorithm to find the shortest route from **A** to **G** in this network. State your shortest route and its length. **(6 marks)**

(b) Arc **FG** is deleted. Write down the new shortest route from **A** to **G**. **(2 marks)**

Route inspection

The route inspection problem is sometimes called the CHINESE POSTMAN problem. You need to work out the SHORTEST PATH through a network that TRAVERSES every arc.

Route inspection algorithm

1. **Find all the ODD vertices.**
   There will usually be FOUR.

2. **Write down all possible pairings of the odd vertices.**
   FOUR odd vertices → THREE pairings

3. **Choose the pairing with the MINIMUM TOTAL DISTANCE.**

4. **Double up the arcs linking these pairs of vertices to create a TRAVERSABLE network.**
   The total length of the route will be the TOTAL WEIGHT of the original network PLUS the weight of the extra arcs.

Odd or even?

A network is TRAVERSABLE if all the vertices have EVEN VALENCY. You can start at any point, traverse the arcs ONCE EACH, and end up where you started.

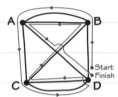

Not traversable – every vertex has ODD valency.

Adding arcs gives every vertex EVEN valency, so the graph is TRAVERSABLE.

Have a look at page 120 for the definition of valency.

Worked example

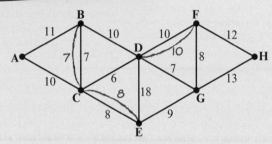

[The weight of the network is 129 miles]

The diagram models a network of canals. The number on each arc gives the length, in miles, of that canal. Brett needs to travel along each canal to check that it is in good repair. He wishes to minimise the length of his route.

Use the route inspection algorithm to find the length of his route. State the arcs that should be repeated. You should make your method and working clear. **(6 marks)**

Odd vertices: B, F, D, E. Possible pairings:
BF + DE = 20 + 14 = 34
<u>BE + DF = 15 + 10 = 25</u>
BD + EF = 10 + 17 = 27
Link vertices B and E by repeating arcs BC and CE
Link vertices D and F by repeating arc DF
Length of route = 129 + 25 = 154 miles

Route inspection checklist

☑ Unless you're told otherwise, routes start and finish at the SAME VERTEX.

☑ Show all the possible pairings and their total distances.

☑ State the REPEATED ARCS and the TOTAL LENGTH of the route.

There are **four** odd vertices, so there are three possible **complete pairings**:

BF and DE   BE and DF   BD and EF

For each one, work out the shortest distance between each pair of vertices. The shortest distance between **D** and **E** is via vertex **C**.

BE and DF is the pairing with the minimum total distance – double up the arcs linking these vertices. Add their weights to the weight of the original network to find the length of Brett's route.

The safest way to make your reasoning clear is to give a **numerical** answer. Calculate the length of the shortest route with the new canal.

Now try this

Look at the network in the Worked example. A canal between **B** and **F**, of length 12 miles, is to be opened and needs to be included in Brett's inspection route. Determine if the addition of this canal will increase or decrease the length of Brett's minimum route. You must make your reasoning clear. **(2 marks)**

Activity networks

An activity network shows you the order in which certain activities have to be carried out in a project. Here is an activity network together with its PRECEDENCE TABLE.

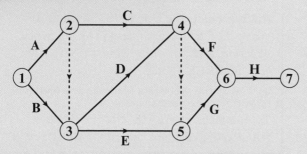

Each ARC represents a different activity.

Activity C DEPENDS on activity A – it can only be started after activity A has been completed.

This is the SINK NODE – all activities have been completed.

This is the SOURCE NODE – no activities have been completed.

This is a DUMMY activity – it shows that activity D depends on activity A as well as activity B.

NODE 4 represents the EVENT that all activities except E have been completed.

The precedence table shows the IMMEDIATELY PRECEDING activities for each activity.

Activity	Preceded by
A	–
B	–
C	A
D	A, B
E	C, D

Worked example

This activity network models a project. The activities are represented by arcs.

(a) Explain the significance of the dotted line from event **2** to event **3**. **(2 marks)**

The dotted line represents a dummy activity. Activities D and E depend on A as well as B, but activity C only depends on A.

Make sure you describe the **effect** of the dummy activity, as well as writing down the word 'dummy'.

(b) Complete the precedence table below. **(3 marks)**

Activity	Preceded by
A	–
B	–
C	A
D	A, B
E	A, B
F	C, D
G	C, D, E
H	F, G

You only fill in the **immediately preceding** activities in a precedence table. Activity **F** is dependent on activities **A**, **B**, **C** and **D**, but you only need to fill in **C** and **D** in the table. Be careful with activity **G**. The **dummy** from node **4** to node **5** means that activity **G** is immediately preceded by activities **C** and **D** as well as activity **E**.

Now try this

A project is modelled by the activity network shown on the right. Complete the precedence table below. **(3 marks)**

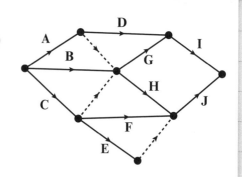

Activity	Preceded by
A	
B	
C	
D	
E	

Activity	Preceded by
F	
G	
H	
I	
J	

Early and late times

The WEIGHT of each arc in an ACTIVITY NETWORK tells you how long that activity takes to complete (its DURATION). You can use the durations to find the early and late times for each node (or event) in the network.

Activity A has a duration of 3 days.

The SOURCE NODE always has an early time and late time of ZERO.

The EARLY TIME of an event is the earliest time you can arrive at this node having completed all preceding activities.
The LATE TIME is the latest time you can leave this node WITHOUT DELAYING the total completion time for the project.

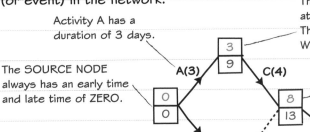

You can complete A and C in 7 days, but you need to have completed B before you reach this node, so the early time for this event is 8 days.

The SINK NODE always has the same early and late times – this project will take a minimum of 18 days to complete.

Worked example

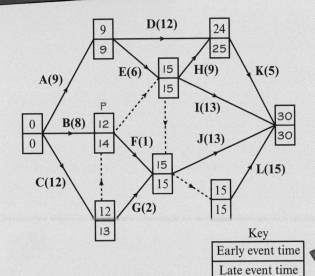

Key

| Early event time |
| Late event time |

The network shows the activities that need to be carried out to complete a building project. Each activity is represented by an arc. The number in brackets is the duration of the activity in days.

Complete the diagram to show the early and late times for this network. **(3 marks)**

Calculating early and late times

Always calculate the EARLY TIMES first. Work FORWARDS through the network starting with an early time of ZERO at the SOURCE NODE.

Look at all the preceding activities and find the LONGEST route to that event.

To calculate the LATE TIMES, work BACKWARDS from the SINK NODE.

EXAM ALERT!

Be careful with **dummies**. Activity **B** can be completed in 8 days, but there is a dummy activity showing that activity **F** is dependent on **B and C**. You need to 'wait' until activity **C** is complete before you can proceed, so the **early time** for node P is 12 days.

Students have struggled with this topic in recent exams – be prepared!

Now try this

The activity network shows the tasks that Fred needs to carry out to complete a woodworking project. Each task is represented by an arc. The number in brackets is the duration of the task in hours. Complete the diagram to show the early and late times for this network. **(3 marks)**

Check it!
At every node, your early time must be less than or equal to your late time.

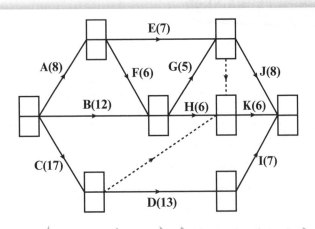

Critical paths

Finding critical paths tells you which activities in a project are the most time sensitive.

1 A CRITICAL ACTIVITY is one whose duration cannot be increased without increasing the duration of the whole project.

2 A CRITICAL PATH from the source node to the sink node ONLY CONTAINS critical activities.

There can be more than one critical path in an activity network.

3 A CRITICAL EVENT lies on the critical path.

For all critical events: EARLY TIME = LATE TIME

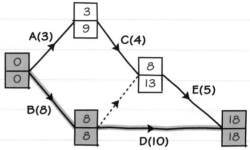

The critical path and critical events are shown in purple on this activity network.

Worked example

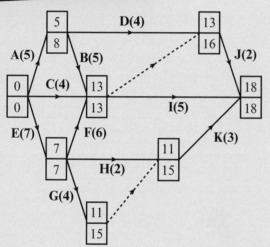

This activity network models a project.

(a) Calculate the total float on activities **C**, **D** and **I**. **(4 marks)**

Activity C: 13 − 0 − 4 = 9

Activity D: 16 − 5 − 4 = 7

Activity I: 18 − 13 − 5 = 0

(b) List the critical activities. **(2 marks)**

E, F and I

Total float

The total float on an activity is the maximum length of time it can be delayed without delaying the whole project.

$$\text{TOTAL FLOAT} = \text{LATEST END TIME} - \text{EARLIEST START TIME} - \text{DURATION}$$

The total float of a CRITICAL ACTIVITY is ZERO.

Here are the key values for calculating the total float for activity D:

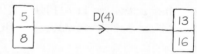

Make sure you show your calculations for the total float.

Be careful – an activity that connects two critical events is not necessarily a critical activity. In this network, activity **C** links two critical events but its total float is **not zero**, so it is **not** a critical activity.

Now try this

The activity network models a project.

(a) Complete the diagram to show the early and late times for this network. **(3 marks)**

(b) List the critical activities. **(2 marks)**

(c) Calculate the total float on activities **E**, **H** and **M**. **(4 marks)**

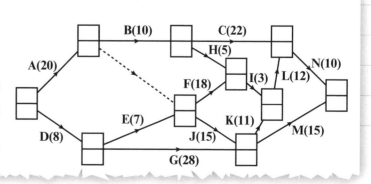

Gantt charts

A Gantt chart is sometimes called a CASCADE CHART. It shows the EARLIEST possible START and LATEST possible FINISH times of all the activities in an activity network.

Here is a simple activity network with its accompanying Gantt chart.

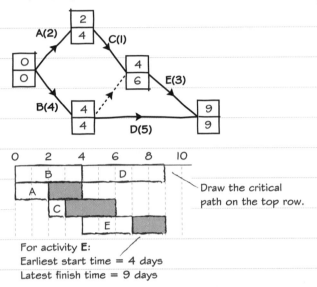

Draw the critical path on the top row.

For activity E:
Earliest start time = 4 days
Latest finish time = 9 days

Gantt chart checklist

✓ Make sure you draw a GANTT chart and not a scheduling diagram.
  Scheduling diagrams are covered on page 130.

✓ Draw CRITICAL ACTIVITIES first, then ALL the other activities in ALPHABETICAL order.

✓ Non-critical activities have a WHOLE ROW each.

✓ Work out the TOTAL FLOAT for each activity.
  The shaded area for each activity is its TOTAL FLOAT.

✓ Check that you have included every activity on your Gantt diagram.

Worked example

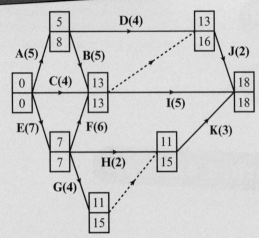

Draw a Gantt chart for this project on the grid below. **(4 marks)**

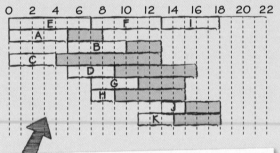

This is the same activity network that is used in the Worked example on page 128. Have a look for a reminder about critical activities.

Now try this

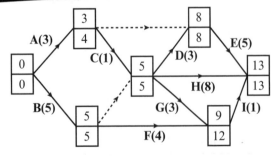

The diagram shows an activity network that models a project. The number in brackets shows the time needed, in days, to complete each activity.

(a) Find **two** critical paths through this network.
    (3 marks)

(b) Draw a Gantt (cascade) chart for this project on the grid on the right. **(4 marks)**

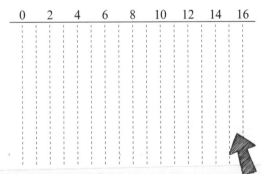

Start by drawing the activities on both critical paths. Draw one critical path on the top row of your chart, and any extra critical activities on the second row:

B		H	
	D	E	

Scheduling

You can use a SCHEDULING DIAGRAM to work out how many WORKERS are needed to complete a project. You assume that each activity requires exactly one worker.

Scheduling diagrams

Each row in a scheduling diagram shows the activities completed by ONE WORKER. This is a scheduling diagram for the activity network at the top left of page 129.

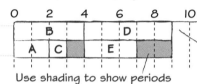

Use shading to show periods of INACTIVITY for a worker.

One worker can do ALL activities on the CRITICAL PATH.

Lower bounds

You can use this formula to work out a LOWER BOUND for the number of workers needed to complete a project:

$$\text{LOWER BOUND} = \frac{\text{SUM OF ALL ACTIVITY TIMES}}{\text{LENGTH OF CRITICAL PATH}}$$

Round up to the nearest whole number.

For the example on the left:
$15 \div 9 = 1.66...$ so the lower bound is 2 workers. The scheduling diagram shows that it can ACTUALLY be done with two workers.

Worked example

Look at the activity network and Gantt chart for the project in the Worked example on page 129.

(a) State the activities that **must** be happening at time 8.5 **(1 mark)**

F, B

(b) Calculate a lower bound for the number of workers needed to finish the project in minimum time. **(2 marks)**

$$\frac{7+6+5+5+5+4+4+4+2+2+3}{18}$$

$= 47 \div 18 = 2.61...$

Lower bound = 3 workers

(c) Schedule the activities using the minimum number of workers so that the project is completed in the minimum time. **(4 marks)**

For part (a), look at the Gantt chart on page 129:

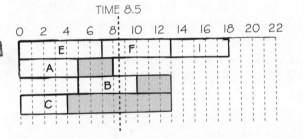
TIME 8.5

Checking for precedence

Don't schedule an activity to begin BEFORE all its preceding activities have FINISHED. For example, in this scheduling for the Worked example, activities J and K have been swapped:

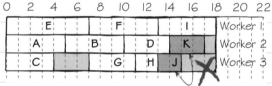

All the activities are taking place within the times shown on the Gantt chart. BUT activity J DEPENDS on activity D. Worker 2 won't finish activity D until time 14, so activity J CANNOT START until then.

Now try this

Look at the activity network in the Now try this section at the bottom of page 129.

(a) Calculate a lower bound for the number of workers needed to finish this project in minimum time. **(2 marks)**

(b) Schedule the activities to show that the project is completed in the minimum time with this number of workers. **(4 marks)**

130

Linear programming 1

Linear programming is a way of MAXIMISING or MINIMISING a variable, subject to certain CONSTRAINTS. Constraints are usually given as INEQUALITIES. Here is an example.

Andrew needs to buy at least 20 pies for a party. He needs at least twice as many meat pies as veggie pies, and he knows there will be at least five vegetarians. He wants to MINIMISE the cost of the pies.

Meat pies £2.50

Veggie pies £2.00

Here is the problem formulated as a LINEAR PROGRAMMING problem.

Let m = number of meat pies bought

Let v = number of veggie pies bought

Let C = total cost in pounds

Minimise $C = 2.5m + 2v$

Subject to
$$m \geqslant 2v$$
$$m + v \geqslant 20$$
$$v \geqslant 5$$
$$m \geqslant 0$$

This is the OBJECTIVE FUNCTION – you need to MAXIMISE or MINIMISE it.

These are the CONSTRAINTS – m and v are called DECISION VARIABLES.

Worked example

Class 8B has decided to sell apples and bananas at morning break this week to raise money for charity. The profit on each apple is 20p, the profit on each banana is 15p. They have done some market research and formed the following constraints.

- They will sell at most 800 items of fruit during the week.
- They will sell at least twice as many apples as bananas.
- They will sell between 50 and 100 bananas.

Assuming they will sell all their fruit, formulate the above information as a linear programming problem, letting a represent the number of apples they sell and b represent the number of bananas they sell. Write your constraints as inequalities. **(7 marks)**

Total profit in pounds, $P = 0.2a + 0.15b$

Maximise P subject to $a + b \leqslant 800$
$$a \geqslant 2b$$
$$50 \leqslant b \leqslant 100$$
$$a \geqslant 0$$

Make sure you write down the word 'maximise' to show this is a maximisation problem.

EXAM ALERT!

If you're **formulating** a linear programming problem you will often need to give a **non-negativity** constraint. You can't sell a negative number of apples or bananas. You already have $50 \leqslant b \leqslant 100$, so add $a \geqslant 0$ as a constraint to make sure that a and b are both non-negative. And don't try to **solve** the problem – you've only been asked to **formulate** it.

Students have struggled with this topic in recent exams – be prepared!

You have to **define** your variables before you start. You could do it like this:

Let x = number of type A mp3 players produced

Let y = number of type B mp3 players produced

Now try this

A company manufactures two types of mp3 player, type A and type B. The company decides that each month

- at least 200 type A mp3 players should be produced
- the number of type A mp3 players should be between 10% and 40% of the total number of mp3 players produced
- a maximum of 3000 mp3 players can be produced.

The company makes a profit of £75 on each type A mp3 player produced and a profit of £55 on each type B mp3 player produced. The firm wishes to maximise its monthly profit.

Formulate this situation as a linear programming problem, defining your variables. **(7 marks)**

Linear programming 2

You can draw a graph to represent a linear programming problem with TWO DECISION VARIABLES. The decision variables are the axis labels on the graph. You draw the CONSTRAINTS as inequalities on the graph. Use SHADING to show the region you're NOT interested in. The region of the graph that satisfies all the constraints is called the FEASIBLE REGION.

If an inequality is STRICT (< or >) use a dotted line to show that the points on the line are not included.

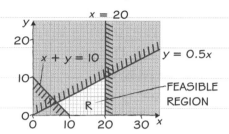

This graph shows the constraints:
$x + y \geqslant 10$ $y \leqslant 0.5x$ $x \leqslant 20$ $y \geqslant 0$

Worked example

A linear programming problem is modelled by the following constraints:
$$4x + y \leqslant 100$$
$$x + y \geqslant 40$$
$$y \geqslant 2x$$
$$x, y \geqslant 0$$

Use the grid below to represent these inequalities graphically. Hence determine the feasible region and label it R.

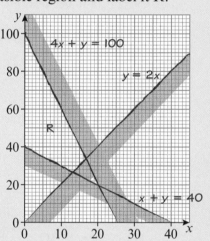

If you have to draw a graph of a linear programming problem in your D1 exam, you will be given a grid. Write the constraints as equations and draw their graphs. Identify the regions you are **not** interested in, and shade them to show this. Be careful – the feasible region won't necessarily be 'inside' all the lines. Here it is bounded by the three lines and the y-axis.

Make sure you take a **30 cm** ruler into the exam with you. If you don't draw your lines long enough on a linear programming graph, you might not be able to identify the correct feasible region.

Drawing $ax + by = c$

In linear programming problems you often have to draw graphs like $4x + y = 100$
These are STRAIGHT-LINE GRAPHS.
The easiest way to draw them is to set $x = 0$ and $y = 0$ to find the points where the graph crosses the axes. When $x = 0$, $y = 100$, and when $y = 0$, $4x = 100$, so $x = 25$.

There is more about equations of lines on page 14.

Now try this

This graph is being used to solve a linear programming problem. Two of the constraints have been drawn on the graph and the rejected regions shaded.

(a) Write down the constraints shown on the graph.

(4 marks)

Two further constraints are:
$$x + y \geqslant 20$$
$$3x + 4y \leqslant 120$$

(b) Add two lines and shading to the graph to represent these constraints. Hence determine the feasible region and label it R.

(4 marks)

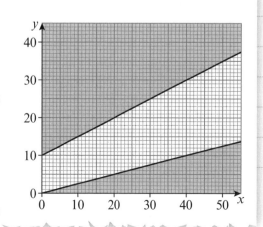

Objective lines

If you have drawn the FEASIBLE REGION for a LINEAR PROGRAMMING problem on a graph, you can use your graph to find an optimal (maximum or minimum) solution. For a reminder about formulating linear programming problems and drawing their graphs look at pages 131 and 132.

Ruler method

The OBJECTIVE LINE method of solving a linear programming problem is sometimes called the RULER method. Follow these steps to solve a problem with OBJECTIVE FUNCTION $ax + by$.

1 Choose a value P and draw the straight line $ax + by = P$ on your graph. This is the OBJECTIVE LINE or PROFIT LINE.

2 Line up your RULER on this line, then slide it PARALLEL to the objective line throughout.

3 The FIRST point in the feasible region that the ruler touches will MINIMISE the objective function.

4 The LAST point the ruler touches will MAXIMISE the objective function.

Worked example

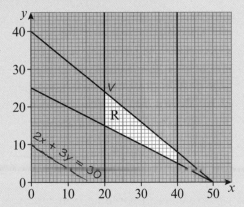

This diagram is being used to solve the following linear programming problem:

Maximise $2x + 3y$

Subject to $20 \leqslant x \leqslant 40$
$\qquad\qquad x + 2y \geqslant 50$
$\qquad\qquad 4x + 5y \leqslant 200$

The feasible region is shown.

(a) Use the objective line method to find the optimal vertex, and label it V.

(3 marks)

(b) Find the values of x and y that maximise the objective function
$P = 2x + 3y$ **(3 marks)**

Intersection of
$x = 20$ and $4x + 5y = 200$
$4 \times 20 + 5y = 200$

$\qquad\qquad 5y = 120$

$\qquad\qquad\qquad y = 24$ and $x = 20$

Choose a value to set $2x + 3y$ equal to. $2x + 3y = 30$ would be a good choice. Make sure you **draw** and **label** the objective line, before using your ruler to find the optimal solution.

You want to **maximise** the objective function, so you are looking for the **last vertex** in the feasible region as you slide your ruler to the **right**. Make sure you keep your ruler **parallel** to the objective line throughout.

It's safest to use a **transparent, 30 cm** ruler to make sure you don't miss the optimal vertex.

Now try this

Look at the diagram in the Worked example.

(a) Use the objective line method to find values of x and y that **minimise** the objective function $P = 2x + 3y$ subject to the constraints given in the question. Label the optimal vertex W. **(4 marks)**

(b) Use the objective line method to find values of x and y that **maximise** the objective function $Q = x + y$ subject to the constraints given in the question. **(6 marks)**

Vertex testing

If you have drawn the FEASIBLE REGION for a LINEAR PROGRAMMING problem on a graph (see page 132 for a reminder), you can use vertex testing (or POINT TESTING) to find the optimal solution.

Worked example

This graph is being used to solve a linear programming problem, subject to the following constraints:

$$y \leq 2x + 10$$
$$6x + 3y \leq 180$$
$$x \geq 10$$
$$y \geq 0$$

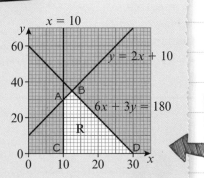

The feasible region is labelled R.

Use the vertex testing method to maximise the objective function $P = 5x + 3y$, and write down the corresponding values of x and y. **(6 marks)**

To find vertex B: $y = 2x + 10$ ①
                $6x + 3y = 180$ ②

Substitute ① into ②: $6x + 3(2x + 10) = 180$
                      $12x + 30 = 180$
                  $x = 12.5$ $y = 35$

Vertex	x	y	$P = 5x + 3y$
A	10	30	140
B	12.5	35	167.5
C	10	0	50
D	30	0	150

Maximum value of $P = 167.5$ when $x = 12.5$ and $y = 35$

Golden rule

In a linear programming problem, the MAXIMUM or MINIMUM value for the objective function MUST OCCUR at one of the VERTICES of the feasible region.

Label the vertices on the diagram to make your working clearer. You need to find the values of x and y at each vertex. You can either read these off the graph, or solve simultaneous equations.

EXAM ALERT!

If you are asked to use **vertex testing** or **point testing** to find a maximum or minimum solution, you need to test **every vertex** of the feasible region, even if it seems obvious that they won't give an optimal solution. It doesn't matter how you find the coordinates of the vertices (reading off the graph is sometimes the easiest way) but you must write down:

- the coordinates of each vertex
- the value of the objective function at each vertex.

Students have struggled with this topic in recent exams – be prepared!

Integer solutions

Some linear programming problems require integer solutions. The easiest way to find these is to find the optimal vertex then test nearby points with INTEGER COORDINATES. For each point:

✓ find the value of the objective function

✓ check whether the point satisfies all the constraints.

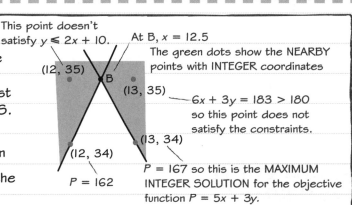

This point doesn't satisfy $y \leq 2x + 10$.

At B, $x = 12.5$

The green dots show the NEARBY points with INTEGER coordinates

(12, 35)

(13, 35) $6x + 3y = 183 > 180$ so this point does not satisfy the constraints.

(13, 34)

(12, 34) $P = 162$

$P = 167$ so this is the MAXIMUM INTEGER SOLUTION for the objective function $P = 5x + 3y$.

Now try this

Look at the diagram given in the Worked example above. Use the vertex testing method to maximise the objective function $Q = 4x + y$ subject to the constraints given, and write down the corresponding values of x and y. **(4 marks)**

Matchings on graphs

A BIPARTITE GRAPH has two sets of nodes. Arcs can ONLY be drawn BETWEEN the two sets – there are no arcs connecting nodes within the same set.

For a reminder about GRAPH notation have a look at page 120.

Modelling with bipartite graphs

Bipartite graphs are useful for assigning people to certain activities or tasks. This bipartite graph for a farm shows which workers are qualified to operate which pieces of machinery.

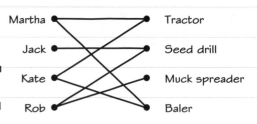

Martha is qualified to operate the tractor or the baler. Jack is only qualified to operate the seed drill.

Matchings

Most questions about BIPARTITE GRAPHS involve finding a matching. A matching is a subgraph of a bipartite graph. You choose arcs that match ONE PERSON to ONE TASK.

✓ Each arc must be in the original graph.

✓ Every person is matched to AT MOST one task.

✓ Every task has AT MOST one person matched to it.

A matching must be ONE-TO-ONE. This means the degree of every vertex in a matching is either ZERO or ONE. If the degree is zero then that person or task remains unmatched.

A complete matching is only possible if both sets contain the SAME NUMBER of nodes. Even then, a complete matching isn't always possible.

Here are TWO possible matchings for the bipartite graph above.

 This is a PARTIAL or INCOMPLETE matching because not every person or task is matched.

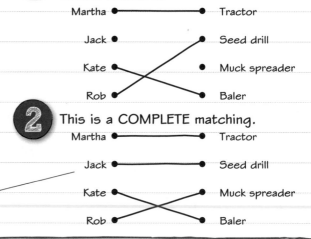

2 This is a COMPLETE matching.

Worked example

Define the terms

(a) bipartite graph   **(2 marks)**

A graph consisting of two sets of vertices, X and Y. Edges can only join vertices in X to vertices in Y – not vertices within a set.

(b) matching.   **(2 marks)**

A one-to-one pairing of some or all of the vertices in set X with vertices in set Y.

Notation for paths and matching

On page 136 you need to write down matchings and paths on bipartite graphs. The easiest way to show a matching is by using = and − to show whether an arc is included:

Kate = Baler   This arc IS included.

Kate − Tractor   This arc IS NOT included.

Now try this

A manager wants to allocate five tasks, 1, 2, 3, 4 and 5, to five workers, Aimee (A), Ben (B), Carla (C), Dhruv (D) and Eric (E). This table shows which tasks each worker is able to carry out.

Worker	Aimee (A)	Ben (B)	Carla (C)	Dhruv (D)	Eric (E)
Tasks	2, 3, 4	1, 2	5	3, 5	2, 4, 5

(a) Draw a bipartite graph to model this situation.   **(2 marks)**

(b) Find a matching which allocates tasks to at least four of the workers.   **(2 marks)**

Maximum matchings

A maximum matching for a BIPARTITE GRAPH contains the maximum number of arcs possible.

Maximum matching algorithm

To find a maximum matching in a bipartite graph:

1 Start with the INITIAL MATCHING given in the question.

2 Find an ALTERNATING PATH.
If there is no alternating path then you already have a maximum matching, so STOP.

3 CHANGE THE STATUS to swap the arcs on your alternating path in or out of the matching.

4 Write down the new arcs, plus any unchanged arcs, to create an IMPROVED MATCHING.

5 Go back to step 2, replacing the initial matching with your improved matching.

Alternating paths

If you have an INITIAL MATCHING in a bipartite graph, then an alternating path:

✓ STARTS and FINISHES at UNMATCHED nodes

✓ alternates between arcs that are in the initial matching and arcs that are not.

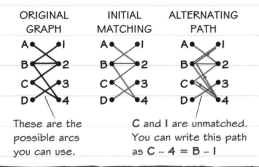

These are the possible arcs you can use.

C and I are unmatched. You can write this path as C – 4 = B – I

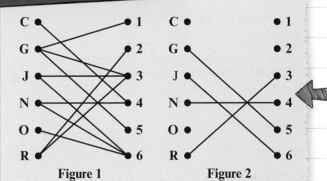

Figure 1   **Figure 2**

Figure 1 shows the possible allocations of six workers, Charlie (**C**), George (**G**), Jack (**J**), Nurry (**N**), Olivia (**O**) and Rachel (**R**), to six tasks, **1**, **2**, **3**, **4**, **5** and **6**. Figure 2 shows an initial matching.

(a) Starting from this initial matching, use the maximum matching algorithm to find an improved matching. You should give the alternating path you use and list your improved matching. **(3 marks)**

Alternating path: O − 6 = J − 3 = R − 2

Change status: O = 6 − J = 3 − R = 2

New matching: O = 6, J = 3, R = 2,
         G = 5, N = 4

(b) Explain why it is not possible to find a complete matching. **(2 marks)**

Tasks I and 5 can only be allocated to George, but it is not possible for him to do both.

The **new** arcs given by the change of status of the alternating path are:

O = 6, J = 3, R = 2

The nodes G, N, 4 and 5 weren't used in the alternating path, so you need to include the **unchanged** arcs G = 5 and N = 4 in your improved matching as well.

EXAM ALERT!

Make sure you write your alternating path clearly and show the **change of status** step. The safest way to do this is to write 'change status' and list the alternating path with **all** the symbols swapped.

Students have struggled with this topic in recent exams – be prepared!

Now try this

Look at the Worked example. After training, Charlie adds task **5** to his possible allocations. Taking the improved matching found in part (a) of the Worked example as the new initial matching, use the maximum matching algorithm to find a complete matching. Give the alternating path you use and list your complete matching. **(3 marks)**

Which algorithm?

The key to success in your D1 exam is learning the different algorithms, and remembering what you need to write down to SHOW THAT YOU UNDERSTAND how they work.

Problem	Algorithm	Key things to show	Page
SORTING a list into alphabetical or numerical order	Bubble sort	✓ FULL LIST after each pass ✓ State when list is SORTED	115
	Quick sort	✓ All PIVOTS	116
LOCATING an item in an ordered list	Binary search	✓ All PIVOTS ✓ Which part of list is REJECTED	117
PACKING items into equal-sized bins	First-fit	✓ Exactly which ITEMS are placed in which BIN and in which ORDER	118
	First-fit decreasing		119
	Full bins		119
Finding a MINIMUM SPANNING TREE for a network	Kruskal's algorithm	✓ Arcs you INCLUDE and arcs you REJECT in the right ORDER	122
	Prim's algorithm	✓ Arcs you add IN THE ORDER they are added	123
Finding the SHORTEST DISTANCE between two nodes in a network	Dijkstra's algorithm	✓ VERTICES NUMBERED in the order you consider them ✓ All WORKING VALUES in the correct ORDER ✓ List of vertices to describe SHORTEST ROUTE	124
Finding the shortest route to TRAVERSE all ARCS in a network	Route inspection	✓ All possible PAIRINGS of odd vertices and the MINIMUM DISTANCE added by each one ✓ New TOTAL WEIGHT of network with the extra arcs needed	125
MATCHING the maximum number of people to tasks	Maximum matching	✓ ALTERNATING PATH ✓ STATUS CHANGE ✓ IMPROVED matching	136

Worked example

What is an algorithm?   **(2 marks)**

A set of instructions you can follow to solve a problem.

 Algorithms are usually designed so that it is clear what should be done at each step. This makes them easy for computer programs to carry out.

Now try this

Draw lines to match each problem to the most appropriate algorithm.

Allocating tasks to workers based on their qualifications •

Working out how to cut different lengths of wallpaper from the smallest number of rolls •

Finding a particular name in a database arranged in alphabetical order •

Finding the shortest route between two stations in a railway network •

• Dijkstra's algorithm

• First-fit bin-packing

• Maximum matching

• Binary search

You are the examiner!

CHECKING YOUR WORK is one of the key skills you will need for your D1 exam. Each of these three students has made key mistakes in their working. Can you spot them all?

1

Max Lauren John Hannah Kieran Tara Richard Imogen

(a) Use a quick sort to produce a list of these names in ascending alphabetical order. You must make your pivots clear. **(5 marks)**

(b) Use the binary search algorithm on your list from part (a) to try to locate the name 'Hannah'. **(4 marks)**

(a)
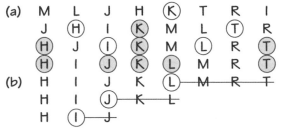

(b)   H   I   J   K   (L)   M   R   T
      H   I   (J)   K   L
      H   (I)   J

First pivot = L → Reject M to T

Second pivot = J → Reject K to L

Third pivot = I → Reject J

H is found.

2

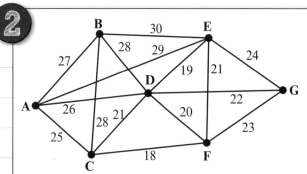

(a) State two differences between Kruskal's algorithm and Prim's algorithm for finding a minimum spanning tree. **(2 marks)**

(b) Listing the arcs in the order that you consider them, find a minimum spanning tree for the network above using
(i) Prim's algorithm
(ii) Kruskal's algorithm. **(6 marks)**

(a) Prim adds points to the tree but Kruskal adds edges.

(b) (i)
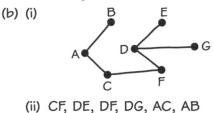

(ii) CF, DE, DF, DG, AC, AB

3

A firm is planning to produce two types of radio, type A and type B. Market research suggests that, each week

• at least 50 type A radios should be produced
• the number of type A radios should be between 20% and 40% of the total number of radios produced.

Each type A radio requires 3 switches and each type B radio requires 2 switches. The firm can only buy 200 switches each week.

The profit on each type A radio is £15.

The profit on each type B radio is £12.

The firm wishes to maximise its weekly profit.

Formulate this situation as a linear programming problem, defining your variables. **(7 marks)**

x = type A, y = type B

Maximise $P = 15x + 12y$ subject to

$x \geqslant 50$

$0.2(x + y) < x < 0.4(x + y)$

$3x + 2y \leqslant 200$

Checking your work

If you have any time left at the end of your exam, you should check back through your working.

☑ Check you have answered EVERY PART and given all the information asked for.

☑ Check that you have used the METHOD or ALGORITHM asked for in the question.

☑ Make sure you've given all the information you need to SHOW how the algorithm works.

☑ Make sure everything is EASY TO READ.

Now try this

Find the mistakes in each student's answer on this page, and write out the correct working for each question. Turn over for the answers.

You are still the examiner!

BEFORE looking at this page, turn back to page 138 and try to spot the key mistake in each student's working. Use this page to CHECK your answers – the corrections are shown in red, and these answers are now 100% CORRECT.

1 Max Lauren John Hannah Kieran Tara Richard Imogen

(a) Use a quick sort to produce a list of these names in ascending alphabetical order. You must make your pivots clear. **(5 marks)**

(b) Use the binary search algorithm on your list from part (a) to try to locate the name 'Hannah'. **(4 marks)**

(a)
```
M   L   J   H  (K)  T   R   I
    J  (H)  I  (K)  M   L  (T)  R
   (H)  J  (I) (K)  M  (L)  R  (T)
   (H)     (I)(J) (K) (L)  M  (R) (T)
   (H)     (I)(J) (K) (L) (M) (R) (T)
```
(b)
```
H   I   J   K  (L)  M   R   T
H   I  (J)  K̶   L̶
H  (I)  J̶
(H)
```

First pivot = L → Reject M̶ L to T

Second pivot = J → Reject K̶ J to L̶ K

Third pivot = I → Reject J̶ I

Fourth pivot H so H is found.

Top tip
(a) If you use **quick sort** you need to keep going until **every item** has been selected as a pivot.
(b) In a **binary search** you always **reject the pivot** if it is not the item you're looking for.
For more on this look at pages 116 and 117.

2

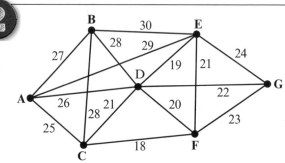

(a) State two differences between Kruskal's algorithm and Prim's algorithm for finding a minimum spanning tree. **(2 marks)**

(b) Listing the arcs in the order that you consider them, find a minimum spanning tree for the network above using
(i) Prim's algorithm
(ii) Kruskal's algorithm. **(6 marks)**

          nodes
(a) Prim adds p̶o̶i̶n̶t̶s̶ to the tree but Kruskal adds edges. With Prim's algorithm the tree grows in a connected way.

(b) (i) AC, CF, DF, DE, DG, AB

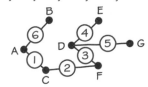

(ii) CF, DE, DF, not CD, DG, not FG, not EG, AC, not AD, AB

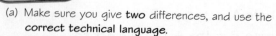

Top tip
(a) Make sure you give **two** differences, and use the **correct technical language**.
(b) For Prim's algorithm you need to specify the **order** the arcs are chosen in. For Kruskal's algorithm, you need to show which arcs are **rejected**, and in which order.
These algorithms are covered on pages 122 and 123.

3 A firm is planning to produce two types of radio, type A and type B. Market research suggests that, each week

- at least 50 type A radios should be produced
- the number of type A radios should be between 20% and 40% of the total number of radios produced.

Each type A radio requires 3 switches and each type B radio requires 2 switches. The firm can only buy 200 switches each week.

The profit on each type A radio is £15.

The profit on each type B radio is £12.

The firm wishes to maximise its weekly profit.

Formulate this situation as a linear programming problem, defining your variables. **(7 marks)**

x̶ ̶=̶ ̶t̶y̶p̶e̶ ̶A̶,̶ ̶y̶ ̶=̶ ̶t̶y̶p̶e̶ ̶B̶

Let x = number of type A radios and
Let y = number of type B radios

Maximise $P = 15x + 12y$ subject to

$x \geqslant 50$

$0.2(x + y) < x < 0.4(x + y)$

$3x + 2y \leqslant 200$

$y \geqslant 0$

Top tip
If you have to **define the variables** in a linear programming problem you need to be very **precise**. And don't forget to include any **non-negativity** constraints.
Revise linear programming problems on page 131.

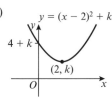

Worked solutions

CORE MATHEMATICS 1

1 Index laws

1. $x(4x^{-\frac{1}{2}})^3 = x^1(4^3x^{-\frac{3}{2}})$
   $= 64x^{-\frac{3}{2}+1} = 64x^{-\frac{1}{2}}$

2. $(9y^{10})^{\frac{3}{2}} = 9^{\frac{3}{2}}y^{10\times\frac{3}{2}}$
   $= (\sqrt{9})^3y^{15} = 27y^{15}$

3. $\dfrac{5 + 2\sqrt{x}}{x^2} = \dfrac{5}{x^2} + \dfrac{2x^{\frac{1}{2}}}{x^2}$
   $= 5x^{-2} + 2x^{\frac{1}{2}-2}$
   $= 5x^{-2} + 2x^{-\frac{3}{2}}$

2 Expanding and factorising

1. $(x + 2)(x + 1)^2 = (x + 2)(x^2 + 2x + 1)$
   $= x^3 + 2x^2 + x + 2x^2 + 4x + 2$
   $= x^3 + 4x^2 + 5x + 2$
   $b = 4, c = 5, d = 2$

2. $3x^3 - 2x^2 - x = x(3x^2 - 2x - 1)$
   $= x(3x + 1)(x - 1)$

3. $25x^2 - 16 = (5x + 4)(5x - 4)$

3 Surds

1. $(7 + \sqrt{2})(7 - \sqrt{2}) = 49 + 7\sqrt{2} - 7\sqrt{2} - 2 = 47$

2. $\sqrt{98} = \sqrt{49} \times \sqrt{2} = 7\sqrt{2}$

3. (a) $\dfrac{8}{3 + \sqrt{5}} = \dfrac{8(3 - \sqrt{5})}{(3 + \sqrt{5})(3 - \sqrt{5})} = \dfrac{24 - 8\sqrt{5}}{4} = 6 - 2\sqrt{5}$

   (b) $\dfrac{4 + \sqrt{5}}{2 - \sqrt{5}} = \dfrac{(4 + \sqrt{5})(2 + \sqrt{5})}{(2 - \sqrt{5})(2 + \sqrt{5})} = \dfrac{13 + 6\sqrt{5}}{-1} = -13 - 6\sqrt{5}$

4 Quadratic equations

1. $2(x - 3)^2 + 3x = 14$
   $2(x^2 - 6x + 9) + 3x = 14$
   $2x^2 - 12x + 18 + 3x = 14$
   $2x^2 - 9x + 4 = 0$
   $(2x - 1)(x - 4) = 0$
   $x = \frac{1}{2}$ or $x = 4$

2. (a) $x^2 - 10x + 7 = (x - 5)^2 - 5^2 + 7$
   $= (x - 5)^2 - 18$

   (b) $x^2 - 10x + 7 = 0$
   $(x - 5)^2 - 18 = 0$
   $(x - 5)^2 = 18$
   $x - 5 = \pm\sqrt{18}$
   $= \pm 3\sqrt{2}$
   $x = 5 \pm 3\sqrt{2}$

5 The discriminant

1. $(-2)^2 - 4 \times 3 \times (-5) = 64$

2. $b^2 - 4ac = 0$
   $2^2 - 4p \times (-3) = 0$
   $4 + 12p = 0$
   $p = -\frac{1}{3}$

3. (a) $(k + 5)^2 - 4 \times 1 \times 2k = k^2 + 10k + 25 - 8k$
   $= k^2 + 2k + 25$

   (b) $k^2 + 2k + 25 = (k + 1)^2 - 1^2 + 25$
   $= (k + 1)^2 + 24$

   (c) $(k + 1)^2 \geqslant 0$ for all k, so discriminant > 0 for all k, so
   $f(x) = 0$ has distinct real roots.

6 Sketching quadratics

1. (a)
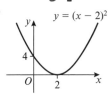
$y = (x - 2)^2$

   (b)
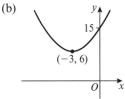
$y = (x - 2)^2 + k$

2. (a) $x^2 + 6x + 15 = (x + 3)^2 - 3^2 + 15$
   $= (x + 3)^2 + 6$

   (b)

   (c) $6^2 - 4 \times 1 \times 15 = 36 - 60 = -24 < 0$
   No real solutions, hence graph does not touch x-axis.

7 Simultaneous equations

1. $x + y = 5$ ①
   $x^2 + 2y^2 = 22$ ②
   From ①: $x = 5 - y$
   Substitute into ②: $(5 - y)^2 + 2y^2 = 22$
   $25 - 10y + y^2 + 2y^2 = 22$
   $3y^2 - 10y + 3 = 0$
   $(3y - 1)(y - 3) = 0$
   $y = \frac{1}{3} \Rightarrow x = 5 - \frac{1}{3} = \frac{14}{3}$
   $y = 3 \Rightarrow x = 5 - 3 = 2$
   Solutions: $x = \frac{14}{3}, y = \frac{1}{3}$ and
   $x = 2, y = 3$

2. (a) $y = x + 6$ ①
   $xy - 2x^2 = 7$ ②
   Substituting ① into ②: $x(x + 6) - 2x^2 = 7$
   $x^2 + 6x - 2x^2 = 7$
   $-x^2 + 6x - 7 = 0$
   $x^2 - 6x + 7 = 0$

   (b) $(x - 3)^2 - 3^2 + 7 = 0$
   $(x - 3)^2 = 2$
   $x = 3 \pm \sqrt{2}$
   $x = 3 + \sqrt{2} \Rightarrow y = 9 + \sqrt{2}$
   $x = 3 - \sqrt{2} \Rightarrow y = 9 - \sqrt{2}$
   Solutions: $x = 3 + \sqrt{2}, y = 9 + \sqrt{2}$ and
   $x = 3 - \sqrt{2}, y = 9 - \sqrt{2}$

8 Inequalities

1. $x(x - 5) < 14$
   $x^2 - 5x - 14 < 0$
   $(x - 7)(x + 2) < 0$

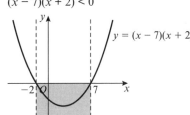
$y = (x - 7)(x + 2)$

   $-2 < x < 7$

2. (a)
$$b^2 - 4ac > 0$$
$$(k - 3)^2 - 4 \times 1 \times (-4k) > 0$$
$$k^2 - 6k + 9 + 16k > 0$$
$$k^2 + 10k + 9 > 0$$

(b) $(k + 9)(k + 1) > 0$

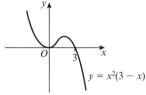

$$k < -9 \text{ or } k > -1$$

9 Sketching cubics

1.

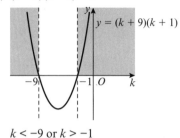

2. (a) $x^3 - 9x = x(x^2 - 9) = x(x + 3)(x - 3)$

(b)

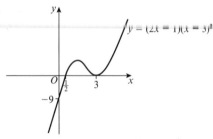

3.

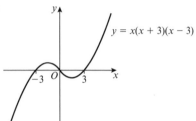

10 Transformations 1

(a)

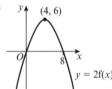

(b)

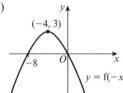

(c)

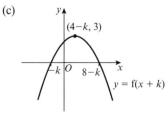

11 Transformations 2

(a)

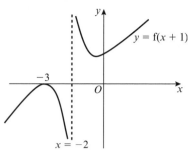

(b) When $x = 0$, $f(x + 1) = f(1)$
$$f(1) = \frac{(1 + 2)^2}{1 + 1} = \frac{9}{2} = 4\frac{1}{2}$$
$(-3, 0)$ and $\left(0, 4\frac{1}{2}\right)$

12 Sketching $y = \dfrac{k}{x}$

1.

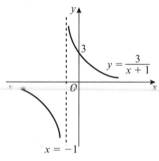

$$y = -\frac{4}{x}$$

2. (a)   (b) $\dfrac{3}{0 + 1} = 3$

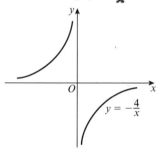 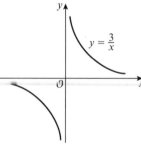

(c) $y = 0$ and $x = -1$

13 Intersecting graphs

(a)

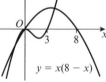

(b)
$$x^2(x - 3) = x(8 - x)$$
$$x(x - 3) = 8 - x \qquad x \neq 0$$
$$x^2 - 2x - 8 = 0$$
$$(x + 2)(x - 4) = 0$$
$$x = -2 \Rightarrow y = -2 \times (8 - (-2)) = -20$$
or $x = 4 \Rightarrow y = 4 \times (8 - 4) = 16$
$(0, 0)$, $(-2, -20)$, $(4, 16)$

14 Equations of lines

1.
$$y - y_1 = m(x - x_1)$$
$$y - (-5) = -\frac{1}{3}(x - 6)$$
$$3y + 15 = -x + 6$$
$$x + 3y + 9 = 0$$

2. $m = \dfrac{y_2 - y_1}{x_2 - x_1} = \dfrac{11 - 2}{8 - (-4)} = \dfrac{3}{4}$

$y - y_1 = m(x - x_1)$

$y - 11 = \dfrac{3}{4}(x - 8)$

$y = \dfrac{3}{4}x + 5$

3. (a) $3(1) + 4(5) - k = 0$

$k = 23$

(b) $3y + 4x - 23 = 0$

$3y = -4x + 23$

$y = -\dfrac{4}{3}x + \dfrac{23}{3}$

Gradient $= -\dfrac{4}{3}$

15 Parallel and perpendicular

1. (a) $10 - 3x = 10 - 3(4) = 10 - 12 = -2$

(b) $m = -\dfrac{1}{-3} = \dfrac{1}{3}$

$y - y_1 = m(x - x_1)$

$y - (-2) = \dfrac{1}{3}(x - 4)$

$3y + 6 = x - 4$

$x - 3y - 10 = 0$

2. $4x - 5(0) - 1 = 0 \Rightarrow x = \dfrac{1}{4}$

A is the point $(\dfrac{1}{4}, 0)$

$4x - 5y - 1 = 0 \Rightarrow y = \dfrac{4}{5}x - \dfrac{1}{5}$

Gradient of $L_1 = \dfrac{4}{5}$

Gradient of $L_2 = -\dfrac{5}{4}$

$y - y_1 = m(x - x_1)$

$y - 0 = -\dfrac{5}{4}(x - \dfrac{1}{4})$

$y = -\dfrac{5}{4}x + \dfrac{5}{16}$

16 Lengths and areas

(a) $x - 2(0) + 6 = 0 \Rightarrow x = -6$

P is $(-6, 0)$

$(0) - 2y + 6 = 0 \Rightarrow y = 3$

Q is $(0, 3)$

$PQ = \sqrt{6^2 + 3^2} = \sqrt{45} = \sqrt{9 \times 5} = 3\sqrt{5}$

(b) $x - 2y + 6 = 0 \Rightarrow y = \dfrac{1}{2}x + 3$

Gradient of $L_1 = \dfrac{1}{2}$

Gradient of $L_2 = -2$

$y - 3 = -2(x - 0)$

$y = -2x + 3$

(c) $0 = -2x + 3 \Rightarrow x = \dfrac{3}{2}$

R is $(\dfrac{3}{2}, 0)$

$PR = 6 + \dfrac{3}{2} = \dfrac{15}{2}$

Area $= \dfrac{1}{2} \times \dfrac{15}{2} \times 3 = \dfrac{45}{4}$

17 Arithmetic sequences

1. (a) $\quad a + 8d = 3 \quad$ ①

$a + 10d = -4 \quad$ ②

(b) ② − ①: $\quad 2d = -7$

$d = -\dfrac{7}{2}$

$\Rightarrow a + 8(-\dfrac{7}{2}) = 3$

$a - 28 = 3$

$a = 31$

2. $p^2 + 1 + 6p = 24$

$p^2 + 6p - 23 = 0$

$(p + 3)^2 - 32 = 0$

$p + 3 = \pm\sqrt{32}$

$p = -3 + 4\sqrt{2}$ because $p > 0$.

3. (a) $300 + 4 \times 20 = 380$

(b) $300 + (n - 1) \times 20 = 20n + 280$

18 Recurrence relationships

1. (a) $a_2 = 2(5) - 4 = 6$

$a_3 = 2(6) - 4 = 8$

(b) $a_4 = 2(8) - 4 = 12$

$a_5 = 2(12) - 4 = 20$

$\displaystyle\sum_{r=1}^{5} a_r = 5 + 6 + 8 + 12 + 20 = 51$

2. (a) $x_2 = 2p - 1$

(b) $x_3 = px_2 - 1$

$= p(2p - 1) - 1$

$= 2p^2 - p - 1$

(c) $\quad 2p^2 - p - 1 = 9$

$2p^2 - p - 10 = 0$

$(2p - 5)(p + 2) = 0$

$\underline{p = \dfrac{5}{2}}$ or $p = -2$

19 Arithmetic series

1. $\dfrac{1}{2}(20)[2(-3) + (20 - 1)d] = 320$

$10(-6 + 19d) = 320$

$-6 + 19d = 32$

$19d = 38$

$d = 2$

2. $S = 1 + 2 + \dots + (n - 1) + n \quad$ ①

$S = n + (n - 1) + \dots + 2 + 1 \quad$ ②

① + ②: $2S = (n + 1) + (n + 1) + \dots + (n + 1)$

$2S = n(n + 1)$

$S = \dfrac{1}{2}n(n + 1)$

20 Sequence and series problems

(a) $25 + (n - 1) \times 6 = 6n + 19$

(b) $\dfrac{1}{2}n[2a + (n - 1)d] = \dfrac{1}{2}n[2(25) + 6(n - 1)]$

$= 25n + 3n(n - 1)$

$= 3n^2 + 22n$

(c) $6n + 19 = 79$

$6n = 60$

$n = 10$

$S_{10} = 3(10)^2 + 22(10)$

$= 300 + 220$

$= 520$

21 Differentiation 1

1. $y = \dfrac{x^2 + 6x + 9}{x} = x + 6 + 9x^{-1}$

$\dfrac{dy}{dx} = 1 - 9x^{-2}$

2. (a) $\dfrac{2 + 5\sqrt{x}}{x} = 2x^{-1} + 5x^{-\frac{1}{2}}$

(b) $y = 3x^2 + 1 - 2x^{-1} - 5x^{-\frac{1}{2}}$

$\dfrac{dy}{dx} = 6x + 2x^{-2} + \dfrac{5}{2}x^{-\frac{3}{2}}$

22 Differentiation 2

1. (a) $f'(x) = 9x^2 + 5$

(b) $9x^2 + 5 = 41$

$9x^2 = 36$

$x^2 = 4$

$x = \pm 2$

So $x = 2$ because $x > 0$.

2. $\dfrac{dy}{dx} = 4x - 8x^{-3}$

$\dfrac{d^2y}{dx^2} = 4 + 24x^{-4}$

3. (a) $y = x^3 + 2x^2 - 3x$

$\dfrac{dy}{dx} = 3x^2 + 4x - 3$

(b)

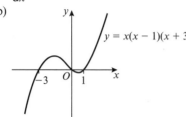

$y = x(x-1)(x+3)$

(c) At $(-3, 0)$: $\dfrac{dy}{dx} = 3(-3)^2 + 4(-3) - 3 = 27 - 12 - 3 = 12$

At $(0, 0)$: $\dfrac{dy}{dx} = 3(0)^2 + 4(0) - 3 = -3$

At $(1, 0)$: $\dfrac{dy}{dx} = 3(1)^2 + 4(1) - 3 = 4$

23 Tangents and normals

$\dfrac{dy}{dx} = \sqrt{4} + \dfrac{8}{4^2} - 5 = 2 + \dfrac{1}{2} - 5 = -\dfrac{5}{2}$

Gradient of tangent $= -\dfrac{5}{2}$

Gradient of normal $= \dfrac{2}{5}$

$y - y_1 = m(x - x_1)$

$y - 11 = \dfrac{2}{5}(x - 4)$

$5y - 55 = 2x - 8$

$2x - 5y + 47 = 0$

24 Integration

1. $x - \dfrac{3x^4}{4} + c = x - \dfrac{3}{4}x^4 + c$

2. $\int(9x^2 + 6x + 1)\,dx = \dfrac{9x^3}{3} + \dfrac{6x^2}{2} + x + c$

$= 3x^3 + 3x^2 + x + c$

3. $y = 6x^2 + 5x^{\frac{3}{2}}$

$\int(6x^2 + 5x^{\frac{3}{2}})\,dx = \dfrac{6x^3}{3} + \dfrac{5x^{\frac{5}{2}}}{\left(\frac{5}{2}\right)} + c$

$= 2x^3 + 2x^{\frac{5}{2}} + c$

25 Finding the constant

1. $f'(x) = 3 - \dfrac{2}{x^2} - \dfrac{3\sqrt{x}}{x^2}$

$= 3 - 2x^{-2} - 3x^{-\frac{3}{2}}$

$f(x) = 3x - \dfrac{2x^{-1}}{-1} - \dfrac{3x^{-\frac{1}{2}}}{\left(-\frac{1}{2}\right)} + c$

$= 3x + \dfrac{2}{x} + \dfrac{6}{\sqrt{x}} + c$

$f(4) = 17$

So $3(4) + \dfrac{2}{4} + \dfrac{6}{\sqrt{4}} + c = 17$

$12 + \dfrac{1}{2} + 3 + c = 17$

$c = \dfrac{3}{2}$

$f(x) = 3x + \dfrac{2}{x} + \dfrac{6}{\sqrt{x}} + \dfrac{3}{2}$

2. (a) $\dfrac{dy}{dx} = \dfrac{(x^2 + 5)^2}{x^2}$

$= \dfrac{x^4 + 10x^2 + 25}{x^2}$

$= x^2 + 10 + 25x^{-2}$

(b) $y = \dfrac{x^3}{3} + 10x + \dfrac{25x^{-1}}{-1} + c$

$= \dfrac{1}{3}x^3 + 10x - \dfrac{25}{x} + c$

At $x = 1$, $y = -13$:

$\dfrac{1}{3}(1)^3 + 10(1) - \dfrac{25}{(1)} + c = -13$

$\dfrac{1}{3} + 10 - 25 + c = -13$

$c = 2 - \dfrac{1}{3} = \dfrac{5}{3}$

$y = \dfrac{1}{3}x^3 + 10x - \dfrac{25}{x} + \dfrac{5}{3}$

CORE MATHEMATICS 2

28 The factor theorem

1. (a) $f(2) = 2^3 - 7(2)^2 - 14(2) + 48$

$= 8 - 28 - 28 + 48$

$= 0$

So $(x - 2)$ is a factor.

(b)

2	1	-7	-14	48
	$\downarrow$	2	-10	-48
	1	-5	-24	0

$f(x) = (x - 2)(x^2 - 5x - 24)$

$= (x - 2)(x - 8)(x + 3)$

2. (a) $f(-4) = 0$

$2(-4)^3 - 3(-4)^2 - 65(-4) - a = 0$

$-128 - 48 + 260 - a = 0$

$a = 84$

(b)

-4	2	-3	-65	-84
	$\downarrow$	-8	44	84
	2	-11	-24	0

$f(x) = (x + 4)(2x^2 - 11x - 21)$

$= (x + 4)(2x + 3)(x - 7)$

29 The remainder theorem

1. (a) $f(-3) = 4$

$k(-3)^3 + 2(-3)^2 - 7(-3) + 19 = 4$

$-27k + 18 + 21 + 19 = 4$

$-27k = -54$

$k = 2$

(b) (i) $f(2) = 2(2)^3 + 2(2)^2 - 7(2) + 19$

$= 16 + 8 - 14 + 19 = 29$

(ii) $f\left(-\dfrac{5}{2}\right) = 2\left(-\dfrac{5}{2}\right)^3 + 2\left(-\dfrac{5}{2}\right)^2 - 7\left(-\dfrac{5}{2}\right) + 19$

$= -\dfrac{125}{4} + \dfrac{25}{2} + \dfrac{35}{2} + 19$

$= 17\dfrac{3}{4}$

2. $f(-1) = -2$

$1 + 2 - a + b = -2$

$a - b = 5$ ①

$f(2) = 4$

$16 - 16 + 2a + b = 4$

$2a + b = 4$ ②

① + ②: $3a = 9$

$a = 3$

Substituting into ①: $b = 3 - 5$

$= -2$

30 Equation of a circle

(a) $AB = \sqrt{(2-(-6))^2 + (4-0)^2} = \sqrt{80} = 4\sqrt{5}$

(b) $\left(\dfrac{-6+2}{2}, \dfrac{0+4}{2}\right) = (-2, 2)$

(c) Centre $(-2, 2)$, radius $2\sqrt{5}$

$(x-(-2))^2 + (y-2)^2 = (2\sqrt{5})^2$

$(x+2)^2 + (y-2)^2 = 20$

31 Circle properties

(a) $(x-5)^2 + (y+2)^2 = 100$

(b) $(-1-5)^2 + (6+2)^2 = (-6)^2 + 8^2 = 36 + 64 = 100$

So $(-1, 6)$ lies on C.

(c) Radius between $(-1, 6)$ and $(5, -2)$ has gradient

$\dfrac{(-2)-6}{5-(-1)} = \dfrac{-8}{6} = -\dfrac{4}{3}$

Tangent is perpendicular to radius, so has gradient $\dfrac{3}{4}$.

$y - y_1 = m(x - x_1)$

$y - 6 = \dfrac{3}{4}(x+1)$

$4y - 24 = 3x + 3$

$3x - 4y + 27 = 0$

32 Geometric sequences

1. $u_n = 420 \times \left(\dfrac{5}{6}\right)^{19} = 13.1$ (3 s.f.)

2. (a) $\dfrac{k}{k-6} = \dfrac{2k+5}{k}$

$k^2 = (2k+5)(k-6)$

$k^2 = 2k^2 - 7k - 30$

$k^2 - 7k - 30 = 0$

(b) $(k+3)(k-10) = 0$

k is positive, so $k = 10$

(c) $r = \dfrac{k}{k-6} = \dfrac{10}{4} = \dfrac{5}{2}$

33 Geometric series

1. $S_{20} = \dfrac{7\left(1 - \left(\frac{3}{2}\right)^{20}\right)}{1 - \frac{3}{2}} = 46\,540$ (nearest whole number)

2.

$S_n = 1 + 2 + 4 + 8 + \dots + 2^{n-1}$ ①

$2S_n = 2 + 4 + 8 + 16 + \dots + 2^n$ ②

②－①: $S_n = 2^n - 1$

34 Infinite series

1. $a = 15$, $r = \dfrac{12}{15} = \dfrac{4}{5}$

$S_\infty = \dfrac{15}{1 - \frac{4}{5}} = 75$

2. $a = 2$, $r = k$

$S_\infty = \dfrac{2}{1-k} = 3k + 4$

$2 = (3k+4)(1-k)$

$2 = 4 - k - 3k^2$

$3k^2 + k - 2 = 0$

$(3k-2)(k+1) = 0$

S_∞ exists, so $-1 < k < 1$, so k cannot equal -1.

$k = \dfrac{2}{3}$

35 Binomial expansion

1. (a) $(1+3x)^9 = 1^9 + \binom{9}{1} \times 1^8 \times 3x + \binom{9}{2} \times 1^7 \times (3x)^2$

$+ \binom{9}{3} \times 1^6 \times (3x)^3 + \dots$

$= 1 + 27x + 324x^2 + 2268x^3 + \dots$

(b) $(2+5x)^4 = 2^4 + \binom{4}{1} \times 2^3 \times 5x + \binom{4}{2} \times 2^2 \times (5x)^2$

$+ \binom{4}{3} \times 2 \times (5x)^3 + \dots$

$= 16 + 160x + 600x^2 + 1000x^3 + \dots$

(c) $(3-x)^{12} = 3^{12} + \binom{12}{1} \times 3^{11} \times (-x) + \binom{12}{2} \times 3^{10} \times (-x)^2$

$+ \binom{12}{3} \times 3^9 \times (-x)^3 + \dots$

$= 531\,441 - 2\,125\,764x + 3\,897\,234x^2$

$- 4\,330\,260x^3 + \dots$

2. (a) $(2+kx)^5 = 2^5 + \binom{5}{1} \times 2^4 \times kx + \binom{5}{2} \times 2^3 \times (kx)^2 + \dots$

$= 32 + 80kx + 80k^2x^2 + \dots$

(b) $80k = 48$

$k = \dfrac{3}{5}$

(c) $80k^2 = 80 \times \left(\dfrac{3}{5}\right)^2 = \dfrac{144}{5}$

36 Solving binomial problems

1. (a) x^3 term $= \binom{30}{3} \times 1^{27} \times (2x)^3 = 32\,480x^3$

$p = 32\,480$

(b) x^4 term $= \binom{30}{4} \times 1^{26} \times (2x)^4 = 438\,480x^4$

$q = 438\,480$ and $\dfrac{q}{p} = \dfrac{438\,480}{32\,480} = \dfrac{27}{2}$

2. (a) $\left(1 + \dfrac{x}{4}\right)^{12} = 1^{12} + \binom{12}{1} \times 1^{11} \times \left(\dfrac{x}{4}\right) + \binom{12}{2} \times 1^{10} \times \left(\dfrac{x}{4}\right)^2$

$+ \binom{12}{3} \times 1^9 \times \left(\dfrac{x}{4}\right)^3 + \dots$

$= 1 + 3x + \dfrac{33}{8}x^2 + \dfrac{55}{16}x^3 + \dots$

(b) $x = 0.1$ so $\left(1 + \dfrac{x}{4}\right)^{12} = (1.025)^{12}$

$(1.025)^{12} \approx 1 + 3 \times (0.1) + \dfrac{33}{8} \times (0.1)^2 + \dfrac{55}{16} \times (0.1)^3 + \dots$

$= 1.3447$ (4 d.p.)

37 Radians, arcs and sectors

(a) $l = r\theta$

$27 = 12\theta$

$\theta = \dfrac{27}{12} = 2.25$ rad

(b) $A = \dfrac{1}{2}r^2\theta$

$= \dfrac{1}{2} \times 12^2 \times 2.25$

$= 162 \text{ cm}^2$

38 Cosine rule

(a) $a^2 = b^2 + c^2 - 2bc\cos A$

$PR^2 = 26^2 + 15^2 - 2 \times 26 \times 15 \times \cos 0.8$

$= 357.5687\dots$

$PR = 18.9$ cm (3 s.f.)

(b) $\cos \angle PQR = \dfrac{QR^2 + QP^2 - PR^2}{2 \times QR \times QP}$

$= \dfrac{20^2 + 13^2 - 18.9^2}{2 \times 20 \times 13} = 0.4065\dots$

$\angle PQR = \cos^{-1}(0.4065\dots) = 1.15$ rad (3 s.f.)

39 Sine rule

$\angle CAB = \pi - \dfrac{\pi}{3} - \dfrac{\pi}{5} = \dfrac{7\pi}{15}$

$\dfrac{AC}{\sin B} = \dfrac{BC}{\sin A}$

$\dfrac{AC}{\sin \frac{\pi}{3}} = \dfrac{13}{\sin \frac{7\pi}{15}}$

$AC = \dfrac{13 \sin \frac{\pi}{3}}{\sin \frac{7\pi}{15}} = 11.3$ cm (3 s.f.)

40 Areas of triangles

(a) $A = \dfrac{1}{2}r^2\theta$

$= \dfrac{1}{2} \times 2.08^2 \times 1.05$

$= 2.27 \text{ m}^2$ (2 d.p.)

(b) $\angle BCA = \angle CAD = 1.05\,\text{rad}$
$AC = AD = 2.08$ (radii of same circle)

$$\frac{\sin \angle ABC}{2.08} = \frac{\sin 1.05}{1.95}$$

$$\sin \angle ABC = \frac{2.08 \sin 1.05}{1.95} = 0.9252\ldots$$

$\angle ABC = 1.1816\ldots\,\text{rad}$

$\angle BAC = \pi - 1.05 - 1.1816\ldots = 0.91\,\text{rad (2 d.p.)}$

(c) Area of triangle $= \frac{1}{2}ab\sin\theta$
$= \frac{1}{2} \times 1.95 \times 2.08 \times \sin 0.91$
$= 1.6009\ldots$

Total area $= 1.6009\ldots + 2.27 = 3.87\,\text{m}^2$ (2 d.p.)

41 Trigonometric graphs

(i) (a)

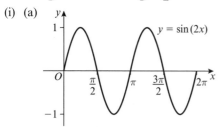

(b) $(0, 0)$, $(\frac{\pi}{2}, 0)$, $(\pi, 0)$, $(\frac{3\pi}{2}, 0)$, $(2\pi, 0)$

(ii) (a)

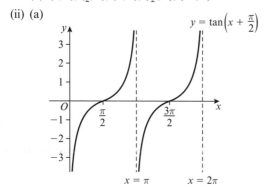

(b) $(\frac{\pi}{2}, 0)$, $(\frac{3\pi}{2}, 0)$; asymptotes at $x = 0$, $x = \pi$ and $x = 2\pi$

42 Trigonometric equations 1

1. (a)

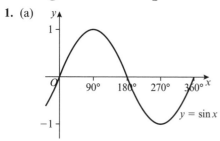

(b) $\sin^{-1}(-0.3) = -17.5°$ (1 d.p.)
$-17.5 + 360 = 342.5$
$180 - (-17.5) = 197.5$
$x = 342.5°, 197.5°$ (1 d.p.)

2. (a) $3\cos\theta = 1$
$\cos\theta = \frac{1}{3}$
$\cos^{-1}(\frac{1}{3}) = 1.23\,\text{rad (2 d.p.)}$
$\theta = 1.23\,\text{rad}, -1.23\,\text{rad (2 d.p.)}$

(b) $\tan\theta + 2 = 0$
$\tan\theta = -2$
$\tan^{-1}(-2) = -1.11\,\text{rad (2 d.p.)}$
$-1.11 + \pi = 2.03$
$\theta = -1.11\,\text{rad}, 2.03\,\text{rad (2 d.p.)}$

43 Trigonometric identities

1. $3\cos^2 x - 9 = 11\sin x$
$3(1 - \sin^2 x) - 9 = 11\sin x$
$3 - 3\sin^2 x - 9 = 11\sin x$
$3\sin^2 x + 11\sin x + 6 = 0$
$(3\sin x + 2)(\sin x + 3) = 0$
$\sin x$ cannot equal -3, so $\sin x = -\frac{2}{3}$
$\sin^{-1}(-\frac{2}{3}) = -0.7297\ldots\,\text{rad}$
$-0.7297\ldots + 2\pi = 5.5534\ldots$
$\pi - (-0.7297\ldots) = 3.8713\ldots$
$x = 5.553\,\text{rad}, 3.871\,\text{rad (3 d.p.)}$

2. (a) $5\sin x = 2\tan x$
$5\sin x = \frac{2\sin x}{\cos x}$
$5\sin x\cos x = 2\sin x$
$5\sin x\cos x - 2\sin x = 0$
$\sin x(5\cos x - 2) = 0$

(b) $\sin x = 0 \Rightarrow x = 0°, 180°$
$5\cos x - 2 = 0 \Rightarrow \cos x = \frac{2}{5}$
$\cos^{-1}(\frac{2}{5}) = 66.42\ldots°$
$360 - 66.42\ldots = 293.57\ldots$
$x = 0°, 180°, 66.4°, 293.6°$ (1 d.p.)

44 Trigonometric equations 2

1. (a) $\sin(x - 40°) = -\frac{1}{2}, 0 \leq x < 360°$
$-40° \leq x - 40° < 320°$
$\sin^{-1}(-\frac{1}{2}) = -30°$
$180 - (-30) = 210$
$x - 40 = -30, 210$
$x = 10°, 250°$

(b) $\cos(2x) = \frac{\sqrt{3}}{2}, 0 \leq x < 360°$
$0 \leq 2x < 720°$
$\cos^{-1}\left(\frac{\sqrt{3}}{2}\right) = 30°$
$30 + 360 = 390$
$360 - 30 = 330$
$330 + 360 = 690$
$2x = 30, 330, 390, 690$
$x = 15°, 165°, 195°, 345°$

2. $\cos\left(2x - \frac{\pi}{6}\right) = \frac{1}{2}, 0 \leq x < \pi$
$-\frac{\pi}{6} \leq 2x - \frac{\pi}{6} < \frac{11\pi}{6}$
$\cos^{-1}(\frac{1}{2}) = \frac{\pi}{3}$
$2\pi - \frac{\pi}{3} = \frac{5\pi}{3}$
$2x - \frac{\pi}{6} = \frac{\pi}{3}, \frac{5\pi}{3}$
$x = \frac{\pi}{4}, \frac{11\pi}{12}$

45 Logarithms

1. (a) $y = 3^{-1} = \frac{1}{3}$
(b) $p^3 = 8 \Rightarrow p = 2$
(c) $\log_4 8 = \frac{3}{2}$

2. (a) $\log_a(5^2) = \log_a 25$
(b) $\log_a(2 \times 9) = \log_a 18$
(c) $\log_a(4^3) - \log_a 8 = \log_a\left(\frac{4^3}{8}\right) = \log_a 8$

3. $\log_a b = \frac{\log_b b}{\log_b a} = \frac{1}{\log_b a}$
$(\log_a b)(\log_b a) = 1$

46 Equations with logs

1. $\log_2(x+1) - \log_2 x = \log_2 5$

$$\log_2\left(\frac{x+1}{x}\right) = \log_2 5$$

$$\frac{x+1}{x} = 5$$

$$x+1 = 5x$$

$$x = \tfrac{1}{4}$$

2. $\log_6(x-1) + \log_6 x = 1$

$$\log_6[(x-1)x] = 1$$

$$x(x-1) = 6$$

$$x^2 - x - 6 = 0$$

$$(x+2)(x-3) = 0$$

$x = 3$ because $\log_6(-2)$ is not defined.

3. $\log_3(x-1) = -1$

$$x-1 = \tfrac{1}{3}$$

$$x = \tfrac{4}{3}$$

4. $2\log_4 x - \log_4(x-3) = 2$

$$\log_4(x^2) - \log_4(x-3) = 2$$

$$\log_4\left(\frac{x^2}{x-3}\right) = 2$$

$$\frac{x^2}{x-3} = 16$$

$$x^2 = 16x - 48$$

$$x^2 - 16x + 48 = 0$$

$$(x-12)(x-4) = 0$$

$$x = 12 \text{ or } x = 4$$

47 Exponential equations

1. (a) $2^b = 15$

$$b = \log_2 15 = 3.91 \text{ (3 s.f.)}$$

(b) $6^x = 0.4$

$$x = \log_6 0.4 = -0.511 \text{ (3 s.f.)}$$

2. (a) $\qquad 3^{2x} + 3^x = 6$

$$(3^x)^2 + 3^x - 6 = 0$$

$$(3^x - 2)(3^x + 3) = 0$$

$$3^x = 2 \Rightarrow x = \log_3 2 = 0.63 \text{ (2 d.p.)}$$

(b) The other factor gives $3^x = -3$, but 3^x is positive for all values of x so this solution does not exist.

3.

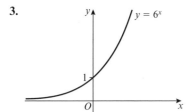

48 Series and logs

1. (a) $200 \times (1.4)^{k-1} > 600$

$$(1.4)^{k-1} > 3$$

$$\log(1.4)^{k-1} > \log 3$$

$$(k-1)\log 1.4 > \log 3$$

$$k - 1 > \frac{\log 3}{\log 1.4}$$

$$k > \frac{\log 3}{\log 1.4} + 1$$

(b) $k > 4.265...$

$$k = 5$$

2. $S_n = \dfrac{a(1-r^n)}{1-r} = \dfrac{4\left(1 - \left(\frac{9}{10}\right)^n\right)}{1 - \frac{9}{10}}$

$$\frac{4\left(1 - \left(\frac{9}{10}\right)^n\right)}{1 - \frac{9}{10}} > 30$$

$$4\left(1 - \left(\tfrac{9}{10}\right)^n\right) > 3$$

$$1 - \left(\tfrac{9}{10}\right)^n > \tfrac{3}{4}$$

$$\left(\tfrac{9}{10}\right)^n < \tfrac{1}{4}$$

$$\log\left(\tfrac{9}{10}\right)^n < \log\tfrac{1}{4}$$

$$n\log\tfrac{9}{10} < \log\tfrac{1}{4}$$

$$n > \frac{\log\frac{1}{4}}{\log\frac{9}{10}} \text{ (with a change of direction because } \log\tfrac{9}{10} \text{ is negative)}$$

$$n > 13.157$$

$$n = 14$$

49 Stationary points 1

1. $y = x^2 - 8x + 3$

$$\frac{dy}{dx} = 2x - 8$$

When $\dfrac{dy}{dx} = 0$, $2x - 8 = 0$

$$x = 4$$

$$y = 4^2 - 8(4) + 3$$

$$= 16 - 32 + 3 = -13$$

Turning point is at $(4, -13)$.

2. $y = x^3 - 5x^2 + 8x + 1$

$$\frac{dy}{dx} = 3x^2 - 10x + 8$$

When $\dfrac{dy}{dx} = 0$, $3x^2 - 10x + 8 = 0$

$$(3x - 4)(x - 2) = 0$$

Stationary points at $x = \tfrac{4}{3}$ and $x = 2$.

50 Stationary points 2

(a) $y = 5x^2 - 3x - x^3$

$$\frac{dy}{dx} = 10x - 3 - 3x^2$$

When $\dfrac{dy}{dx} = 0$, $10x - 3 - 3x^2 = 0$

$$3x^2 - 10x + 3 = 0$$

$$(3x - 1)(x - 3) = 0$$

A: $x = \tfrac{1}{3}$, $y = 5(\tfrac{1}{3})^2 - 3(\tfrac{1}{3}) - (\tfrac{1}{3})^3 = -\tfrac{13}{27}$, coordinates $(\tfrac{1}{3}, -\tfrac{13}{27})$

B: $x = 3$, $y = 5(3)^2 - 3(3) - 3^3 = 9$, coordinates $(3, 9)$

(b) $\dfrac{d^2y}{dx^2} = 10 - 6x$

At B, $x = 3$, so $\dfrac{d^2y}{dx^2} = 10 - 6 \times 3 = -8$

$\dfrac{d^2y}{dx^2} < 0$ so B is a maximum.

51 Max and min problems

1. (a) $P = 80x - \dfrac{x^2}{50}$

$$\frac{dP}{dx} = 80 - \frac{x}{25}$$

(b) When $\dfrac{dP}{dx} = 0$, $80 - \dfrac{x}{25} = 0$

$$80 = \frac{x}{25}$$

$$x = 2000$$

$$\frac{d^2P}{dx^2} = -\frac{1}{25} < 0$$

Hence P is a maximum at $x = 2000$.

2. (a) $\pi r^2 x = 100$

$$x = \frac{100}{\pi r^2}$$

$$A = \pi r^2 + 2\pi r x$$

$$= \pi r^2 + 2\pi r\left(\frac{100}{\pi r^2}\right)$$

$$= \pi r^2 + \frac{200}{r}$$

(b) $A = \pi r^2 + 200 r^{-1}$

$$\frac{dA}{dr} = 2\pi r - \frac{200}{r^2}$$

When $\frac{dA}{dr} = 0$, $2\pi r - \frac{200}{r^2} = 0$

$$2\pi r = \frac{200}{r^2}$$

$$2\pi r^3 = 200$$

$$r^3 = \frac{100}{\pi}$$

$$r = \sqrt[3]{\frac{100}{\pi}} = 3.17 \ (3 \text{ s.f.})$$

(c) $\frac{d^2 A}{dr^2} = 2\pi + \frac{400}{r^3}$

When $r = 3.17$, $\frac{d^2 A}{dr^2} = 2\pi + \frac{400}{3.17^3} = 18.84... > 0$

So A is a minimum.

(d) $A = \pi r^2 + \frac{200}{r} = \pi(3.17)^2 + \frac{200}{3.17} = 94.7 \text{ m}^2 \ (3 \text{ s.f.})$

52 Definite integration

1. $\int_1^3 \left(3x^2 - 7 + \frac{6}{x^2}\right) dx = \left[x^3 - 7x - \frac{6}{x}\right]_1^3$

$$= (27 - 21 - 2) - (1 - 7 - 6)$$

$$= 4 - (-12)$$

$$= 16$$

2. $\int_1^2 \left(6x^{-3} - 2x^{-\frac{1}{2}}\right) dx = \left[\frac{-3}{x^2} - 4\sqrt{x}\right]_1^2$

$$= \left(\frac{-3}{4} - 4\sqrt{2}\right) - (-3 - 4)$$

$$= \frac{25}{4} - 4\sqrt{2}$$

53 Area under a curve

$y = x^3 - 6x^2 + 8x$

A_1 above the x-axis:

$$\int_1^2 (x^3 - 6x^2 + 8x) \, dx = \left[\frac{1}{4}x^4 - 2x^3 + 4x^2\right]_1^2$$

$$= (4 - 16 + 16) - \left(\frac{1}{4} - 2 + 4\right)$$

$$= 1.75$$

A_2 below the x-axis:

$$\int_2^4 (x^3 - 6x^2 + 8x) \, dx = \left[\frac{1}{4}x^4 - 2x^3 + 4x^2\right]_2^4$$

$$= (64 - 128 + 64) - (4 - 16 + 16)$$

$$= -4$$

So $A_2 = 4$

Total area $= 1.75 + 4 = 5.75$

54 More areas

(a) $5x - x^2 = x$

$5 - x = 1, x \neq 0$

$x = 4$

Coordinates of A are $(4, 4)$.

(b) Area of R = area under curve − area of triangle

Area under curve:

$$\int_0^4 (5x - x^2) \, dx = \left[\frac{5}{2}x^2 - \frac{1}{3}x^3\right]_0^4$$

$$= \left(40 - \frac{64}{3}\right) - (0)$$

$$= 18\frac{2}{3}$$

Area of triangle $= \frac{1}{2} \times 4 \times 4 = 8$

Area of $R = 18\frac{2}{3} - 8 = 10\frac{2}{3}$

55 The trapezium rule

(a)

x	0	1	2	3	4	5
y	0	2	3.464	4.243	4	0

(b) $n = 5, a = 0, b = 5$

$$h = \frac{5 - 0}{5} = 1$$

$$\int_0^2 y \, dx \approx \frac{1}{2} \times 1 \times [(0 + 0) + 2(2 + 3.464 + 4.243 + 4)]$$

$$= 13.707$$

MECHANICS 1

58 Constant acceleration 1

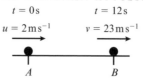

$t = 0\,\text{s}$ $t = 12\,\text{s}$

$u = 2\,\text{m s}^{-1}$ $v = 23\,\text{m s}^{-1}$

A B

(a) $s = ?, u = 2, v = 23, a = ?, t = 12$

$$v = u + at$$

$$23 = 2 + 12a$$

$$12a = 21$$

$$a = 1.75 \text{ m s}^{-2}$$

(b) $s = ?, u = 2, v = 23, a = 1.75, t = 12$

$$s = \frac{1}{2}(u + v)t$$

$$= \frac{1}{2}(2 + 23) \times 12$$

$$= 150 \text{ m}$$

59 Constant acceleration 2

$t = 0\,\text{s}$ $t = 30\,\text{s}$

$u = 16\,\text{m s}^{-1}$

A B

    $\leftarrow$ 300 m $\rightarrow$

(a) $s = 300, u = 16, v = ?, a = ?, t = 30$

$$s = ut + \frac{1}{2}at^2$$

$$300 = 16 \times 30 + \frac{1}{2} \times a \times 30^2$$

$$a = -0.4 \text{ m s}^{-2}$$

The boat decelerates at 0.4 m s^{-2}.

(b) $s = 300, u = 16, v = ?, a = -0.4, t = 30$

$$v^2 = u^2 + 2as$$

$$= 16^2 + 2 \times (-0.4) \times 300$$

$$= 16$$

$$v = 4 \text{ m s}^{-1}$$

(c) $s = ?, u = 4, v = 0, a = -0.4, t = ?$

$$v^2 = u^2 + 2as$$

$$0^2 = 4^2 + 2 \times (-0.4) \times s$$

$$0.8s = 16$$

$$s = 20 \text{ m}$$

60 Motion under gravity

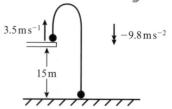

$3.5\,\text{m s}^{-1}$ $-9.8\,\text{m s}^{-2}$

15 m

(a) $s = ?, u = 3.5, v = 0, a = -9.8, t = ?$

$v^2 = u^2 + 2as$

$0^2 = 3.5^2 + 2 \times (-9.8) \times s$

$19.6s = 12.25$

$s = 0.625\,m$

Greatest height above water $= 15 + 0.625 = 15.625\,m.$

(b) $s = -15, u = 3.5, v = ?, a = -9.8, t = ?$

$v^2 = u^2 + 2as$

$= 3.5^2 + 2 \times (-9.8) \times (-15)$

$= 306.25$

$v = \pm17.5$

The diver hits the water with speed $17.5\,m\,s^{-1}.$

(c) $s = -15, u = 3.5, v = -17.5, a = -9.8, t = ?$

$v = u + at$

$-17.5 = 3.5 + (-9.8) \times t$

$9.8t = 21$

$t = 2.1428... = 2.1\,s\ (2\ s.f.)$

61 Speed–time graphs

(a)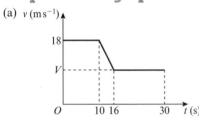

(b) Area under graph $= 455$

$18 \times 10 + \frac{1}{2}(18 + V) \times 6 + 14 \times V = 455$

$180 + 54 + 3V + 14V = 455$

$17V = 221$

$V = 13$

62 Other motion graphs

(a) (i)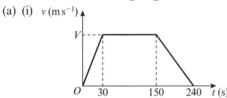

(ii)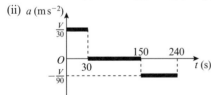

(b) $\frac{1}{2}(240 + 120)V = 3270$

$180V = 3270$

$V = 18.1666... = 18.2$

63 Forces

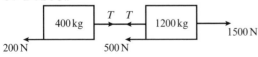

(a) Using $F = ma$ (whole system):

$1500 - 500 - 200 = (400 + 1200)a$

$800 = 1600a$

$a = 0.5\,m\,s^{-2}$

(b) Using $F = ma$ (trailer):

$T - 200 = 400 \times 0.5$

$T = 400\,N$

64 Resolving forces

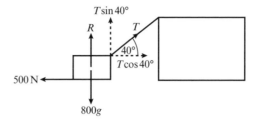

(a) Using $F = ma$ (car):

$T\cos 40° - 500 = 800 \times 2.5$

$T\cos 40° = 2500$

$T = 3263.5... = 3260\,N\ (3\ s.f.)$

(b) $R(\uparrow)$: $T\sin 40° + R = 800g$

$R = 800g - 3263.5...\sin 40°$

$= 5742.2... = 5700\,N\ (2\ s.f.)$

65 Friction

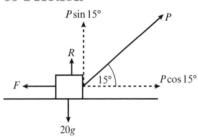

(a) $R(\rightarrow)$: $\qquad P\cos 15° - F = 0$

$F = \mu R = 0.5R$ so

$\qquad\qquad P\cos 15° - 0.5R = 0 \qquad ①$

$R(\uparrow)$: $\qquad P\sin 15° + R - 20g = 0$

$\qquad\qquad P\sin 15° + R = 20g \qquad ②$

$2 \times ①$: $\qquad 2P\cos 15° - R = 0$

$+ ②$: $\qquad\quad \underline{P\sin 15° + R = 20g}$

$\qquad 2P\cos 15° + P\sin 15° = 20g$

$\qquad P(2\cos 15° + \sin 15°) = 20g$

$\qquad\qquad P = 89.4703... = 89\ (2\ s.f.)$

(b) The normal reaction will increase from $20g - P\sin 15°$ to $20g$.

66 Sloping planes

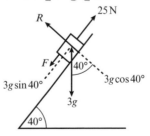

(a) $R(\searcher)$: $R - 3g\cos 40° = 0$

$R = 22.5217... = 23\,N\ (2\ s.f.)$

(b) $R(\nearrow)$: Using $F = ma$:

$25 - 3g\sin 40° - F = 3a$

$F = \mu R = 0.2R$ so

$25 - 3g\sin 40° - 0.2 \times 22.5217... = 3a$

$1.5977... = 3a$

$a = 0.5325 = 0.53\,m\,s^{-2}\ (2\ s.f.)$

67 Pulleys

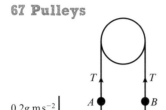

$0.2g\,\mathrm{m\,s^{-2}}$

(a) $R(\downarrow)$: Using $F = ma$ for particle A:
$$4g - T = 4 \times 0.2g$$
$$T = 4g - 0.8g$$
$$= 3.2g = 31\,\mathrm{N}\ (2\ \text{s.f.})$$

(b) Using $F = ma$ for particle B:
$$mg - T = m \times (-0.2g)$$
$$1.2mg = T$$
$$m = \frac{3.2g}{1.2g}$$
$$= \frac{8}{3} = 2.7\ (2\ \text{s.f.})$$

(c) For first 1 second of motion:
$$s = x,\ u = 0,\ v = y,\ a = 0.2g,\ t = 1$$
$$s = ut + \tfrac{1}{2}at^2$$
$$= 0 + \tfrac{1}{2} \times 0.2g \times 1$$
$$= 0.98\,\mathrm{m}$$
$$v = u + at$$
$$= 0 + 0.2g \times 1$$
$$= 1.96\,\mathrm{m\,s^{-1}}$$

For motion after 1 second:
$$s = -0.98,\ u = 1.96,\ v = ?,\ a = -9.8\,\mathrm{m\,s^{-2}},\ t = ?$$

$1.96\,\mathrm{m\,s^{-1}}$ $-9.8\,\mathrm{m\,s^{-2}}$

$0.98\,\mathrm{m}$

$$s = ut + \tfrac{1}{2}at^2$$
$$-0.98 = 1.96t - 4.9t^2$$
$$4.9t^2 - 1.96t - 0.98 = 0$$
$$t = \frac{-(-1.96) \pm \sqrt{(-1.96)^2 - 4 \times 4.9 \times (-0.98)}}{2 \times 4.9}$$
$$= -0.2898\ldots\ \text{or}\ 0.6898\ldots$$

Particle B returns to its initial position after $0.69\,\mathrm{s}$ (2 s.f.).

68 Connected particles 1

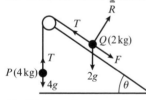

(a) $R(\nearrow)$: $R - 2g\cos\theta = 0$
Using $\cos\theta = \frac{4}{5}$ $R = 1.6g$
So $F = \mu R = \frac{1}{4} \times 1.6g = 0.4g$
$R(\nwarrow)$: Using $F = ma$ on Q:
$$T - F - 2g\sin\theta = 2a$$
Using $\sin\theta = \frac{3}{5}$ $T - 0.4g - 1.2g = 2a$
$$T - 1.6g = 2a \qquad ①$$
$R(\downarrow)$: Using $F = ma$ on P:
$$4g - T = 4a \qquad ②$$
$① + ②$: $2.4g = 6a$
$$a = 0.4g = 3.9\,\mathrm{m\,s^{-2}}\ (2\ \text{s.f.})$$

(b) For first 0.6 second of motion:
$$s = ?,\ u = 0,\ v = ?,\ a = 0.4g,\ t = 0.6$$
$$v = u + at$$
$$= 0.4g \times 0.6$$
$$= 0.24g\,\mathrm{m\,s^{-1}}$$
$R(\nwarrow)$: After P hits floor, using $F = ma$ on Q:
$$2g\sin\theta + F = 2a$$
Using $\sin\theta = \frac{3}{5}$ $2a = 1.2g + 0.4g$
$$= 1.6g$$
$$a = 0.8g\,\mathrm{m\,s^{-2}}$$

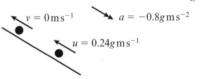
$v = 0\,\mathrm{m\,s^{-1}}$ $a = -0.8g\,\mathrm{m\,s^{-2}}$ $u = 0.24g\,\mathrm{m\,s^{-1}}$

For motion after 0.6 seconds:
$$u = 0.24g,\ v = 0,\ s = ?,\ a = -0.8g,\ t = T\ (\text{to find})$$
$$v = u + aT$$
$$0 = 0.24g - 0.8gT$$
$$0.8gT = 0.24g$$
$$T = 0.3\,\mathrm{s}$$

Particle Q reaches its highest point up the slope after a further $0.3\,\mathrm{s}$.

69 Connected particles 2

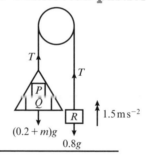
$(0.2 + m)g$ $0.8g$ $1.5\,\mathrm{m\,s^{-2}}$

(a) $R(\uparrow)$: Using $F = ma$ for particle R:
$$T - 0.8g = 0.8 \times 1.5$$
$$T = 0.8g + 1.2$$
$$= 9.04\,\mathrm{N}$$
$R(\downarrow)$: Using $F = ma$ for particles P and Q combined:
$$(0.2 + m)g - T = (0.2 + m) \times 1.5$$
$$0.2g + mg - 9.04 = 0.3 + 1.5m$$
$$1.96 + 9.8m - 9.04 = 0.3 + 1.5m$$
$$8.3m = 7.38$$
$$m = 0.88915\ldots = 0.89\ (2\ \text{s.f.})$$

(b)
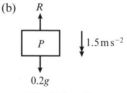
R P $1.5\,\mathrm{m\,s^{-2}}$ $0.2g$

$R(\downarrow)$: Using $F = ma$ on block P:
$$0.2g - R = 0.2 \times 1.5$$
$$R = 0.2g - 0.3$$
$$= 1.66\,\mathrm{N}$$
So the force exerted on P by Q is $1.7\,\mathrm{N}$ (2 s.f.).

70 Collisions and momentum

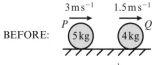

BEFORE:

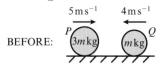

AFTER:

$5 \times 3 + 4 \times 1.5 = 9v$

$21 = 9v$

$v = \frac{7}{3} = 2.33 \text{ m s}^{-1}$ (3 s.f.)

71 Impulse

BEFORE:

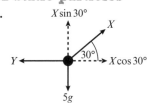

AFTER:

(a) $3m \times 5 - m \times 4 = 3m \times 1.4 + m \times v$

$15m - 4m = 4.2m + mv$

$v = 6.8 \text{ m s}^{-1}$

(b) $6.8m + 4m = 8.1$

$10.8m = 8.1$

$m = 0.75$

72 Static particles

1.

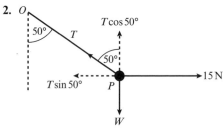

(a) $R(\uparrow)$: $X \sin 30° - 5g = 0$

$X = 10g = 98$

(b) $R(\leftarrow)$: $Y - X \cos 30° = 0$

$Y = 10g \cos 30°$

$= 49\sqrt{3} = 85$ (2 s.f.)

2.

(a) $R(\leftarrow)$: $T \sin 50° - 15 = 0$

$T = \dfrac{15}{\sin 50°}$

$= 19.5811... = 19.6 \text{ N}$ (3 s.f.)

(b) $R(\downarrow)$: $W - T \cos 50° = 0$

$W = 19.5811... \cos 50°$

$= 12.5864...$

$= 13 \text{ N}$ (2 s.f.)

73 Limiting equilibrium

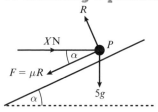

$R(\searrow)$: $R - X \sin \alpha - 5g \cos \alpha = 0$

Using $\sin \alpha = \frac{3}{5} = 0.6$ and $\cos \alpha = \frac{4}{5} = 0.8$:

$R - 0.6X = 4g$ ①

$R(\nearrow)$: $X \cos \alpha - F - 5g \sin \alpha = 0$

Using $F = \mu R = 0.5R$:

$0.8X - 0.5R = 3g$ ②

①: $R - 0.6X = 4g$

$+ 2 \times$②: $\underline{1.6X - R = 6g}$

$X = 10g = 98$ (2 s.f.)

74 Moments 1

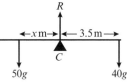

Taking moments about C:

$\circlearrowleft 40g \times 3.5 = 50g \times x \circlearrowright$

$140g = 50gx$

$x = 2.8$

75 Moments 2

(a)

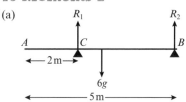

Taking moments about B:

$\circlearrowleft R_1 \times 3 = 6g \times 2.5 \circlearrowright$

$R_1 = 5g \text{ N}$

(b)

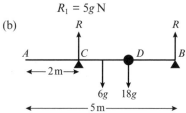

$R(\uparrow)$: $2R - 6g - 18g = 0$

$R = 12g$

Taking moments about B:

$\circlearrowleft R \times 3 = 6g \times 2.5 + 18g \times BD \circlearrowright$

$36g = 15g + 18g \times BD$

$BD = \frac{7}{6} \text{ m}$

$AD = 5 - \frac{7}{6} = 3\frac{5}{6} \text{ m or } 3.83 \text{ m}$

76 Centres of mass

(a)

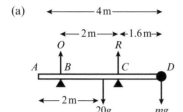

Taking moments about D:

$\circlearrowright R \times 1.6 = 20g \times 2 \circlearrowleft$

$R = 25g$

$R(\uparrow): R - 20g - mg = 0$

$25g - 20g - mg = 0$

$m = 5$

(b)

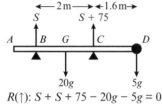

$R(\uparrow): S + S + 75 - 20g - 5g = 0$

$2S = 25g - 75$

$= 170$

$S = 85$

Taking moments about C:

$\circlearrowright S \times 2 + 5g \times 1.6 = 20g \times GC \circlearrowleft$

$170 + 8g = 20g \times GC$

$GC = 1.2673... = 1.3\,\text{m} \ (2\text{ s.f.})$

$DG = 1.6 + 1.3 = 2.9\,\text{m} \ (2\text{ s.f.})$

77 Vectors

(a) $|\mathbf{v}| = \sqrt{(-10)^2 + (-5)^2} = 11.2\,\text{km h}^{-1} \ (3\text{ s.f.})$

(b) $\mathbf{r} = \mathbf{r_0} + \mathbf{v}t$

$= (12\mathbf{i} + 25\mathbf{j}) + 3(-10\mathbf{i} - 5\mathbf{j})$

$= -18\mathbf{i} + 10\mathbf{j}$

78 Vectors and bearings

(a)

$\tan\theta = \frac{1}{4}$ so $\theta = 14.03...°$

Bearing is $360° - 14.03...° = 346°$ (nearest degree).

(b) $\mathbf{r}_A = (3\mathbf{i} - 8\mathbf{j}) + t(-\mathbf{i} + 4\mathbf{j})$

$= (3 - t)\mathbf{i} + (-8 + 4t)\mathbf{j}$

$\mathbf{r}_B = (-21\mathbf{i} + 16\mathbf{j}) + t(5\mathbf{i} - 2\mathbf{j})$

$= (-21 + 5t)\mathbf{i} + (16 - 2t)\mathbf{j}$

Equating $\mathbf{i}$ components: $3 - t = -21 + 5t$

$24 = 6t$

$t = 4$

$\mathbf{j}$ components when $t = 4$:

$A: -8 + 4t = -8 + 16 = 8$

$B: 16 - 2t = 16 - 8 = 8$

So the particles collide when $t = 4$ at the point with position vector $(-\mathbf{i} + 8\mathbf{j})\,\text{m}$.

79 Forces as vectors

(a) $\sqrt{(-4)^2 + 1^2} = \sqrt{17} = 4.12\,\text{m s}^{-1}$

(b) $\mathbf{v} = \mathbf{u} + \mathbf{a}t$

$(6\mathbf{i} - 5\mathbf{j}) = (-4\mathbf{i} + \mathbf{j}) + 5\mathbf{a}$

$5\mathbf{a} = (10\mathbf{i} - 6\mathbf{j})$

$\mathbf{a} = (2\mathbf{i} - 1.2\mathbf{j})\,\text{m s}^{-2}$

$\mathbf{F} = m\mathbf{a}$

$= 2.5(2\mathbf{i} - 1.2\mathbf{j})$

$= (5\mathbf{i} - 3\mathbf{j})\,\text{N}$

(c) $\mathbf{v} = \mathbf{u} + \mathbf{a}t$

$= (-4\mathbf{i} + \mathbf{j}) + t(2\mathbf{i} - 1.2\mathbf{j})$

$= [(-4 + 2t)\mathbf{i} + (1 - 1.2t)\mathbf{j}]\,\text{m s}^{-1}$

Parallel to $\mathbf{i}$ so $\mathbf{j}$ component $= 0$

$1 - 1.2t = 0$

$t = 0.833\,\text{s}$

80 Vectors and resultants

(a) $\mathbf{R} = \mathbf{F_1} + \mathbf{F_2} = (2\mathbf{i} - 6\mathbf{j}) + (3\mathbf{i} + k\mathbf{j})$

$= [5\mathbf{i} + (-6 + k)\mathbf{j}]$

$5 = -(-6 + k)$

$k = 1$

(b) $\mathbf{F_1} + \mathbf{F_2} + \mathbf{F_3} = 0$

$(2\mathbf{i} - 6\mathbf{j}) + (3\mathbf{i} + \mathbf{j}) + (p\mathbf{i} + q\mathbf{j}) = 0$

$\mathbf{i}$ components: $2 + 3 + p = 0$, so $p = -5$

$\mathbf{j}$ components: $-6 + 1 + q = 0$, so $q = 5$

81 Modelling assumptions

(a) You can ignore friction.

(b) The weight of each block acts at a single point.

(c) The accelerations of P and Q have the same magnitude.

(d) You can ignore the weight of the string.

(e) The tension in the string is equal at P and at Q.

STATISTICS 1

84 Mean

(a) $251 + 19 + 22 + 15 + 21 + 16 = 344$

$\frac{344}{20} = 17.2\,°\text{C}$

(b) The mean will go down because $16 < 17.2$.

85 Median and quartiles

(a) 25

(b) $4 + 16 + 13 + 9 + 7 + 0 + 1 = 50$

$\frac{50}{4} = 12.5: Q_1 = $ 13th value $= 25$

$\frac{50}{2} = 25: Q_2 = $ half way between 25th and 26th values $= 33$

$\frac{3(50)}{4} = 37.5: Q_3 = $ 38th value $= 43$

86 Linear interpolation

$\frac{178}{4} = 44.5: Q_1 = 14.5 + (44.5 - 29) \times \frac{3}{64} = 15.23 \ (2\text{ d.p.})$

$\frac{178}{2} = 89: Q_2 = 14.5 + (89 - 29) \times \frac{3}{64} = 17.31 \ (2\text{ d.p.})$

$\frac{3(178)}{4} = 133.5: Q_3 = 17.5 + (133.5 - 93) \times \frac{2}{55} = 18.97 \ (2\text{ d.p.})$

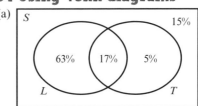

87 Standard deviation 1

$\sum x = 875$

$\text{Variance} = \dfrac{30\,911}{26} - \left(\dfrac{875}{26}\right)^2 = 56.30325\ldots$

SD = 7.50 (3 s.f.)

88 Standard deviation 2

(a) $\dfrac{1+3}{2} = 2, \dfrac{11+20}{2} = 15.5$

(b) $\sum fx = 471.5, \sum f = 100$

$\text{Variance} = \dfrac{3492.25}{100} - \left(\dfrac{471.5}{100}\right)^2 = 12.6912\ldots$

SD = 3.56 (3 s.f.)

89 Box plots and outliers

(a) (i) 20 m

(ii) Upper quartile (Q_3)

(b) It is an outlier. It is a non-typical data value that is usually more than $1.5 \times (Q_3 - Q_1)$ above Q_3.

90 Histograms

(a) $63.5 - 57.5 = 6$

$57.5 - 54.5 = 3$

55–57 bar will be 2 cm wide.

(b) Area of $6 \times 4 = 24\,\text{cm}^2$ represents 30 apples.

$\dfrac{24}{30} \times 12 = 9.6$, so 12 apples represented by area of $9.6\,\text{cm}^2$.

$\dfrac{9.6}{2} = 4.8$ so bar is 4.8 cm high.

91 Skewness

10.3 10.5 10.7 11.3 11.6 11.8 11.9 12.5 12.8 13.5 14.1 15.2

$Q_1 = $ half way between 3rd and 4th values = 11.0

$Q_2 = $ half way between 6th and 7th values = 11.85

$Q_3 = $ half way between 9th and 10th values = 13.15

$Q_3 - Q_2 = 13.15 - 11.85 = 1.3$

$Q_2 - Q_1 = 11.85 - 11.0 = 0.85$

Hence $Q_3 - Q_2 > Q_2 - Q_1$ so positive skew

92 Comparing distributions

(a) $n = 18, Q_1 = 195, Q_2 = 201.5, Q_3 = 206$

(b) (i) $\dfrac{3617}{18} = 200.9444\ldots = 201$ m (3 s.f.)

(ii) $\text{Variance} = \dfrac{727\,823}{18} - \left(\dfrac{3617}{18}\right)^2 = 55.9413\ldots$

SD = 7.48 (3 s.f.)

(c) Median for Team A (201.5 cm) > Median for Team B (194 cm)

IQR for Team A (11 cm) > IQR for Team B (8 cm)

Team A shows negative skew ($Q_2 - Q_1 = 6.5 > 4.5 = Q_3 - Q_2$).

Team B shows negative skew ($Q_2 - Q_1 = 5 > 3 = Q_3 - Q_2$).

93 Drawing Venn diagrams

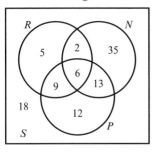

94 Using Venn diagrams

(a)
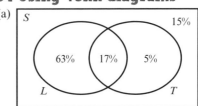

(b) $P(L \cap T') = 0.63$

95 Conditional probability

$P(\text{Cheese} \mid \text{Avocado or Bacon}) = \dfrac{1+2+11}{4+1+2+8+11+5} = \dfrac{14}{31}$

96 Probability formulae

(a) $P(C \cap V) = P(C) \times P(V \mid C)$

$\qquad = \dfrac{2}{3} \times \dfrac{7}{25}$

$\qquad = \dfrac{14}{75}$

(b) $P(C \cup V) = P(C) + P(V) - P(C \cap V)$

$\qquad = \dfrac{2}{3} + \dfrac{2}{5} - \dfrac{14}{75}$

$\qquad = \dfrac{22}{25}$

$P(C' \cap V') = 1 - P(C \cup V)$

$\qquad = 1 - \dfrac{22}{25} = \dfrac{3}{25}$

97 Independent events

(a) $P(A \cup B) = P(A) + P(B) - P(A \cap B)$

$\qquad = P(A) + P(B) - P(A) \times P(B)$

$\dfrac{3}{4} = \dfrac{2}{5} + P(B) - \dfrac{2}{5}P(B)$

$\qquad = \dfrac{2}{5} + \dfrac{3}{5}P(B)$

$P(B) = \dfrac{\frac{3}{4} - \frac{2}{5}}{\frac{3}{5}} = \dfrac{7}{12}$

(b) $P(A' \cap B) = P(A') \times P(B)$

$\qquad = \left(1 - \dfrac{2}{5}\right) \times \dfrac{7}{12}$

$\qquad = \dfrac{7}{20}$

(c) $P(B' \mid A) = P(B') = 1 - \dfrac{7}{12} = \dfrac{5}{12}$

98 Tree diagrams

(a)
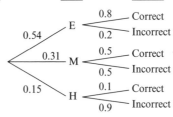

(b) $P(\text{Correct}) = 0.54 \times 0.8 + 0.31 \times 0.5 + 0.15 \times 0.1 = 0.602$

(c) $P(H' \mid \text{Correct}) = \dfrac{P(H' \cap \text{Correct})}{P(\text{Correct})}$

$\qquad = \dfrac{0.54 \times 0.8 + 0.31 \times 0.5}{0.602}$

$\qquad = 0.97508\ldots = 0.975$ (3 s.f.)

99 Correlation

(a) $S_{ll} = 81\,938.5 - \dfrac{2015^2}{50} = 734$

$S_{lw} = 7332.5 - \dfrac{2015 \times 176.5}{50} = 219.55$

(b) $r = \dfrac{219.55}{\sqrt{734 \times 72.25}} = 0.95338\ldots = 0.953$ (3 s.f.)

100 Understanding the PMCC

Set A: 0.72 because it shows positive correlation.

Set B: -0.48 because it shows weak negative correlation.

Set C: -0.93 because it shows strong negative correlation.

101 Regression lines

(a) $S_{xy} = 2972.76 - \dfrac{42.01 \times 338.72}{10} = 1549.79728$

(b) $b = \dfrac{S_{xy}}{S_{xx}} = \dfrac{1549.79728}{205.09} = 7.5566\ldots$

$\bar{x} = \dfrac{42.01}{10} = 4.201 \qquad \bar{y} = \dfrac{338.72}{10} = 33.872$

$a = 33.872 - 7.5566\ldots \times 4.201 = 2.12643\ldots$

$y = 2.13 + 7.56x$

102 Using regression lines

(a) $83.17 + 22.03 \times 2.9 = 147.057$

147 mm is a good estimate.

(b) This estimate is reliable because 2.9 years is within the range of data values (interpolation).

(c) $r = \dfrac{29.85}{\sqrt{1.355 \times 726.68}} = 0.951$ (3 s.f.)

(d) Yes. Strong positive linear correlation, so the data are well approximated by linear regression model.

103 Coding

(a) $\bar{x} = \dfrac{668}{10} = 66.8$

Variance $= \dfrac{47\,870}{10} - \left(\dfrac{668}{10}\right)^2 = 324.76$

SD $= 18.0$ (3 s.f.)

(b) $r = \dfrac{2485.8}{\sqrt{3247.6 \times 3204.0}} = 0.771$ (3 s.f.)

(c) Mean $= 1.1(66.8 - 8)$

$= 64.68$

SD $= 1.1 \times 18.0$

$= 19.8$ (3 s.f.)

(d) $r = 0.771$ (3 s.f.)

104 Random variables

1. (a)

y	2	3	4	5
$P(Y = y)$	$\frac{1}{30}$	$\frac{2}{15}$	$\frac{3}{10}$	$\frac{8}{15}$

(b) $P(Y > 3) = P(Y = 4) + P(Y = 5) = \frac{3}{10} + \frac{8}{15} = \frac{5}{6}$

2. (a) $0.1 + a + 0.15 + 2a + 0.15 = 1$

$3a = 0.6$

$a = 0.2$

(b) $P(3X + 1 \leqslant 6) = P(X \leqslant \frac{5}{3})$

$= P(X = -2) + P(X = -1) + P(X = 0) + P(X = 1)$

$= 0.1 + 0.2 + 0.15 + 0.4$

$= 0.85$

105 Cumulative distribution

(a) $a = 0.2$, $b = 0.1$, $c = 0.3$, $d = 0.6$, $e = 1$

(b) $P(2X - 1 > 4) = P(X > \frac{5}{2})$

$= P(X = 3) + P(X = 4)$

$= 0.1 + 0.3$

$= 0.4$

106 Expectation and variance

1. (a)

x	1	2	3	4
$P(X = x)$	$\frac{1}{22}$	$\frac{2}{11}$	$\frac{7}{22}$	$\frac{5}{11}$

(b) $E(X) = 1 \times \frac{1}{22} + 2 \times \frac{2}{11} + 3 \times \frac{7}{22} + 4 \times \frac{5}{11}$

$= \frac{35}{11}$

(c) $E(X^2) = 1^2 \times \frac{1}{22} + 2^2 \times \frac{2}{11} + 3^2 \times \frac{7}{22} + 4^2 \times \frac{5}{11}$

$= \frac{120}{11}$

$\text{Var}(X) = \frac{120}{11} - \left(\frac{35}{11}\right)^2 = 0.7851\ldots$

$= 0.785$ (3 s.f.)

2. (a) $0.25 + 0.1 + a + b = 1 \Rightarrow a + b = 0.65$

$0 \times 0.25 + 1 \times 0.1 + 2a + 3b = 1.5 \Rightarrow 2a + 3b = 1.4$

(b) $\qquad a + b = 0.65 \qquad ①$

$\qquad 2a + 3b = 1.4 \qquad ②$

$-2 \times ①: \quad \underline{2a + 2b = 1.3}$

$\qquad\qquad\qquad b = 0.1$

$\Rightarrow \qquad\qquad a = 0.55$

107 Functions of random variables

1. (a) $E(1 - 3X) = 1 - 3E(X) = 1 - 3(-0.4) = 2.2$

(b) $\text{Var}(3X - 10) = 3^2\text{Var}(X) = 9 \times 5.8 = 52.2$

2. (a) $E(Y) = 1 \times \frac{1}{10} + 4 \times \frac{2}{10} + 9 \times \frac{3}{10} + 16 \times \frac{4}{10}$

$= 10$

$E(2Y + 1) = 2E(Y) + 1$

$= 2 \times 10 + 1$

$= 21$

(b) $E(Y^2) = 1^2 \times \frac{1}{10} + 4^2 \times \frac{2}{10} + 9^2 \times \frac{3}{10} + 16^2 \times \frac{4}{10}$

$= 130$

$\text{Var}(Y) = 130 - 10^2$

$= 30$

$\text{Var}(5 - Y) = (-1)^2\text{Var}(Y) = 30$

108 Normal distribution 1

1. $P(X < 3.2) = P\left(Z < \dfrac{3.2 - 3}{0.5}\right)$

$= P(Z < 0.4)$

$= 0.6554$

2. (a) $P(X < 80) = P\left(Z < \dfrac{80 - 70}{6}\right)$

$= P(Z < 1.67)$

$= 0.9525$

(b) $0.9525 \times 0.9525 = 0.90725\ldots = 0.907$ (3 s.f.)

109 Normal distribution 2

(a) $P(X > 500) = P\left(Z > \dfrac{500 - 410}{125}\right)$

$= P(Z > 0.72)$

$= 1 - P(Z < 0.72)$

$= 1 - 0.7642$

$= 0.2358$

(b) $P(X < 350) = P\left(Z < \dfrac{350 - 410}{125}\right)$

$= P(Z < -0.48)$

$= 1 - P(Z < 0.48)$

$= 1 - 0.6844$

$= 0.3156$

(c) $P(380 < X < 420) = P\left(\dfrac{380 - 410}{125} < Z < \dfrac{420 - 410}{125}\right)$

$= P(-0.24 < Z < 0.08)$

$= P(Z < 0.08) - P(Z < -0.24)$

$= P(Z < 0.08) - [1 - P(Z < 0.24)]$

$= 0.5319 - (1 - 0.5948)$

$= 0.1267$

110 Finding unknown values

(a) $\qquad P(432 < W < w) = 0.3$

$\qquad P(-0.18 < Z < z) = 0.3$

$\qquad P(Z < z) - P(Z < -0.18) = 0.3$

$\qquad P(Z < z) - [1 - P(Z < 0.18)] = 0.3$

$\qquad P(Z < z) - (1 - 0.5714) = 0.3$

$\qquad\qquad P(Z < z) = 0.7286$

$\Rightarrow z = 0.61$ (2 d.p.)

$\dfrac{w - 450}{100} = 0.61 \Rightarrow w = 511$

(b) $0.3 \times 0.7 + 0.7 \times 0.3 = 0.42$

111 Finding μ and σ

$P(W < 175) = P\left(Z < \dfrac{175 - \mu}{\sigma}\right) = 0.2$

$\Rightarrow \dfrac{175 - \mu}{\sigma} = -0.8416$

$\qquad \mu = 175 + 0.8416\sigma$

$P(W > 230) = P\left(Z > \dfrac{230 - \mu}{\sigma}\right) = 0.1$

$\Rightarrow \dfrac{230 - \mu}{\sigma} = 1.2816$

$\qquad \mu = 230 - 1.2816\sigma$

So $175 + 0.8416\sigma = 230 - 1.2816\sigma$

$\Rightarrow 2.1232\sigma = 55$

$\qquad \sigma = 25.9042\ldots$

$\qquad = 25.9$ (3 s.f.)

So $\mu = 175 + 0.8416 \times 25.9042\ldots$

$\qquad = 196.801\ldots$

$\qquad = 197$ (3 s.f.)

DECISION MATHEMATICS 1

114 Flow charts

(a)

X	N	$\dfrac{X}{N}$ an integer?	$N^2 > X$?	Output
13	2	No	No	
	3	No	No	
	4	No	Yes	Yes

(b) Whether X is a prime number.

(c) (i) Yes (ii) No

The algorithm stops when $N^2 > X$ because factors occur in pairs. For every factor a of X there is a corresponding factor b with $ab = X$. If a is greater than $\sqrt{X}$ then b must be less than $\sqrt{X}$, and vice versa.

115 Bubble sort

71 65 80 75 79 65 63 85 82 69 70

65 71 75 79 65 63 80 82 69 70 85

65 71 75 65 63 79 80 69 70 82 85

65 71 65 63 75 79 69 70 80 82 85

65 65 63 71 75 69 70 79 80 82 85

65 63 65 71 69 70 75 79 80 82 85

63 65 65 69 70 71 75 79 80 82 85

List is sorted.

116 Quick sort

23 25 17 12 22 ⟨20⟩ 19 26 29 21 13

17 12 ⟨19⟩ 13 ⟨20⟩ 23 25 22 ⟨26⟩ 29 21

17 ⟨12⟩ 13 ⟨19⟩ ⟨20⟩ 23 25 ⟨22⟩ 21 ⟨26⟩ ⟨29⟩

⟨12⟩ 17 ⟨13⟩ ⟨19⟩ ⟨20⟩ ⟨21⟩ ⟨22⟩ 23 ⟨25⟩ ⟨26⟩ ⟨29⟩

⟨12⟩ ⟨13⟩ ⟨17⟩ ⟨19⟩ ⟨20⟩ ⟨21⟩ ⟨22⟩ ⟨23⟩ ⟨25⟩ ⟨26⟩ ⟨29⟩

117 Binary search

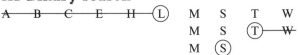

First pivot = Ladybird → Reject A to L

Second pivot = Termite → Reject T to W

Third pivot = Sandfly → Sandfly found

118 Bin packing 1

(a) $47 + 71 + 39 + 19 + 22 + 27 + 6 + 80 + 55 + 32 + 28 + 32 + 41 + 50 = 549$

$549 \div 90 = 6.1$

Lower bound = 7 tapes

(b) Tape 1: 47 39

Tape 2: 71 19

Tape 3: 22 27 6 32

Tape 4: 80

Tape 5: 55 28

Tape 6: 32 41

Tape 7: 50

(c) $7 \times 90 = 630$

$630 - 549 = 81$ minutes wasted

119 Bin packing 2

(a) 0.6 4.0 2.5 3.2 1.0 ⟨2.6⟩ 0.4 0.3 4.0 0.5

4.0 ⟨3.2⟩ 4.0 ⟨2.6⟩ 0.6 2.5 1.0 ⟨0.4⟩ 0.3 0.5

4.0 ⟨4.0⟩ ⟨3.2⟩ ⟨2.6⟩ 0.6 2.5 ⟨1.0⟩ 0.5 ⟨0.4⟩ ⟨0.3⟩

⟨4.0⟩ ⟨4.0⟩ ⟨3.2⟩ ⟨2.6⟩ ⟨2.5⟩ ⟨1.0⟩ 0.6 ⟨0.5⟩ ⟨0.4⟩ ⟨0.3⟩

⟨4.0⟩ ⟨4.0⟩ ⟨3.2⟩ ⟨2.6⟩ ⟨2.5⟩ ⟨1.0⟩ ⟨0.6⟩ ⟨0.5⟩ ⟨0.4⟩ ⟨0.3⟩

(b) Length 1: 4.0

Length 2: 4.0

Length 3: 3.2 0.6

Length 4: 2.6 1.0 0.4

Length 5: 2.5 0.5 0.3

(c) $0.6 + 4.0 + 2.5 + 3.2 + 1.0 + 2.6 + 0.4 + 0.3 + 4.0 + 0.5 = 19.1$

$19.1 \div 4 = 4.775$

Lower bound = 5, so this does use the minimum number of 4 m lengths.

120 Graphs

(a) 3

(b) (i) e.g. **BE, EA, AD** (ii) e.g. **A → E → C**

(c) (i) e.g. (ii)

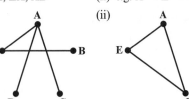

121 Drawing networks

(a) e.g.

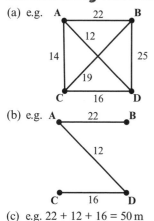

(b) e.g.

A $\underline{\quad 22 \quad}$ B

12

C $\underline{\quad 16 \quad}$ D

(c) e.g. 22 + 12 + 16 = 50 m

122 Kruskal's algorithm

e.g. **EC** (5) ✓, **BC** (6) ✓, **BE** (8) ✗, **DG** (8) ✓, **EF** (9) ✓,
AB (11) ✓, **AF** (13) ✗, **BF** (13) ✗, **GF** (14) ✓, **CG** (14) ✗,
CD (15) ✗. All vertices connected.

123 Prim's algorithm

(a)

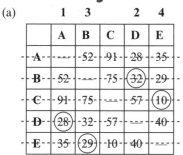

	1	3	2	4
	A	B	C	D	E

(table with crossed out rows A, B, C, D, E)

AD, DB, BE, EC

(b) e.g.

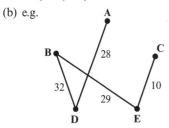

Total weight = 28 + 32 + 29 + 10 = 99

124 Dijkstra's algorithm

(a)

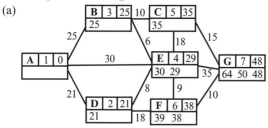

Shortest route = **ADEFG** of length 48

(b) Shortest route via **E** = 29 + 35 = 64
Shortest route via **C** = 35 + 15 = 50
Shortest route = **ABCG** of length 50

125 Route inspection

New total weight of network = 129 + 12 = 141 miles
Odd vertices: **D** and **E**
Shortest route **D** → **E** = 14 miles
New minimum route = 141 + 14 = 155 miles > 154 miles
Brett's route will increase.

126 Activity networks

Activity	Preceded by
A	–
B	–
C	–
D	A
E	C

Activity	Preceded by
F	C
G	A, B, C
H	A, B, C
I	D, G
J	H, F, E

127 Early and late times

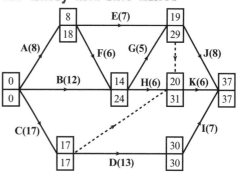

128 Critical paths

(a)

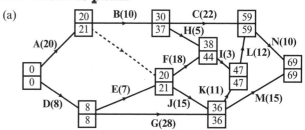

(b) **D, G, K, L, N**

(c) Activity **E**: 21 − 8 − 7 = 6
Activity **H**: 44 − 30 − 5 = 9
Activity **M**: 69 − 36 − 15 = 18

129 Gantt charts

(a) **B** → **H** and **B** → **D** → **E**

(b)

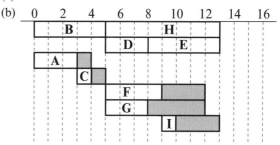

130 Scheduling

(a) $\dfrac{5 + 8 + 3 + 5 + 3 + 1 + 4 + 3 + 1}{13} = 2.53...$

Lower bound = 3 workers

(b) e.g.

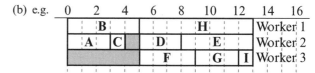

131 Linear programming 1

Let x = number of type A mp3 players produced

Let y = number of type B mp3 players produced

Maximise $P = 75x + 55y$

Subject to
$$x \geqslant 200$$
$$0.1(x + y) < x$$
$$0.4(x + y) > x$$
$$x + y \leqslant 3000$$

132 Linear programming 2

(a) Top line: $y = 0.5x + 10$

Constraint: $y \leqslant 0.5x + 10$

Bottom line: $y = 0.25x$

Constraint: $y \geqslant 0.25x$

(b)

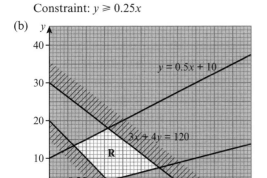

133 Objective lines

(a)

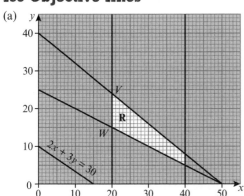

Intersection of $x = 20$ and $2y + x = 50$

$2y + 20 = 50$

$y = 15, x = 20$

(b)

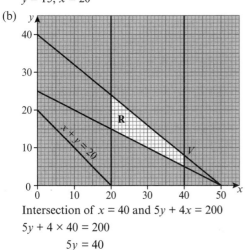

Intersection of $x = 40$ and $5y + 4x = 200$

$5y + 4 \times 40 = 200$

$5y = 40$

$y = 8, x = 40$

134 Vertex testing

Vertex	x	y	$Q = 4x + y$
A	10	30	70
B	12.5	35	85
C	10	0	40
D	30	0	120

Maximum value of $Q = 120$ when $x = 30$ and $y = 0$

135 Matchings on graphs

(a)

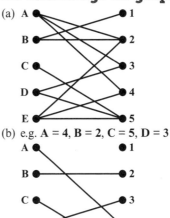

(b) e.g. **A = 4, B = 2, C = 5, D = 3**

136 Maximum matchings

Alternating path: **C − 5 = G − 1**

Change status: **C = 5 − G = 1**

New matching: **C = 5, G = 1, J = 3, N = 4, O = 6, R = 2**

137 Which algorithm?

Allocating tasks to workers based on their qualifications

Working out how to cut different lengths of wallpaper from the smallest number of rolls

Finding a particular name in a database arranged in alphabetical order

Finding the shortest route between two stations in a railway network

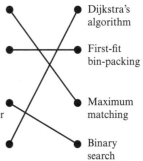

Dijkstra's algorithm

First-fit bin-packing

Maximum matching

Binary search

Published by Pearson Education Limited, Edinburgh Gate, Harlow, Essex, CM20 2JE.

www.pearsonschoolsandfecolleges.co.uk

Copies of official specifications for all Edexcel qualifications may be found on the Edexcel website: www.edexcel.com

Text © Harry Smith and Pearson Education Limited 2013
Edited by Project One Publishing Solutions, Scotland
Typeset and illustrated by Tech-Set Ltd, Gateshead
Original illustrations © Pearson Education Limited 2013
Cover illustration by Miriam Sturdee

The rights of Harry Smith to be identified as author of this work have been asserted by him in accordance with the Copyright, Designs and Patents Act 1988.

First published 2013

17 16 15 14 13
10 9 8 7 6 5 4 3 2 1

British Library Cataloguing in Publication Data
A catalogue record for this book is available from the British Library

ISBN 978 1 447 96164 2

Printed in Slovakia by Neografia

Acknowledgements
The following Edexcel examination questions are reproduced with permission from Edexcel:
Question 1 on page 26 © Edexcel 2011; Question 2 on page 26 © Edexcel 2009; Question 3 on page 26 © Edexcel 2012;
Question 4 on page 26 © Edexcel 2009; Question 5 on page 26 © Edexcel 2006; Worked example on page 55 © Edexcel 2008;
Question 1 on page 56 © Edexcel 2012; Question 2 on page 56 © Edexcel 2006; Question 3 on page 56 © Edexcel 2013;
Question 4 on page 56 © Edexcel 2009; Question 5 on page 56 © Edexcel 2005; Worked example on page 58 © Edexcel 2005;
Worked example on page 59 © Edexcel 2006; Worked example on page 60 © Edexcel 2008; Worked example on page 61 © Edexcel 2010;
Worked example on page 63 © Edexcel 2012; Worked example on page 65 © Edexcel 2010; Worked example on page 66 © Edexcel 2009;
Worked example on page 71 © Edexcel 2010; Worked example on page 73 © Edexcel 2007; Worked example on page 75 © Edexcel 2006;
Worked example on page 76 © Edexcel 2012; Worked example on page 78 © Edexcel 2011; Worked example on page 79 © Edexcel 2007;
Worked example on page 80 © Edexcel 2012; Question 1 on page 82 © Edexcel 2006; Question 2 on page 82 © Edexcel 2009;
Question 3 on page 82 © Edexcel 2009; Worked example on page 103 © Edexcel 2011; Worked example on page 125 © Edexcel 2012;
Worked example on page 131 © Edexcel 2008; Worked example on page 136 © Edexcel 2013; Question 1 on page 138 © Edexcel 2009;
Question 2 on page 138 © Edexcel 2008; Question 3 on page 138 © Edexcel 2011.

Every effort has been made to trace the copyright holders and we apologise in advance for any unintentional omissions. We would be pleased to insert the appropriate acknowledgement in any subsequent edition of this publication.

In the writing of this book, no Edexcel examiners authored sections relevant to examination papers for which they have responsibility.